The Perfect Portfolio

A REVOLUTIONARY APPROACH TO PERSONAL INVESTING

Leland B. Hevner
President, National Association
of Online Investors

WILEY

John Wiley & Sons, Inc.

Published by John Wiley & Sons, Inc., Hoboken, New Jersey.
Published simultaneously in Canada.

For general information on our other products and services or for technical
support, please contact our Customer Care Department within the United States
at (800) 762-2974, outside the United States at (317) 572-3993 or fax (317)
572-4002.

Wiley also publishes its books in a variety of electronic formats. Some content that
appears in print may not be available in electronic books. For more information
about Wiley products, visit our web site at www.wiley.com.

Library of Congress Cataloging-in-Publication Data:
Hevner, Leland B., 1952–
    The perfect portfolio : a revolutionary approach to personal investing /
Leland B. Hevner.
        p.   cm.
    Includes bibliographical references and index.
    ISBN 978-0-470-40174-3 (cloth/website : alk. paper)
        1. Investments.   2. Portfolio management.   3. Finance, Personal.   I. Title.
    HG4521.H557   2009
    332.6—dc22

                                                                    2008040638

Printed in the United States of America.
10   9   8   7   6   5   4   3   2   1

Contents

"Do not believe in anything simply because you have heard it. Do not believe in anything simply because it is spoken and rumored by many. Do not believe in anything simply because it is found written in your religious books. Do not believe in anything merely on the authority of your teachers and elders. Do not believe in traditions because they have been handed down for many generations. But after observation and analysis, when you find that anything agrees with reason and is conducive to the good and benefit of one and all, then accept it and live up to it."

Buddha (Hindu Prince Gautama Siddharta, the founder of Buddhism, 563–483 B.C.)

Foreword

I first met Leland Hevner in 2002 at my former job as a *Wall Street Journal* reporter for CNBC. I interviewed Leland for a televised investor education segment, and soon found myself calling him frequently for interviews because his advice was always both insightful and immensely practical. Most of all, Leland was a welcome addition to the discussion because he was an advocate for Main Street, not Wall Street. His goal in these interviews was to translate the investing topics being discussed into plain English and to make them relevant to the average person with money to invest.

When I wrote my first book, *Investing Success*, published in 2004, I again drew upon Leland's wisdom to explain common investing mistakes that people make—and how they could fix or avoid those mistakes. As we maintain contact over the years, I have come to appreciate Leland's dedication to providing individuals with comprehensive, objective, and actionable investing education. The study courses he has created for the National Association of Online Investors are a resource that I often recommend to people when I conduct my own investment workshops and investor empowerment activities.

In *The Perfect Portfolio*, Leland does more than simply show readers how to navigate the personal investing landscape as it exists today. He goes one step further and boldly advocates making significant changes to this landscape. He challenges the validity and relevance of existing investing concepts such as asset class definition, portfolio design theory, and even the very definition of investing risk. And in doing so he presents new ways of thinking and new methods that make the world of personal investing simpler and less intimidating to individuals seeking to take more personal control of their portfolios.

I applaud the author's willingness in this book to challenge conventional investing concepts that have been taught by "experts" as indisputable facts for decades. I also applaud his recognition that individuals are truly capable of making their own investing decisions if given the appropriate knowledge, structure, and resources. Readers will undoubtedly appreciate his innovative use of an online supplement that makes *The Perfect Portfolio* more than just a book but rather a total learning experience.

Today's markets are rife with challenges that confound novice and professional investors alike. Thankfully, *The Perfect Portfolio* provides the type of outside-the-box thinking that can enable individual investors to not only cope with these challenges but also to view them as profit making opportunities. I firmly believe that anyone with money to invest will benefit from reading this book. *The Perfect Portfolio* is an easy-to-follow road map to being a successful investor in up and down markets.

LYNNETTE KHALFANI-COX
The Money Coach
www.TheMoneyCoach.net

Preface

The investing environment that we, as individual investors, face today is not a friendly place. Equity prices are buffeted by factors that were inconceivable just a few years ago. Yet while markets have changed dramatically, the investing theories, methods, and resources we have available to cope with them have not. We are essentially stuck using twentieth-century tools for dealing with twenty-first-century investing challenges, and these tools no longer work.

The time has come to pause, take a deep breath, and rethink the totality of how we view and interact with equities markets. It is time to recognize that much of what we have been taught about how to invest has become obsolete. To survive and thrive in today's new investing environment, a completely new approach to personal investing is needed. Providing this new approach is the purpose of this book.

The New Face of Investing Today

In the good old days (not many years ago), investors had a reasonable chance of predicting stock prices by analyzing company financial statements. Not too long ago, we could trust with some degree of confidence what a CEO was saying about the health and earnings potential of his or her company. And most of us can remember a time when news items in the financial media had at least been fact-checked. In other words, in the not too distant past, we had a legitimate chance of being successful investors by doing some good old-fashioned homework using basic equity analysis methods and tools. Unfortunately, those days are gone.

Today, a host of factors influence stock prices that have nothing to do with corporate fundamentals. And these factors are almost impossible for us to analyze using the resources available to us. What are these new factors? Let's look at just a few.

- **The Web.** This vehicle of mass communication has changed everything. Some of the effects are good, and some are bad. Among the good effects are that individuals have access to massive amounts of investment-related information, and they can use this input to trade equities from the comfort of their homes. Among the bad effects are that much of the information investors are exposed to on the Web is misleading at best and fraudulent at worst. Anyone can post rumors, opinions, and bogus analysis on the Web that can be made to look like legitimate news. The Web then proliferates these postings with the speed of light, and they are read by millions of people who often place trades without questioning what they read. By creating and spreading misinformation on the Web, anyone with a computer and an Internet connection can cause millions of people to make uninformed trading decisions and in this manner manipulate stock prices easily and cheaply.

- **The short attack industry.** Short selling is now a major factor that can dramatically influence the price of any stock. In today's markets, major traders such as hedge funds are making tens of billions of dollars through the practice of borrowing shares of a company stock and immediately selling these shares at current market prices. They hope that the stock price will go down so they can buy back the shares at a lower price, return the borrowed shares, and pocket the price difference. This is called shorting a stock and it is a legal activity. What short attackers do, however, is abuse this activity by orchestrating a massive smear campaign against a stock they have shorted in order to rapidly drive down its price. As a part of this effort, they may spread false rumors about the stock on the Web, create and distribute bogus financial analysis reports, and even influence mainstream media reporters to write negative articles about the company they are shorting. A short attack can destroy the value of a stock, and there is no way for us as individual investors to predict which companies are in the crosshairs.

- **Government activism.** As I write these words, the government is rampaging through the equities markets like a bull in a china shop. Legislators have voted to inject hundreds of billions of dollars into the financial system without a clear plan for how the money will be spent. This is all in response to a problem that the government itself created by insisting (under threat of prosecution) that banks give home mortgages to people who could not afford them (subprime loans). Anytime the government interferes with the free market, bad things happen; and unfortunately signs currently point to increasing government activism. This is another factor that can dramatically affect stock prices, but that defies analysis using investing tools and analysis techniques currently available to us.

* **Speculation.** In commodities markets, the activity of speculators has a significant effect on the prices of such assets as gold, oil, and food, all of which are vital to the health of our overall economy. Speculative price swings in these commodities affect the earnings and thus the prices of a full range of stocks. As I write these words, in the past six months the price of a barrel of oil has moved from $80 to $140 and back to $60. Such violent price movements are not totally attributable to factors that can be analyzed, such as supply and demand. Much of this price volatility is due to speculation, and this is yet another factor that cannot be analyzed and quantified with any degree of confidence.

These are only a few examples of stock price influences that we, as individual investors, cannot analyze with the methods and tools we have at our disposal today. Fundamental stock analysis does not and cannot take into account any of the factors discussed above and this is why it is very difficult, if not impossible, for individuals to make informed investing decisions in today's markets. This is why a comprehensive new approach to investing is desperately needed in today's new and challenging market environment.

A New Approach to Investing

In the face of these new market dynamics and the inability of existing investing tools to deal with them, what can we do? We have three choices.

One option is to whine, complain, and say that the factors listed earlier, and others like them, are illegal or unfair and that government regulators should step in and make everything right. This course of action and $5 will buy you a cup of coffee. It is not going to happen.

A second option is to develop revised theories, methods, and tools that will enable us to analyze the new market influences such as those just described. But this would be an unbelievably difficult task to accomplish, if it were even possible at all. The new problems that plague the market today simply defy any type of rational analysis. This option is a dead end.

The third choice is to develop an updated, and improved approach to personal investing. This approach would recognize the new factors influencing equity markets and provide an updated set of tools, concepts, and methods for dealing with them.

This third option, consisting of creating a completely new approach to personal investing, is the only viable choice for enabling us to succeed in today's markets. This is the option presented in *The Perfect Portfolio*.

Why Should You Complete This Book?

As I write these words soon after the stock market crash of 2008, panic reigns in markets. Stock prices have collapsed based on a number of factors that I have just discussed and others. It is understandable that individual investors don't know what to do in current chaotic market conditions. What is more interesting to me is that financial advisers and market mavens don't know what to do, either.

The current market malaise is shining a bright light on the financial services industry. We are discovering that the so-called experts are really no more capable of creating and managing an effective portfolio of investments in today's new market environment than you are, and that placing absolute trust in financial professionals to manage your investments is a very risky strategy indeed.

What is becoming increasingly clear is that it is up to you to take more personal control of your portfolio in order to protect and grow your wealth. To do so, you must have the knowledge, structure, methods, and tools needed to make effective investing decisions in current markets. By reading *The Perfect Portfolio* you will gain all of these elements necessary for investing success.

Regaining personal control of your portfolio and becoming empowered to succeed in today's personal investing environment are two of the many reasons why you should, and must, complete this book.

How Is This Book Organized?

I have taught personal investing at the college level for more than 10 years. During this time, I have created dozens of lesson plans. Input from hundreds of students has shown me the presentation design that is most effective. The organization of this book is based on this feedback.

The Perfect Portfolio is divided into three Parts, each containing several chapters, and a Summary. An overview of how the book content is organized is presented in the following paragraphs.

Part I: The Problem, the Solution, and Getting Started—Chapters 1 to 3. I start in Chapter 1 by illustrating the problems faced by individual investors today. For this purpose, I present actual questions from students in the classes I teach. With the problems defined, I then discuss a comprehensive approach for solving them in Chapter 2. Here I explain the Perfect Portfolio Methodology (PPM). It calls for your portfolio to be divided into two segments, a Core Segment and a Target Market Segment. Chapter 3 shows you how to start building the Perfect Portfolio by designing its Core Segment, which serves as the foundation of your portfolio and sets the stage for the more powerful Target Market Segment.

Part II: Supercharging Your Portfolio with Target Market Investing—Chapters 4 to 9. While the purpose of the Core Segment is to provide stability to your portfolio, the purpose of the Target Market Segment is to supercharge its returns. In Chapter 4, I provide an overview of this Segment and describe the process used for its design. It will contain five Asset Building Blocks: gold, energy, agricultural commodities, real estate, and emerging markets. These are assets that can have annual returns of 20 percent, 30 percent, 40 percent, and higher! I show you how to invest in these assets in a manner that enables you to take advantage of their incredible returns potential without excessive risk. Chapters 5 through 9 then go into significant detail on how to identify, analyze, select, and monitor investments for each Target Market asset type.

Part III: Creating and Working with Your Perfect Portfolio—Chapters 10 to 12. At this point in the book you will have the knowledge, structure, and tools needed to construct a Perfect Portfolio that meets your investing goals, your unique investing profile and current market conditions. Chapter 10 walks you, step by step, through the total portfolio design process. In Chapter 11, I show you how to monitor, manage, and modify your portfolio on an ongoing basis. And in Chapter 12, I show you areas of the PPM where you can strive for even higher returns by becoming more involved in the investing process. The PPM enables you to aim for virtually any level of return that you are willing to work for.

Summary: Reviewing, Teaching, and Experiencing the Perfect Portfolio Methodology. I end *The Perfect Portfolio* with a review of why I have the audacity to call the PPM approach to investing *revolutionary*. It is an adjective that I don't use lightly. Then I discuss the reactions I get from students in my classes when they are first exposed to the PPM. Your reactions will probably be similar. Next I present a real-life story told to me by a student who actually used the PPM to build her own portfolio. I think you will find this story interesting and the perfect way to illustrate the benefits of using the PPM approach to portfolio design. I close by presenting a final note that asks you to step back and review what you have just learned in *The Perfect Portfolio* and to consider how this knowledge can enable you to become a confident and successful individual investor in markets as they exist today and as they will exist in the future.

A Prerequisite for Continuing: An Open Mind

Many students enter the classrooms where I teach the Perfect Portfolio Methodology (PPM) with a host of preconceptions. They believe that they are about to learn how to find and analyze stocks, dissect mutual funds and fund styles, build portfolios with three asset classes, and be shown why buy-and-hold is the preferred investing strategy. Who can blame them? For years they have been taught that these activities form the very foundation of effective personal investing.

As my classes begin, therefore, they are literally stunned when I kick to the curb much of conventional investing "wisdom" and replace it with a dramatically different and simpler method for designing a powerful portfolio. They are, at first, skeptical when I teach none of the traditional investing activities they thought they were about to learn. But as classes progress, they see the logic of the PPM and their skepticism gradually turns to excitement. They begin to realize that the investing concepts they have been taught for years have been stifling their ability to become effective investors and that there exists a far better and more logical way for growing their wealth.

It is therefore appropriate for me to give to you the same advice that I give to my new students. Before starting this book, clear your mind of any preconceptions you may now have about how personal investing works. Forget much of what you have been taught for years. Start with a clean slate. In the PPM, you are about to learn an approach to investing that enables you to view the world of personal investing from a totally different angle, one that defies tradition. You will need an open mind to appreciate and absorb this paradigm shift. Allow yourself the freedom to consider and accept change.

Author's Note

The logistics of publishing dictate that the content of a book be completed months before the release date. When dealing with a topic as dynamic as equities markets, this can pose a challenge. In the pages of this book, I walk you through a detailed explanation of a revolutionary approach to investing that I call the Perfect Portfolio Methodology (PPM). To illustrate how to implement this new approach, I have used price charts for various market sectors and asset classes as they existed in July of 2008, when I created the content. At that time stock markets were trending down but not dramatically, and certain market sectors were moving up strongly— as you will see in the example charts presented.

Alas, as I write this note in December of 2008, market conditions have significantly changed. Stocks, both domestic and international, have suffered a significant setback, and sectors/asset types that were moving up when I created the examples in this book have tumbled.

In light of the new market environment that may exist when you read this book, you may be tempted to think that the portfolio creation methodology illustrated here is no longer valid.

Nothing could be further from the truth.

In the time between when I created the illustrations used in the content of this book and now, the PPM has worked perfectly for a portfolio I am managing. As markets began deteriorating, it guided me to decrease my portfolio allocation to stocks, both foreign and domestic, and it also completely eliminated from my portfolio investments in energy, agricultural commodities, and emerging markets. At the same time, the PPM directed me to increase my allocations to cash and gold.

The PPM also enabled me actually to earn significant returns using "short" Exchange Traded Funds for various asset types as they began falling in price. These are investment vehicles that go up in value in direct proportion to the decrease in value of the underlying asset or market index. You will learn how to use them in this book.

Thus, while many investors were being advised to buy-and-hold during the 2008 crash and were losing their collective shirts by so doing, the PPM was automatically moving a portion of my portfolio into an extremely defensive stance with a substantial cash allocation, positioning it perfectly for reentry into equities at the first signs of market recovery. At the same time, another portion of my portfolio was earning returns of 20 percent and higher by taking carefully monitored short positions on the S&P 500 index and specific asset classes as they rapidly declined.

So, as you move through this book you may see positive charts for investments that have since been decimated. Don't worry; the PPM principles you will learn are sufficiently flexible to handle *any* set of market conditions, not just those illustrated in this book. The performance of my own portfolio is proof of this fact.

Market conditions will change. A good portfolio design methodology recognizes and takes advantage of these changes and that is exactly what the Perfect Portfolio Methodology has done for my portfolio. The PPM has proved to be relevant and effective before, during, and after that market crash of 2008. And it will be just as relevant and effective when you read this book, regardless of current market conditions.

—Leland B. Hevner
December 1, 2008

The Perfect Portfolio
Online Supplement

The Perfect Portfolio is more than simply a book. It also includes a supplemental component that you access on the Web. The use of this supplement is not required, yet I encourage you to do so to take full advantage of a richer and more convenient learning experience.

Throughout the book, I will alert you to instances where you will benefit from accessing an online resource found in the supplement.

Accessing the Online Supplement

To access the online supplement enter the following Web address:
www.perfectportfoliobook.com

This entry takes you to a page on the site of the National Association of Online Investors (NAOI), the organization that hosts the supplement. The Web page will display the URL www.naoi.org/members/pportlogin.asp. Don't worry, this is not an error. I have set up the Web address presented above to point to the supplement home page simply because it is easier to remember.

On The Perfect Portfolio supplement's sign-in page, you will be prompted for a User ID and Password. Simply enter the following for each:

- *User ID:* Perfect
- *Password:* Portfolio

Neither of these entries is case sensitive. After logging in, a Home Page will display with these selections:

- *Links by Chapter.* When you click on this link, you will be taken to a page that displays the book's Table of Contents. Clicking on a Chapter link shows you a list of links for the resources that are referenced in the corresponding chapter in this book. Clicking on a link in this list takes you to a resource that can be a worksheet, a calculator, or a third-party Web site.

- *Calculators and Worksheets.* Click on this link to access an area of the site where I have collected all of the calculators and worksheets referenced in this book. They are presented here, all in one place, for your convenience so you do not have to remember in which specific chapter a resource of interest is referenced.
- *Web Link Compilation.* When you click on this link you will access a list of all of the third-party Web sites that I have referenced throughout this book. They are listed here, all in one place, for your convenient access.

Benefits of the Online Supplement

The following is a description of the resources and benefits that you will find in the online supplement.

- *Worksheets:* At various stages of this book, I will suggest that you go to the Web and collect data. For this purpose, you will use specially designed data collection worksheets. You can easily create these worksheets on your own or, for greater convenience, you can access each in the form of a PDF file found in the online supplement and print it.
- *Calculators:* At various points in this book, I show the use of calculators for purposes such as determining the expected returns for various portfolio configurations. These are easy calculations that you can do with your own calculator. A more convenient method, however, is to simply access the online calculators in the supplement.
- *Expanded Information and Education:* This book covers a lot of ground, and if I discussed every topic in detail, it would be over a thousand pages in length. I therefore provide Web sites in the online supplement where you can find more detailed discussions of specific topics. For example, while I discuss in this book the definition of Exchange Traded Funds (ETFs) and how they are used, you may wish to learn more about them. For this purpose, I provide one or more

Web links in the online supplement where you can go to get additional information on ETFs.

- *Updated Web References:* Anytime a hardcopy book lists a Web site address, there is a danger that by the time you read the material, the link is out of date. To guard against this, the online supplement contains Web references that are constantly updated. If a Web site mentioned in this book seems to be no longer valid or doesn't work as described, you can go to the supplement to get updated information.

- *Third Party Tools and Resources:* Everything you need to design, implement, and monitor your unique Perfect Portfolio is presented in this book. The techniques and the tools are easy to understand and simple to use. However, there exist Web-based tools and resources that you may wish to consider to assist you at various steps of the portfolio development process. You will find a list of these resources in the supplement. Keep in mind that these resources are presented only for your consideration and are not a requirement for you to develop your Perfect Portfolio.

It is important to repeat that use of the supplemental online component is optional. It exists for your convenience only. Having said this, I truly believe that a book combined with a closely integrated online component is the future of all financial publications. *The Perfect Portfolio* is at the vanguard of this exciting and inevitable new trend in financial publishing.

Acknowledgments

The inspiration and knowledge required to create a truly effective book on personal investing cannot come from the secretive backrooms of Wall Street insiders, the brightly lit stages of TV pundits/celebrities, or the sterile halls of academia.

No, a book that has the potential to instill widespread confidence among the investing public can only originate from the people it is designed to help—namely, the average person with money to invest.

The Perfect Portfolio was created based in large part on my interaction with individual investors. Fortunately, I have access to a host of them through the personal investing classes I teach and via the multi-thousand-member organization I run, the National Association of Online Investors.

In writing this book, I spent countless hours interviewing people who are faced every day with investing decisions that they are not prepared to make and with financial offerings that they are not prepared to evaluate. They told me of the challenges they encounter as they try to navigate the chaotic world of personal investing in an effort to protect and grow their wealth. They expressed to me their feelings of frustration, despair, and even anger as they watched their savings melt away in portfolios designed by credentialed advisors. And they told me that they would be willing, in fact eager, to become more involved in the investing process if they only knew how.

The almost universal desire of people to cut the cord of dependency on the financial services industry and to regain personal control of their investments, and thus their quality of life, inspired me to create *The Perfect Portfolio*.

I would like to acknowledge the great debt of gratitude that I owe to the many, many people who were willing to share with me their personal investing stories along with suggestions on how their investing lives could be made better. In essence, they told me what to write in this book.

I also wish to thank Ms. Rachelle Cohen, a superb editor and a tremendously supportive friend for her valuable assistance in reviewing the content of this book.

PART I

THE PROBLEM, THE SOLUTION, AND GETTING STARTED

Our journey toward creating the Perfect Portfolio is divided into three Parts as briefly described in the Preface to this book. Part I consists of three chapters.

I start in Chapter 1 with a description of the problems that face individual investors on a daily basis. I illustrate these problems with discussions I have had with students in the college classes I teach.

With the problem defined, I then lay out in Chapter 2 a solution to these problems using a revolutionary new approach to investing that I call the Perfect Portfolio Methodology, or PPM for short.

We begin in Chapter 3 the process of creating a Perfect Portfolio by building its Core Segment, consisting of the traditional asset classes of Cash, Stocks, and Bonds.

After completing Part I of *The Perfect Portfolio,* you will understand the problems that need to be solved, you will understand the new approach to personal investing I am proposing for addressing these problems, and you will know how to build the foundation of the Perfect Portfolio in the form of its Core Segment.

Then in Part II of *The Perfect Portfolio,* you will learn how to supercharge the portfolio's returns potential by adding a Target Market Segment consisting of five new asset classes that I have defined for this approach.

And finally, in Part III, we bring the Core Segment and the Target Market Segment together to form a Perfect Portfolio that meets your unique goals, matches your personal investing style, and works in current market conditions.

CHAPTER 1

The Woeful State of Personal Investing and the Need for Change

A VIEW FROM MAIN STREET

As I fiddle with the overhead projector at the front of the room, people start to file in for the first session of an investing class that I teach at Montgomery College just outside of Washington, D.C. They find their seats, and as I turn to face the group of about 20 people, I see a cross-section of the U.S. public. Most are older and probably retired. Many are middle-aged and in their peak earning years. There are a surprising number of younger people who look like they are fresh out of college and just starting their earning careers. And, as usual, there are more women than men.

I know that these students are not day traders and few, if any, are experienced personal investors. These are average people with money to invest and they simply don't know how to navigate the world of personal investing. I note that many have brought folders with them that I suspect contain broker statements they do not understand. At some point, either before or after class, they will spread these statements in front of me hoping that I will be able to decode them.

The overwhelming majority of people who attend my classes have off-loaded their portfolios, some of which are quite substantial, to advisers and brokers because they have no confidence in their own ability to make investing decisions. But as they have watched their portfolios stagnate or erode while being charged significant fees, these individuals have reached a breaking point. They have had enough of standing on the sidelines and watching their hard-earned savings fade away without understanding how or why. They want to understand and have more personal control of their portfolios, either by making their own investing decisions or at least being able to challenge their adviser's recommendations, but they don't know how. They have found their way to my class hoping against hope that it will be their first step toward becoming a more confident and independent investor.

Yet, students enter the class skeptical. Many believe they are about to hear a sales pitch from a broker or a financial adviser. They have experienced this many times before and are fully prepared to be disappointed if it happens again. Others believe they are about to learn new ways to pick stocks and mutual funds based on an incredibly successful trading system I am promoting. Still others believe I will be trying to persuade them to buy specific stocks or funds on which I receive commissions.

Therefore, my students are typically surprised when I tell them that I am not selling anything, that I am not going to give them specific investment recommendations, and that I will not reveal to them a shortcut to investing riches.

I tell them that I am a professional educator, not a professional salesman, and that what I am about to teach in this class is nothing short of a totally new approach to personal investing. They look at me with surprise when I tell them that this new approach will require that they forget most of what they have learned about investing to this point. I tell them that the only prerequisite to taking this class is that they clear their minds and be open to new investing methods that most of their advisers or brokers will look upon with the utmost of disdain. I tell them that what they learn over the next 12 hours of class work will enable even the least experienced among them to become confident, independent and successful investors. At this point, while many facial expressions show disbelief, I at least have their attention.

What I teach my students in the classroom is what I will teach you in this book. I therefore give you the same advice that I give to my students. Clear your mind of preconceived notions of how personal investing works. Open your mind to new ideas. Don't compare what you read here to what you have read or been told elsewhere until you finish the book. Then decide if this new approach makes sense for you.

You are now a student of a radically new way of investing that takes the power out of the hands of salespeople and third party "experts" and puts it squarely into yours. By picking up *The Perfect Portfolio* you have shown that you are ready, willing, and able to accept the challenge.

The Current State of Personal Investing

Why is a new approach to investing needed? The answer is, unfortunately, because the world of personal investing today is broken. The financial services industry is not meeting the needs of people who are seeking to learn how to take more personal control of their portfolios. As a result, the investing public wants, needs, and demands change.

In my position as a teacher of personal investing and as President of the multi-thousand-member National Association of Online Investors (NAOI), I have the opportunity to interact with the investing public on a daily basis. I talk with hundreds of individual investors every year. I can see in their faces and hear in their voices that they are confused and often intimidated by the world of personal investing as it currently exists. When seeking to learn how to cope with this world, they are confronted with hundreds of investing books, countless newsletters, nonstop seminars for trading systems promising instant success, sales pitches from hoards of financial advisers, and a constant barrage of information from the financial media. The world of personal investing today is simply overwhelming for the average person trying to protect and grow their savings.

When confronted with this chaos, most people simply give up in despair and give their portfolios to financial advisers to manage. In essence, they are entrusting their financial futures to strangers who are far too often salespeople with fancy financial credentials. This situation is clearly unacceptable. But what can we do? What can we change?

I realized early in my teaching career that people did not simply need more investing tools, more information, or more expert financial advice. Rather, the public told me that they needed nothing less than a totally new approach to investing. They wanted a greatly simplified approach that would enable them to take more personal

control of their portfolios and to effectively manage their investments on their own with confidence. To meet this goal, I developed
the revolutionary Perfect Portfolio Methodology (PPM) approach
to investing which I explain in this book.

The PPM greatly simplifies the investing process. It shows you
how to create an incredibly powerful portfolio using only nine key
Asset Building Blocks. It frees you from the tedious process of analyzing individual stocks and mutual fund styles. And it gives you a
logical structure for designing a portfolio that meets your unique
needs and is responsive to changing market conditions. In short, it
fixes what is broken in today's personal investing market.

But before presenting a solution, it is beneficial to understand
the problem the solution is designed to address. The purpose of the
next section of this chapter is to shine a bright light on the obstacles
that individual investors face today. In doing so, I hope to convince
you that a new approach to personal investing is needed. I also show
in this first chapter that a new approach is possible and what it will
look like.

I begin by illustrating the problems faced by average people
with money to invest using the words of students in the personal
investing college classes I teach.

Questions from the Classroom

It is 9 P.M. on a blustery March night. I have just finished a three-
hour session of my class, titled "Effective Investing Using Online
Resources," at Montgomery College on the outskirts of Washington,
D.C. This is one of four weekly sessions that make up the entire
program.

While the class is officially over for the night, I know that it is
not finished. Students are lining up at my desk to speak to me one
on one. Each wants to discuss a personal finance issue that they do
not feel comfortable raising during class. Even though it is late,
everyone is tired, and they are missing *American Idol,* they stand
patiently, folders in hand, waiting for their turn to engage in a private conversation about their mysterious financial situation.

My students know that I am not a registered financial adviser.
I told them at the beginning of the class that I cannot give them
specific investment recommendations. But this is not what they are
seeking. They simply want to talk to a knowledgeable and objective

third party who is not selling anything and whom they feel they can trust. So they wait.

It would not be hard for me to simply list the problems faced by individual investors today. But a sterile list of such items would not do the topic justice. The full scope of the problem is better understood when presented within the context of real-life, human experience. These are experiences that I believe you may be able to identify with on a personal level.

Each of the following questions and related discussions represents a real issue presented to me by a student whom I will refer to by first name only. These are only representative examples of hundreds of similar issues that I address every year. Taken as a whole, they tell me that the world of personal investing today is not a friendly place in which to travel and is in desperate need of change.

Margaret—The Problem with Advisers

Margaret is a 58-year-old teacher who has over $500,000 of investment money. She has entrusted it to an adviser to whom she pays a yearly fee of 2 percent of the total amount invested. The returns she has been receiving have been less than market averages and she is concerned. She knows little about investing (which is why she is attending my class) and has put her complete faith and trust in her adviser. She suspects something is wrong but does not even know the questions to ask of the financial professional with whom she is working. She is afraid to offend him by challenging his judgment. In a one-on-one discussion following the class period, she shows me her latest broker statements and asks for my comments.

A quick scan of her statements reveals a list of rather mundane mutual funds, all of which have a load, which is nothing more than a sales commission to the broker/adviser. I ask to see an investing plan that the adviser has developed defining her investing goals, time horizon, risk tolerance, and so forth. None exists. I ask to see a prospectus for each of the funds in her portfolio. I am handed glossy marketing brochures instead.

Her portfolio is very poorly thought out and ill-designed. It seems there was little effort made to find investments that meet Margaret's unique goals and risk profile. It is clear to me that the main driving force behind this random mix of funds is to earn commissions for her adviser.

While most financial advisers are ethical, many are not, as this example illustrates. Biased advisers looking to maximize their income with commissions are one symptom of a financial services industry that is not serving the public well. Margaret is by no means the only one of my students who has shown me a portfolio that is designed to meet the goals of the adviser as opposed to the goals of the investor.

My advice to Margaret is to use the worksheets and Web sites I provide in class to perform a complete due diligence process on each fund she owns. (I provide many of these same resources to you in upcoming chapters.) I tell her to look at the risk, return history, and expenses of each, and then compare these factors to other funds in the same category. Web resources that I show her make such an analysis quick and simple. Armed with this information, she will be able to sit down with her adviser and have a meaningful discussion. She will be able to ask relevant questions and expect reasonable answers. If she does not get them, I suggest that she either look for another adviser or, better still, implement the new approach to investing that she is learning in my class.

John—The Problem with Expert Stock Recommendations

John is a 42-year-old lawyer. He has an adviser who manages a portion of his portfolio but he also likes to invest some money on his own. He came to me with a list of stocks that he had heard recommended on a Saturday morning TV talk show about investing. I could tell that he wanted me to give my blessing to this list of stocks, as he was quite excited about their potential.

I asked him if he had done his own due diligence on each stock. No, he had not. After all, he had received these recommendations from experts. I asked where in his investment plan these stocks fit. Is he looking for long-term growth or short-term profits? He responded that he just wanted to make some quick money.

I asked if he had thought about a trading plan for each stock that, should he buy it, defined price exit points for stopping losses and taking profits. No, he had not. I asked if the TV program he had seen recommended a different set of stocks every week with the same amount of enthusiasm. Yes, he supposed so. Therefore, I pointed out, the day he watched the show was a major determinant of his investing strategy. He did see the absurdity of this.

John is a smart man. He should know that the financial media are tasked with one objective and one objective only: to attract viewers so they can raise advertising rates. And audience surveys have shown that the financial media (TV, newspapers, radio, magazines) get the most eyeballs when they dole out stock recommendations with great enthusiasm. So they do, dozens per day, hundreds per month, and thousands per year.

Are there really that many excellent stocks so underpriced in the market that they are screaming *"buys"*? The answer is no. And should the stocks you buy depend on the day you watch a TV show or read a magazine? Again, the answer is no. Far too many people believe they can gain an advantage in the market by taking the advice of experts in the financial media. They can't.

My advice to John was to turn off the TV. Barring that, I suggested that he watch investing programs only for their entertainment value and perhaps to get stock buying ideas. He should then perform his own due diligence by researching each stock of interest. He was learning how to do this in my class. John was not particularly happy with my response to his questions but agreed that it made sense.

Here is a second reason why I contend that the world of personal investing is broken. The environment is filled with investing *entertainment* that too often substitutes for serious investing research. The public eats up frenetic stock recommendation shows on TV and often gets financial indigestion by making impulse trades based on what they see and hear.

Suzanne—The Problem with Selling Investments

Suzanne is a high-ranking government employee of Chinese ethnicity who needed more investment income to pay for her son's college tuition. She employed a friend of the family to advise her.

The friend recommended a mutual fund concentrating on Chinese firms and she showed me the fund prospectus. I immediately saw that the risk of the fund in terms of volatility was very high, and probably not appropriate for Suzanne's risk profile.

I pulled up a price chart on my computer for the fund, using a financial Web site, and saw that it had returned over 50 percent during the first six months that she owned the fund. It then started to drop, and at the time of our conversation, it was down 25 percent from her purchase price. She was obviously concerned and asked for my advice.

I see this all too often. People buy investments without a plan for selling them. I teach people to divide their portfolio into two segments: a Core Segment and a Target Market Segment. (I discuss these concepts at length in upcoming chapters.) The Core should contain broad-based mutual funds that are buy-and-hold investments. History shows that over the long term they will go up at a predictable pace and with relatively low risk. I recommend that riskier investments go into the Target Market Segment of the portfolio. Here is where more volatile funds, such as the one Suzanne showed me, should be placed. For each of these riskier investments, a trading plan must be put in place at the same time the investment is purchased.

A trading plan is essentially an exit strategy. Price points need to be set for stopping losses and for taking profits. These investments then need to be monitored and sold based on these exit points. The Web, fortunately, allows this to be accomplished automatically, as you will learn in this book.

Suzanne was unfamiliar with the trading plan concept. She simply bought the China fund with no thought of when to sell. So the fund earned for her a nice profit that she did not take. She held the fund and it fell. Now she wanted to know what to do and her adviser friend offered little help.

Here is yet another area where the financial services industry fails the public. Advisers and so-called experts are very good at promoting the purchase of investments, but they tend to ignore the equally important action of selling them. Even though Web resources are freely available that enable individuals to easily put in place an automated selling plan for each investment they buy, few even consider doing so. As a result, they simply buy and hold volatile investments that should be sold in accordance with a trading plan. All portfolios have a place for buy-and-hold investments and a place for buy-and-sell investments. There is, however, no place for buy-and-forget investments.

My advice to Suzanne was to assume that she had just bought the fund yesterday. We used the Web to look at a price chart for the fund to define exit points. I then showed her how to use a Web resource to place automated stop-loss and take-profit selling points for the fund. While still facing a loss on this fund, she was happy that she now, at least, had a plan for moving forward with not only this investment but also with all others in her portfolio.

Mike—The Problem with Trading System Seminars

Mike is a 62-year-old retired government worker. His wife is also retired, and they live on a fixed income. He came to me very excited about a stock-trading seminar he had attended in the past week. He owned a Web-connected home computer and envisioned a future in which he could use this stock-trading system in his spare time to generate significant income. The initial training session and software for the system cost about $5,000 and monthly data feeds cost about $150. He wanted my opinion on whether he should sign up for the program as he handed me a very, very glossy brochure.

I see this question so often that I should simply tape-record my thoughts and hit the play button. Stock-trading systems and related seminars are very successful and profitable—for the company that sells them. The systems are typically based on the user looking at stock price charts that are overlaid with a variety of indicators. These indicators measure aspects of the price charts such as trends, money flow in or out of the stock, strength of price movement, and so on. This type of activity is called *technical analysis* (TA), and is a very sophisticated technique used by scores of professional investors.

Yet the seminar system made TA look very simple. Mike was told that all he had to do was run a screening program every day to find stocks showing the most promising set of technical indicators and buy the stocks that showed the most green arrows lined up on the chart. This is—I don't know how else to describe it—pure garbage.

Technical analysis and the study of price charts is not an easy field to master. Professional investors spend years learning the craft and use very powerful computers to predict stock price movements based on price and volume indicators. The chances that an average person sitting at a home computer finding stocks poised for major moves upward based on TA that the professionals have missed are slim and none. Mike was about to fall for a pitch that made a very complex effort seem like child's play. He was about to buy snake oil.

Instead of putting it so bluntly, I queried him about the dynamics of the three-hour seminar he attended. Were the presenters all tall, tanned, immaculately dressed men? Yes. Did they seem like they wanted to be your personal friend? Yes. Did they try to get the crowd worked up into a frenzy by soliciting loud group responses to such questions as "Who here wants to be rich?" Yes. Were questions banned during the slide presentation because of time constraints? Yes. Did they present any independent analysis of the performance of stocks that the system rated highest? No. Were slides shown presenting testimonials from incredibly successful traders? Yes. Did the speakers mention the full price of the training, the software, and the ongoing data feeds during the presentation? No. Was there a special discounted price offered if you signed up that night? Yes.

Being a smart man, Mike began to see that he was not thinking clearly. He wanted so badly for this trading system to work that he was oblivious to the overt signs of manipulative marketing. The entire seminar was a well-crafted marketing show aimed at creating massive groupthink and impulse buying. The product just happened to be a stock trading system. It could just as easily have been oil wells in Antarctica.

As a final push that closed the door on this potentially bad decision, I asked Mike to consider why the presenters were traveling the country, staying in hotels, eating rubber chicken, and being away from their families giving these seminars. Why aren't they simply sitting in the comfort of their homes growing rich using the very system they are promoting? I watched, with no particular satisfaction, as Mike threw the brochures in the trash. I was dismayed yet again by another piece of evidence that the world of personal investing is not a friendly place for the individual investor who is desperately seeking answers.

Amy—Where Do I Start?

Amy is just entering the work force after graduating from college. She is 24 years old and starting to earn enough money to put some in an investment account. She tells me that nowhere in school, at any level, had she been taught even the basics of investing. She has seen advertisements for dozens of online brokerages, fund companies, and full service brokers and advisers. She approached me in private to discuss a question that she was embarrassed to ask in class: "Where do I start?"

This is not an embarrassing question at all. It is one that people at all stages of their investing careers should ask if they are not satisfied with the performance of their portfolios.

Amy's question illustrates very clearly two points. First, young people today are not being taught one of life's most important skills, namely how to invest so they can protect and grow the wealth they work so hard to earn. Second, when seeking to start their investing career, they see no clear path to learning how to take personal control of their investments. As a result, most people simply throw up their hands in despair and give their portfolios, and their financial futures, to a third-party adviser.

People like Amy deserve better. My comment to her was "I'm glad you are taking my class on personal investing." I knew that upon completing the class she would be far less vulnerable to the predatory practices that are so prevalent in the financial industry today. And she would have the knowledge, structure, and resources she needed to start a productive investing career with confidence.

A Troubling and Unacceptable Environment

The aforementioned questions are but a few of the hundreds I hear every year from not only my students, but also members of the National Association of Online Investors, of which I am President. I also hear similar questions in social situations and from people I interact with every day outside of my professional activities. These people include store clerks, taxi drivers, waiters/waitresses, people on the subway, and others with whom I engage in even the most casual conversations. The stories I hear are often heartbreaking. Good, honest, hardworking people have strived for years to accumulate savings. Now they need to protect their money and manage their portfolios in a manner that increases their wealth, income, and financial security. Yet the financial services industry slams them with sales pitches and commissioned advice instead of giving them education and empowering their ability to think on their own. This is a disgraceful state of affairs and a problem that must be addressed.

Let's summarize, review, and shine a bright light on the obstacles placed in front of individual investors today:

- *Adviser Bias:* There are good advisers and there are bad advisers. Very few are actually corrupt, but far too many are more concerned with making commissions than with giving good advice. You should always keep in mind that advisers make commissions when you buy what they sell, even if what they sell are not the best investments available for you. Margaret's question illustrated this problem.

- *Expert Opinions and the Financial Media:* Why do we trust people just because they are on TV, on the radio, or quoted in print? Why do we confer on them *expert* status simply because they look good and speak well? It is because we are looking for someone to tell us what to do in a world filled with noise and chaos. We too often want to believe other people so we don't have to think for ourselves. We want to be led when we find ourselves in unfamiliar territory. The fact is that the so-called experts in the financial media are typically little more than entertainers. Relying on them to guide our investing decisions is a recipe for disaster. This was my student John's problem.

- *The Investing Marketing Machine:* The marketing of dubious trading systems and stock investments is a billion-dollar industry. Incredible sums are spent getting glossy brochures into your hands and slick infomercials onto your TV screen. That's the problem. The money is spent on marketing, not on investing research or developing better education and analysis tools. The investing marketing machine is all about separating you from your money, not showing you how to accumulate more money. Always remember this: Any sales pitch that promises quick investment riches with little risk and no work is simply not true. Yet millions of individuals every year forget this bit of common sense and fall prey to the investing marketing machine. And many individual portfolios are ruined in the process. My student Mike almost fell into the jaws of this beast.

- *The Lack of Serious Investing Education:* There is a dirty little secret in the financial services industry today that is so repulsive that it is rarely even hinted at. The success of many financial professionals depends on you, the individual investor, being dumb. That may sound harsh, but as a person who has dealt with financial service organizations for decades, I know it to be true. If the public were well educated in the basics of investing, advisers would not get away with selling inferior products. An educated public would not spend an excessive amount of time looking for stock recommendations on TV and in magazines. And an educated public would certainly see the problems inherent in stock-trading systems that make investing seem as easy as lining up green arrows on a chart. There is little or no incentive, unfortunately, for financial service providers to offer you comprehensive and unbiased investing education. It is bad for business. As a result, quality investor education is virtually nonexistent. The offerings of the National Association of Online Investors, found at naoi.org, are an exception. My student Amy was a victim of the complete lack of serious investor education during her student years.

These problems are symptoms of a financial services industry that is not serving the public well. Instead of providing an education-rich environment where people are encouraged to learn how to invest and how to take personal control of their investments, the industry concentrates on making sales.

The Need for and the Nature of Change

In light of these problems it is obvious that change is needed. But what do we change?

We will not be able to change the financial services industry I have described here. It is a multibillion-dollar industry that is firmly entrenched, and tens of millions of people depend on it in its current form. All we can do about the existing problems in the world of personal investing is to recognize, understand, and avoid them. We cannot change them.

The only change that we, as individual investors, can make is in how we approach the world of investing. We can either let third parties and the financial services industry control our portfolios or we can take charge of creating and securing our own financial future, using an approach that enables us to bypass the pitfalls described earlier in this chapter.

The choice is clear. A totally new approach to personal investing must be developed. What should this approach look like? Answering this question is where we go to next.

Goals of a New Approach to Investing

The overall goal of any new approach to investing must be to enable you to take more control of your portfolio. It must empower you to become more personally involved in the investing process and to make informed investing decisions with confidence. My 10-plus years of working with the investing public have shown me that to be effective this new approach must:

- *Be Easy to Understand:* The study of investing is broad, complex, and intimidating to most people. The new approach must simplify this overwhelming field of study and focus on only the most important factors. It must be short on theory and long on pragmatic actions. It must teach fundamental investing principles in a manner that can easily be understood and in such a way as to enable you to translate this knowledge into concrete actions.
- *Be Simple to Implement:* In today's personal investing environment, when attempting to build a portfolio, you are faced with the daunting task of choosing from among thousands of stocks and mutual funds. The new approach must provide a structure and methodology that enables you to focus on a much smaller and more manageable universe of investments without sacrificing returns potential.
- *Be Easy to Monitor and Change:* The new approach must enable you to use Web-based resources that can automatically monitor your portfolio continuously and trigger alerts to you when changes are needed or attention is required. It must not require that you spend hours per day or per week sitting in front of a computer to monitor and change.
- *Enable Superior Returns without Excessive Risk:* Current portfolio-building theory maintains that higher investment returns come only at the cost of higher risks. It does not take into account the idea that personal involvement in the investing process can reduce risk. The new approach must enable you to achieve higher returns through increased involvement in the investing process instead of requiring that you accept higher risk.
- *Be Responsive to Changing Market Conditions:* Today's market environment is dynamic. A new approach to investing must give you the tools you need to recognize market catalysts when they occur and then enable you to respond quickly and easily to these changes by adjusting your portfolio to either avoid losses or to take advantage of opportunities.

- *Be Customizable:* The new approach must be usable by all investors, from novice to experienced, from conservative to aggressive, and from people who prefer to work totally on their own to people who prefer to work with an adviser. It must enable you to build a portfolio that meets your unique investment goals and investing style.

Input from hundreds of individuals tells me that these are the benefits that the public wants and needs from a new approach to personal investing. They want an approach that will simplify the entire investing process and empower them to take personal control of their portfolios. They want to decrease their dependence on third-party advisers. They want an approach that will enable them to bypass the perils and ignore the chaos of the financial industry that exists today. And they want an approach that will enable them to achieve returns that have the potential to significantly exceed market averages without subjecting them to excessive risk.

These are lofty goals. Is it possible to develop an approach that meets them? The answer, of course, is yes or this book would not exist. The PPM approach you will learn in this book is designed to meet these goals.

Enablers of the New Approach

I have set forth exceptionally high requirements and goals for a new approach to personal investing. New resources and new ways of thinking will be required to meet them. Fortunately, they exist. In this section, I describe three basic enablers of the Perfect Portfolio Methodology that I present in this book. These enablers give you just a hint of what you will learn in the chapters to come.

1. *A New Strategy and Methodology for Portfolio Design:* The problems faced by individual investors today exist in large part because the methods used for designing and building a portfolio are becoming tired and outdated. We have been faced for decades with portfolio construction methodologies that involve complicated asset allocation and diversification theories. We have been asked to sort through thousands of stocks and fund styles to develop a mix of investments that fall on a chart line called *the efficient frontier.* The complexity of this

traditional methodology drives most people directly into the open arms of the adviser community I warned you about earlier in this chapter.

The new portfolio design and construction methodology presented in this book will involve investing in total asset classes and total markets instead of individual stocks and funds. As an example, for the stock component of the Core Segment of the Perfect Portfolio (discussed in Chapters 2 and 3), we will invest in the total U.S. stock market and in the total foreign stock market. For the bond component, we will invest in the total U.S. bond market. In the Target Market Segment of the portfolio (discussed in Part II of this book) we will invest in five asset classes using only one investment for each. By using this strategy, your investment choices are reduced from thousands to a total of nine. Sound radical? Don't worry, I explain the why's and how's in the next chapter.

2. *New Investing Vehicles:* The revolutionary new approach described in this book would not have been easy to implement just a few years ago. Now it is simple because of the availability of a relatively new type of investment called the Exchange Traded Fund, or ETF. An ETF is a single investment that trades like a stock, yet holds a basket of stocks or bonds like a mutual fund. We can thus place entire asset classes and entire markets in our portfolio by purchasing one simple investment. I discuss these new investing vehicles in Chapter 2 and explain how this type of investment is a key enabler of the Perfect Portfolio approach to investing.

3. *Powerful Web Resources:* The third enabler of the new approach is a set of Web investing tools that provide powerful portfolio creation, monitoring, and trading capabilities. It should be no secret that the Web contains a wide array of investing tools. But they are so numerous that many people are overwhelmed when looking to the Web for the resources they need. I point you to the specific Web resources that enable you to implement the Perfect Portfolio Methodology in this book and there are only a few. You will build a Web-based toolkit that consists of the very best resources for finding, analyzing, selecting, and monitoring the best investments for building a Perfect Portfolio that meets your unique goals.

These tools make the Perfect Portfolio approach to investing possible and they are all free to use.

These are the basic enablers that make a new approach to investing possible. You will learn about each in detail in the chapters that follow.

Chapter Summary

I described in this chapter the woeful state of personal investing as it exists today. I have illustrated through the words of my students the incredible obstacles that individuals face as they try to protect and grow the value of their investment portfolios. After reading this chapter, I think you will agree that the world of personal investing is not a friendly place for the average person to navigate and that change is needed.

My purpose has not been to discourage you. My purpose has been simply to describe and highlight the problems that exist. It is only with this understanding that it is possible to define a new approach that enables you to avoid them.

In this chapter, I have also shown the type of change needed. An effective new approach to investing must be simple to understand, easy to implement, and it must empower you to make confident investing decisions on your own. It must free you from dependence on the massive financial services marketing/sales machine that exists today.

In the final part of this chapter, I defined what a new approach must provide to meet the needs of the investing public and I showed that new ways of thinking, new investing vehicles, and powerful Web tools exist that make this new approach possible.

My next goal is to explain this revolutionary approach to personal investing in detail and show you how to implement it. That is the purpose of the chapters that follow.

Let's get started!

2

The Perfect Portfolio Methodology

A REVOLUTIONARY APPROACH TO CREATING A SUPERIOR PORTFOLIO

During the 10-plus years of my career in investor education I have for the most part been teaching the same basic investing concepts. I have presented lessons on how to analyze stocks, the difference between fund styles, the theory behind constructing an efficient portfolio, how to manage risk, and other conventional investing topics. My students were typically very happy with my classes and have expressed a great deal of appreciation for the knowledge they gained by taking them.

Yet, I was not happy. The classes were generating knowledge and appreciation but not excitement. I could not shake the feeling that while the stock market was evolving, traditional investing *wisdom* seemed stuck. Methods and concepts of personal investing were growing tired, worn out, increasingly nonresponsive to people's needs, and out of touch with current market dynamics.

I found that teaching a topic as basic as how to analyze a stock was an excruciating ordeal. Even after using the best Web-based stock analysis resources and spending significant time on research, my students were still faced with a host of unknown factors that could not be analyzed and that could torpedo a stock's price. Also, after years of research and teaching I still couldn't provide a logical rationale for why one fund style should be selected over another. How could anyone predict whether a large-cap growth fund would be a better investment than a small-cap value fund? These are only a few examples of what I viewed as problems as I tried to teach people how to make investing decisions with confidence.

Something was missing in my teaching methodology. Something new was needed that would energize my students and motivate them to confidently take more personal control of their portfolios. With this realization, I became determined to define a better and more effective approach to personal investing, one that would provide not only knowledge, tools, and structure but also generate *excitement.*

In 2007, during the subprime mortgage credit crisis, I observed market dynamics that showed me what a new approach to personal investing should look like. I saw the possibility of a new methodology that was easier to understand, simpler to implement, and provided the potential for returns significantly higher than market averages without excessive risk.

I developed these observations and resulting ideas into a new teaching plan and called it the Perfect Portfolio Methodology, or PPM for short. The purpose of this chapter is to give you an overview of the PPM. I discuss each part of it in detail in the chapters that follow and bring each component of the PPM to life.

In this chapter I give you an overview of the PPM. But before I do, I suggest that you free your mind of preconceptions related to how investing has been taught for decades. Today's investing environment presents individual investors with challenges that were inconceivable just a few short years ago. New factors influence equity prices today that cannot be easily examined with existing analysis theories and methods. New market dynamics require updated ideas, resources, and tools to cope with them. The PPM was created to provide these updates and to bring the entire field of personal investing into the twenty-first century.

The Genesis of a New Approach

As I mentioned earlier, the behavior of the market that I observed during the credit crisis of 2007 gave me the information I needed to develop a better approach to personal investing. The following are a few of the most important dynamics that I saw.

I watched as previously safe stocks and investments, particularly those in the financial sector, became virtually worthless. I realized that there was no way I could have taught students how to predict this behavior in advance. The seeds of disaster were not evident in their financial statements, their price charts, or the comments of their chief executives.

I watched as gold predictably spiked to over $1,000 per ounce as stocks sank and the public docked their investing boats in a safe harbor. I noted an almost exact reverse correlation between the price trends of stocks and gold. When one went up, the other went down. Could I have taught students to anticipate this? Yes, I could have.

I noted the value of energy-based investments march steadily and inevitably higher. This price movement was very predictable as the price of oil skyrocketed because of a number of factors, including the increased demand for energy in developing countries as well as heightened political tensions in the world that threatened oil supplies. Students could read about these factors in any newspaper and see this coming.

I saw the value of real estate investments slump because of bad loans and the derivative investments Wall Street had created based on them. Could I have taught students how to predict this development? I had to admit that I could not. I could, however, have taught them how to limit losses through a risk management plan placed on investments in this area.

I watched as the value of commodity-based investments grew. This seemed to me to be very predictable, because commodities consist of natural resources and foodstuffs that people and businesses need to survive. Regardless of what is happening in the financial sectors, people still need to eat. It seemed logical that the demand for agricultural commodities could only continue to increase along with the prices of the securities that invest in them. Could I teach this? Yes.

In general, I saw that the change in value of certain asset types was far easier to predict than the price of any one stock or any one style of mutual fund. I could read in virtually any newspaper about the worldwide growth in population, the increasing demand for oil by developing countries, the increasing demand for corn in Latin America, and other news stories. If I could relate these publicly available news stories to the assets affected by them, then I would have a solid basis for teaching students how to make profitable investing decisions.

I also observed that the markets were being roiled by trader speculation in all areas including stocks, gold, oil, agricultural commodities, and real estate. Such speculation was influencing assets in ways that individual investors could not analyze. Could I find or develop tools to predict the effects of this factor? No, I could not. But I could show individuals how to protect themselves from speculative "bubbles" in any market by implementing an automated trading plan that, for any asset they bought, could limit losses while letting profits run. The Web tools for doing so existed and were free to use.

After observing all of these factors, it became obvious to me that a dramatically easier and more effective method for building a portfolio would be to understand the macro events and trends occurring in the market and then to invest in entire asset classes or market sectors affected by them. For example, realizing that the demand for energy can only continue to increase, investors would be smart to include an energy component in their portfolio. But instead of going through the difficult process of finding the "best" energy stock, why not just buy an investment that holds a group of stocks that represents the entire energy sector? The same logic would apply to a variety of markets and asset classes.

I saw that to develop an effective new approach to investing based on this thinking, I would first need to define a new set of asset classes, each of which would have a unique response to market and world events. I would need to carefully choose the asset types and markets to include in this new set of asset classes and limit their number to a manageable few. I would then need to identify investing vehicles that would enable investors to easily include each new asset class in their portfolios with one purchase. I would next need to define a structured process for combining the newly minted asset classes in a portfolio in a manner that enabled individuals to match their unique investing goals and investing style as well as to meet current market conditions. Finally, I would need to show people how to use Web resources to automatically monitor their portfolios to enable maximum return while guarding against excessive risk.

With this conceptual model of a new approach to personal investing in place, the genesis of the Perfect Portfolio Methodology was born. Now I needed to transform each concept into reality. That is where we go to next.

Defining New Asset Classes

Investing purists will cringe at what I am about to do. I am going to defy the conventional wisdom that has been taught for decades, and define six new asset classes. Since there is no regulatory body that governs such actions and since by doing so I will greatly enhance your ability to design a powerful and efficient portfolio, I will continue this task without fear or hesitation.

It became apparent to me that a new approach to investing had to give investors more tools to work with when building a portfolio. Current portfolio design theory gives us only three building blocks to combine in order to configure a portfolio: Cash, Stocks, and Bonds. These are the traditional asset classes, defined as such because each tends to behave differently in response to the same market events. For example, when the Federal Reserve raises interest rates, stock prices tend to go down while bond prices tend to go up. In financial and statistical terms, these asset classes are said to have a low correlation.

When you build a portfolio with assets that have low or negative correlations, you reduce its risk. Thus, a portfolio that includes stocks and bonds is less risky than one that includes only stocks. The amount of risk a portfolio has is largely determined by how many asset classes you include and the percentage of your total investment money that you allocate to each. This is called asset allocation, and studies have shown that this factor is the major determinant of how well your portfolio performs in the long term.

As I have watched market dynamics over the years, and particularly in 2007, I was struck by how limited the portfolio design theory taught today really is. As an educator teaching conventional investing theories, I was stuck using only three asset classes to show students how to build an efficient portfolio that was customized to meet their unique needs and current market conditions. More building blocks were needed to enable students to design an optimal portfolio.

My observations of the market and my research into correlation factors told me that a collection of *nine asset types* allowed for the creation of a much more efficient, powerful, and flexible portfolio. My newly defined "asset classes" for portfolio building purposes, are:

- Cash
- U.S. Stocks
- Foreign Stocks
- Bonds
- Gold

- Energy
- Agricultural Commodities
- Real Estate
- Emerging Market Stocks

Why did I pick these asset types? Because after much research, I found that each responds differently to market events. In other words, they have a low correlation with one another. Another reason that I chose these specific assets is that among them are asset types that have the potential for returns that significantly exceed stock market averages. (I discuss the rationale for these selections in more detail in Chapter 4.)

Adding these new asset classes to the portfolio design process seemed to me to be just the kick start needed to reenergize portfolio design methodology. With their use, building a dynamic and powerful portfolio became all of a sudden an activity that students could understand, do on their own, and get excited about!

As you move through this book, you will see the advantages of using these nine asset classes to create incredibly powerful and efficient portfolios that can thrive in any market condition.

Defining Portfolio Building Blocks

I have defined nine asset classes: the three traditional ones and six new ones. As I developed the conceptual model for using them, I also came to the conclusion that to build an optimal portfolio, *these asset types were all that I needed.* So as a part of the Perfect Portfolio Methodology, I defined each to be a *PPM Portfolio Building Block.* This concept is at the heart of my new approach to investing.

The point I am about to make here is extremely important. The Perfect Portfolio Methodology tells you that the decision related to the assets to include in your portfolio has been made for you. *Your unique portfolio need only include a maximum of nine investments, these being the nine asset classes listed above.*

Designing an optimal portfolio configuration is then simply a matter of allocating varying percentages of money to each of these Building Blocks! The allocation percentages for your unique portfolio will depend on a multitude of factors that you will learn in the chapters to come. And you may choose to allocate zero percentage to a particular Building Block if your analysis tells you to do so.

This is an astounding conclusion! The implications are that you will never again need to sort through thousands of stocks and funds to populate your portfolio. You will never again need to go through the excruciating process of performing due diligence on a stock or worry about a fund's style. And you can completely ignore virtually all of the stock and mutual fund advice sources I warned you about in Chapter 1!

I will expand on this revolutionary portfolio building methodology later in this chapter and throughout this book. Before doing so, however, we need to further solidify the concept of the Portfolio Building Block. There will be nine PPM building blocks, one for each of the asset classes listed earlier. Now we need to define how to buy these entire asset classes with the simple purchase of one investment for each.

Building Block Investing Vehicles

When building a portfolio using traditional methods, you are asked to choose from among thousands of stocks and mutual funds. This task is so daunting that most people give up trying to do it themselves and allow a third-party adviser to make selections for them. As I discussed in Chapter 1, this can be bad for your financial health, as too often advisers primarily recommend investments on which they earn commissions, as opposed to investments that are best for you.

This problem is solved under the PPM approach, where you need buy only nine asset types. But how do you purchase entire asset classes or markets? The answer is by using investments that own baskets of stocks or bonds that represent each entire asset class.

For example, to include a domestic stock component in your portfolio, instead of sorting through thousands of stocks and stock funds, you can just buy an investment that holds the top 3,000 stocks in the market. Instead of trying to find the best stock for adding an energy component to your portfolio, you can buy an investment that holds the top 30 energy stocks. The same thinking applies to each of the nine asset classes I have defined.

In this manner, you don't have to go through the agonizing work of analyzing individual stocks or bonds. Plus, by holding a basket of stocks, you almost completely diversify away company risk in your portfolio.

Buying baskets of securities instead of individual securities is a core principle of the PPM. Fortunately, there exist investing vehicles that enable you to do so with ease. They are discussed here.

Index Mutual Funds: Mutual funds are distinct investment types that own baskets of stocks, bonds, or a combination of both. Mutual funds can be either passively managed index funds or actively managed funds. Index funds simply hold the stocks in a defined index. There is no trading of these stocks unless the index changes and this is typically a rare occurrence. This results in fund expenses that are relatively low. Examples of index funds are those that hold all of the stocks in the S&P 500, the DOW 30, or the NASDAQ 100. There are dozens of others. A Russell 3000 index mutual fund is a good candidate for the PPM domestic stock portfolio building block as it, for all practical purposes, holds the entire stock market.

Actively Managed Mutual Funds: Actively managed funds hold stocks and/or bonds that are selected by a fund manager. These funds are characterized by more frequent trading and expenses are typically higher than those for index funds. Actively managed funds make more sense in focused areas of the market such as Emerging Market funds where a good manager can produce superior results by identifying, analyzing, and trading stocks as conditions warrant.

Exchange Traded Funds: ETFs are a relatively new type of investing vehicle and one that you should be aware of and understand completely. Like traditional mutual funds, they enable you to buy a basket of stocks or bonds with one purchase. Unlike traditional mutual funds, however, you can trade them just like stocks. Regular stock trading commissions apply when you buy or sell ETFs. A little more explanation is needed for this type of investment.

There are a growing number of financial companies today that create and manage ETFs, and each company refers to its ETFs by different names. Giant asset manager Barclays Global Investors creates ETFs called iShares, Vanguard offers VIPERS, Merrill Lynch offers HOLDRs, Standard & Poor's offers SPDRs (referred to as *spiders*), and there are others. Whatever they are called, they are all ETFs as defined by the SEC, and they trade in a similar manner.

Creators of ETFs use indexes to define the objective of each ETF just as creators of index mutual funds do. There are ETFs that track just about all index categories from broad-based indexes such as the S&P 500 to more narrowly focused indexes such as a sector index—for example, an Energy Sector ETF—or a single country—for example, a Japan ETF. Also, like mutual funds, ETFs have an expense component that is charged against fund returns. Typically for ETFs, this management expense is significantly lower than for actively managed funds and often even lower than fees charged by traditional index funds.

You can learn more about ETFs by logging in to the online supplement to this book and clicking *Links by Chapter* and then on *Chapter 2* on the Table of Contents Web page.

So, we now have defined nine Portfolio Building Blocks and we have a choice of three investing vehicles for including each in our portfolio. But which investing vehicle is the best for each Building Block?

Choosing the Best Investing Vehicle

As we examine each Portfolio Building Block in more detail in upcoming chapters, we will consider for each whether an index fund, an ETF, or an actively managed fund is the better investment vehicle. To make this decision for each Building Block we will evaluate each investment vehicle type and look at historical returns, risk levels, expenses, and ease of trading. A comparison of these factors will reveal to us the best vehicle to use for the purpose of including that asset class in the portfolio.

Thus, as you build your own unique Perfect Portfolio, you will not only decide which asset classes to buy, but you will also determine for each the best investing vehicle for doing so.

Defining a Portfolio Structure

I have presented the Portfolio Building Block concept. The next step is to define a logical structure for combining these building blocks in an efficient and effective manner. I explain in this section the design framework of the PPM-based portfolio.

We start this process with a significant advantage provided by the PPM. Whereas traditional portfolio theory limits investors to only three asset classes, the PPM gives us nine. We now have a great deal more flexibility to design a portfolio that meets a full range of investing styles and market conditions. We can design a portfolio that is aggressive, conservative, or middle of the road. We can build a portfolio that thrives in a bull market, a bear market, or a neutral market.

Key to the design flexibility of the PPM is putting into place a portfolio framework that divides the portfolio into multiple segments and enables you to define the portfolio's characteristics by altering the percentage of your investment money that you allocate to each. I discuss the concept of portfolio segments next.

Portfolio Segmentation

My research has shown that the optimal way to approach portfolio design begins with dividing the portfolio into two high-level segments. These are the Core Segment and the Target Market Segment. Each has a specific purpose in the PPM portfolio structure. Figure 2.1 presents a simple chart that shows the first-tier division of the PPM portfolio framework.

The Core Segment.   The Core segment will be the foundation of the portfolio. This is essentially the portfolio you would design using today's traditional methodologies. It contains the following building blocks:

- *Cash*—as represented by a Money Market Fund
- *Bonds*—as represented by a Total Bond Market index fund or ETF

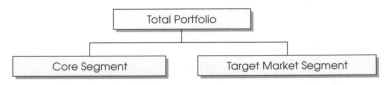

Figure 2.1   The Perfect Portfolio Segments

- *U.S. Stocks*—as represented by a Total U.S. Stock Market index fund or ETF
- *Foreign Stocks*—as represented by a Total Foreign Stock Market index fund or ETF

The Core Segment is the portion of the portfolio that you buy and hold. The portfolio building blocks placed here are broad-based collections of stocks and bonds along with cash. Each noncash investment you place in the Core Segment will hold a basket of hundreds or even thousands of stocks or bonds, and because of this diversity of holdings, the risk profile of each building block will be low.

The investment vehicles used here will typically be index funds or ETFs that require no active management, so expenses will be low. The Core Segment will also require little active monitoring on your part because you will not trade these investments frequently. Remember, these are buy-and-hold investments. In exchange for the lower risk and expenses, however, you will not expect returns that significantly exceed market averages.

The risk-reward profile of the Core can be altered by changing the allocations of money to each of the four Core Building Blocks. Higher returns potential is achieved by allocating more money to the two stock building blocks. This also increases the Core Segment risk. The factors that will determine your allocations to each of the Core Building Blocks will include your risk tolerance, your time horizon, and your view of current market conditions.

You will learn in Chapter 3 how to select specific investments for each of the Building Blocks in the Core Segment and a methodology of assigning allocations of money to each.

The Target Market Segment.   The Target Market Segment makes the PPM portfolio uniquely powerful. This is the segment that enables you to supercharge your portfolio and strive for returns that can significantly exceed market averages without exposing it to excessive risk. The Target Market Segment contains these portfolio building blocks:

- *Gold*—as represented by a gold mutual fund or ETF
- *Energy*—as represented by an energy mutual fund or ETF
- *Agricultural Commodities*—as represented by a commodities mutual fund or ETF

- *Real Estate*—as represented by a real estate mutual fund or ETF
- *Emerging Markets*—as represented by an emerging markets mutual fund or ETF

Securities held in the Target Market Segment will *not* be buy-and-hold investments. They will, instead, be buy-and-sell investments. They will require more active monitoring and a more in-depth knowledge of the factors that can affect their prices. But the reward for this additional involvement in the investing process is the potential for much higher returns.

Major factors that will determine the allocation of your money among these assets will be your view of current economic and market conditions, the current price trends of each asset, and your willingness to become actively involved in the investing process. I describe more fully in Part II of this book how to construct and manage this Segment of the Perfect Portfolio.

The Total Perfect Portfolio Design.   Figure 2.2 is a diagram that shows the structure of the total Perfect Portfolio. Allocations of your investing monies occur at two levels. First, you will allocate money between the Core Segment and the Target Market Segment. Then, you will make second-level allocations among the various Asset Building Blocks within each segment.

As mentioned earlier, Chapter 3 discusses how to build the Core Segment. Part II of this book, consisting of Chapters 6 through 9, discusses how to build your Target Market Segment. Chapter 10 discusses how to bring these two Segments together to form a total Perfect

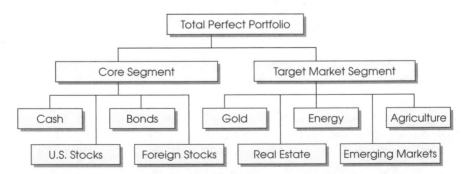

Figure 2.2   The Total Perfect Portfolio Design

Portfolio that is designed to meet your unique needs and current market conditions.

Understanding Your Investing Profile

With the portfolio building blocks and the portfolio structure in place, you now have the tools to design a comprehensive and powerful portfolio. By adjusting the allocations of investment monies to the various Segments and Building Blocks, you have the flexibility to build a portfolio to meet an almost infinite number of investing profiles. To grasp this point more fully, it is important to understand what I mean by *investing profile.*

When you design a portfolio, you will take into consideration a number of factors that make up your unique investing profile. Your profile takes into consideration elements of your investing style (that is, whether you are conservative, moderate, or aggressive) and your perception of external factors that affect the price of assets (that is, whether you think the market is bearish, bullish, or neutral). Here are the three elements I have defined as making up your unique investing profile.

1. *Your Risk-Return Level:* Every investor needs to have investing goals, and inherent in these goals is a portfolio return rate required to meet them. Since a core principle of investing is that higher return rates are associated with higher risk levels, this element of an investing profile can be labeled as your risk-return level. It is an important element in your portfolio design. I give you the tools to define your risk-return level in Chapter 10.
2. *Your Involvement Level:* This factor relates to your willingness to devote time and effort to the investing process. Nowhere in traditional portfolio development theory is this factor considered. In today's investing environment, you have access to incredible Web-based resources that can empower you to increase the returns or lower the risk of your portfolio if you take the time to become involved in the investing process. Your willingness to do so needs to be considered. Your involvement level will therefore affect how you design your portfolio.
3. *Your View of Economic and Market Factors:* An effective portfolio design will take into account current economic and market factors that can affect the price of your investments. Examples

of such factors are interest rates, the price of oil, political instability in the world, and other macro factors. Your assessment of these market catalysts is part of your investing profile and will affect how you configure your portfolio.

The PPM approach gives you the tools you need to configure a portfolio that is tuned to match your unique investing profile. Think of the portfolio structure as containing multiple dials, just like radio knobs that enable you to adjust its frequency and volume. The PPM structure enables you to turn the dials to find the station that matches your profile and the volume with which you are comfortable. You adjust these dials through allocation of investment monies to the various Segments and Building Blocks in the portfolio. I discuss the portfolio configuration dials next.

Configuring the Portfolio to Meet Your Profile

Let's look at the effects of turning the various allocation dials in order to configure a portfolio that matches your investing profile. I discuss this topic in much greater detail in Chapter 10, after you have learned more about each Segment and each Building Block. For now, a simple overview will be sufficient to show you the power of this feature.

Segment Allocation: Segment allocation is the portfolio's top-level tuning dial. Higher allocations of investment money to the Core Segment reduce portfolio risk, lower potential portfolio returns, and lessen the personal involvement required. Higher allocations to the Target Market Segment increase all of these factors. The following list is an example of the percentage of assets that you might allocate to each Segment based on the three investing styles—aggressive, moderate, and conservative. (I discuss Segment allocation in more detail in Chapter 10, where we complete the design of a sample Perfect Portfolio.)

Investing Style	Core Segment	Target Market Segment
Aggressive	30%	70%
Moderate	60%	40%
Conservative	80%	20%

For finer tuning of the portfolio's risk-return profile, you will adjust allocations to the portfolio Building Blocks within each Segment as discussed next.

Allocations within the Core Segment. As stated previously, the choices you have for money allocation in the Core Segment are: Cash, Bonds, U.S. Stocks, and Foreign Stocks. Higher allocations to the stock-related building blocks increase the risk-return characteristics of the Segment. The degree to which this affects the risk-return profile of the entire portfolio depends on how much of your total investment money you have allocated to the Core Segment.

The following list is an example of the percentage of assets that you might allocate within the Core Segment based on the aggressive, moderate, and conservative investing styles. (I discuss the construction of your Core Segment in more detail in Chapter 3.)

Investing Style	Cash	Bonds	Stocks (domestic and foreign)
Aggressive	5%	10%	85%
Moderate	5%	30%	65%
Conservative	10%	45%	45%

Allocations within the Target Market Segment: The third portfolio tuning dial is the allocation of money among the asset types in the Target Market Segment. You will determine allocations here based on your view of the economy, the market, and current price trends for each asset type. For example, if you believe the stock market is headed for a downturn, you may wish to increase your allocation to Gold. If you believe that interest rates are moving down, then you may wish to increase your allocation to Real Estate. If you believe the market is neutral, you may wish to increase your allocation to Agricultural Commodities.

The assets in the Target Market Sector allow you to configure your portfolio to take advantage of current economic and market factors. And there may be times when you assign a zero percentage allocation to any one Target Market building block. It is important to understand that the PPM does not require that you own each Portfolio Building Block in your portfolio at all times.

As with the Core Segment, the extent to which the asset allocations in this Segment affect the profile of the entire portfolio will depend on the amount of total investment money you allocate to this Segment. (I discuss the Target Market Segment in greater depth in the chapters of Part II of this book.)

Portfolio Configuration through Allocation

You can see the tremendous flexibility that the PPM gives you for configuring a portfolio that meets your specific investing profile and market outlook. You change the profile of the portfolio not by searching through thousands of stocks and funds but rather by changing money allocation percentages to the two Segments and to the nine PPM Building Blocks. I provided in the previous section just a quick overview of the portfolio configuration concept. You will learn how to translate these concepts into concrete actions as you move through this book.

Meeting Our Goals for a New Approach

In describing the Perfect Portfolio Methodology in this chapter, I have set forth a revolutionary approach to investing. It is intended to enable you to regain control of your portfolio amid the chaos that reigns in the world of personal investing today.

Does the Perfect Portfolio Methodology meet this goal? I discussed in Chapter 1 that the PPM was developed on the basis of interviews and market surveys that showed me what the public wanted and needed in a new approach to investing. I repeat this list of requirements here and discuss how each has been met by the new PPM approach laid out in this chapter.

- *It Must Be Easy to Understand:* The PPM has only nine investment building blocks, each related to a specific and unique asset class. The chapters that follow in this book will teach you about these asset classes in a very straightforward and understandable manner. The discussion of each will be short on theory and long on practical action. I do not bog down the discussion with complex charts and tables of statistics. I believe that when you complete this book you will agree that the ease-of-understanding requirement has been met.

- *It Must Be Simple to Implement and Change:* As stated earlier, the PPM portfolio will own only nine investments. There is no need to search through thousands of stocks and funds to build your portfolio. You simply need to find the single best investment that represents each Portfolio Building Block and buy it. Changes to the portfolio profile come in the form of modifying allocations to each Segment and to each Building Block. Making changes to the portfolio using this methodology could not be simpler or easier to implement.

- *It Must Be Easy to Monitor:* In Part II of this book, I discuss powerful Web resources that can automatically monitor your total portfolio and each investment in it. These tools are capable of making automated trades or sending you e-mail alerts when action is required. Upon receipt of such an alert, you can do some simple research and make changes, if necessary, by altering allocations to your Portfolio Building Blocks. The PPM does not require you to spend hours per day or week sitting in front of your computer watching your investments. Your attention is only required when your automated monitoring system sends you an alert. And when change is needed, the process of making it is extremely simple.

- *It Must Enable Superior Returns without Excessive Risk:* The PPM enables you to build a portfolio with any risk-return profile that you desire. The most direct way to increase potential returns is by allocating more money to the Target Market Segment. This segment contains five investment types, each having the potential for incredible returns. But along with higher returns come higher risks. So, in upcoming chapters, I show you how to control risk through the implementation of an automated trading plan. The PPM thus gives you the potential for returns that are significantly higher than market averages and the tools to control the related risk so that it does not exceed your risk tolerance level.

- *It Must Be Responsive to Changing Market Conditions:* When your economic outlook and view of the market changes, you can change the profile of your portfolio to match it by simply adjusting allocations of money between the two Segments and among the Portfolio Building Blocks. Should your sense of the market turn bearish, you may wish to increase your allocation to the Gold Building Block. If you are more bullish, you can easily respond by increasing your allocation to Real Estate or Stocks. The PPM portfolio is remarkably easy to adjust in response to market catalysts and your overall sense of the market.

- *It Must Be Customizable for Individual Investing Styles:* You are unique in regard to your financial profile, risk tolerance, willingness to become involved in the investing process, and your market outlook. The PPM enables you to very easily design a portfolio that takes all of these factors into account. The dials that you will use to tune your portfolio to meet any investing profile will be allocations to the different portfolio components discussed earlier.

It seems at first glance that the Perfect Portfolio Methodology meets the goals that the public and I have set for a new approach to investing. I cannot expect you to completely agree with this conclusion at this point. After all, you have just learned the basic concepts of the PPM. The remaining chapters of this book will put flesh on the bones of the approach presented here. After completing these chapters you can decide if the PPM meets the lofty goals I have set for a superior approach to personal investing.

Chapter Summary

I discussed in this chapter a revolutionary approach to investing. It includes the definition of two Portfolio Segments and nine Portfolio Building Blocks, each related to a unique asset type. It also includes a structured process for combining these Building Blocks to create an optimal portfolio for your unique investing profile. The characteristics of the portfolio are changed by altering allocations of money between the Portfolio Segments and among the Building Blocks within each Segment. I call this approach the Perfect Portfolio Methodology, or PPM for short.

I have presented the benefits of the PPM. Among the most dramatic benefits is that you need only include in your portfolio a maximum of nine investments. Using the PPM you do not have to sort through thousands of stocks and funds to find the best investments.

The only analysis and investigation required is directed at finding the best specific investment to represent each of the nine Portfolio Building Blocks. This feature alone eliminates the chaos that has created the ugly personal investing scenarios I described in Chapter 1. Using the PPM, you can ignore all of the marketing hype and avoid all of the adviser bias related to stock and fund selection. This is huge!

But what are you giving up in exchange for this convenience? Virtually nothing. In fact, with the PPM, you significantly increase returns potential, dramatically lower risk factors, and gain the flexibility to easily design a portfolio that meets a full range of investing styles and market conditions. These benefits will become clear as you read the chapters that follow.

My purpose in this chapter has been only to present the basic concepts of the PPM. There is much work yet to be done. You still need to find the best investment for each Portfolio Building Block. You need more knowledge related to each of the nine asset types that make up these Building Blocks. You also need to understand in greater detail the factors to consider when making your portfolio allocation decisions. You will learn all of this in chapters to come.

Is the PPM really a superior approach to investing when compared to the traditional concepts taught today? My experience in the classroom tells me that it is, but it will be up to you to decide. In the classes I teach, we have built test portfolios using the PPM. In each case, these portfolios have performed significantly better than stock market averages and with lower risk. In addition, the PPM concepts are so simple to understand and easy to implement that students are motivated and willing to become more involved in the investing process.

To me, the greatest satisfaction of teaching the Perfect Portfolio Methodology is seeing the enthusiasm it generates. I am confident that this enthusiasm will build for you as well as you progress through the chapters that follow.

CHAPTER 3

Building Your Portfolio's Core Segment
ESTABLISHING A FIRM FOUNDATION

I have defined two Portfolio Segments using the Perfect Portfolio Methodology: a Core Segment and a Target Market Segment. In this chapter, we concentrate on the Core Segment. In Chapter 2, you learned that this segment contains the traditional asset classes of Cash, Stocks (U.S. and Foreign), and Bonds. In the discussion that follows you will learn how to identify, analyze, and select the most promising specific investments for each. Part II of this book discusses finding specific investments for the Target Market Segment.

The Purpose of the Core Segment

Imagine your Perfect Portfolio as a sleek sailing ship. The Core Segment is like the ship's ballast, keeping it stable and safe in choppy waters. The Target Market Segment can be seen as your ship's sails that determine its speed and performance. You configure the power and stability of your unique portfolio ship design by allocating money between these two Segments. The more you allocate to the Core, the more stable your ship will be, but it will be slower. If you want more speed and are willing to spend more time at the helm, then you will allocate more money to your Target Market Segment.

As you will learn in this chapter, building a Core Segment is not complicated. You will have the knowledge and tools you need to do so by the end of this one chapter. The Target Market Segment will take a little more work because it contains more volatile, and more interesting, investments. Discussing how to build the Target Market Segment will take the next six chapters.

The fact that there are fewer pages dedicated to the Core Segment does not mean that it is less important. The Core Segment must be carefully designed to build a firm foundation for your portfolio. Only with this Segment properly constructed will you be free to strive for higher returns in the Target Market Segment.

The overall influence that your Core Segment will have on your total portfolio's risk-return profile will depend on how much money you allocate to the Core as opposed to the Target Market Segment. Using Segment allocations to design a total Perfect Portfolio that meets your unique needs is discussed in Chapter 10.

Characteristics of the Core Segment

As discussed in Chapter 2, the Core Segment is the buy-and-hold portion of your portfolio. It will contain the four building blocks shown in Figure 3.1.

The Perfect Portfolio Methodology (PPM) suggests that even though you will periodically monitor their performance, you will not actively trade the investments in this Segment. You simply select the best investment for each Building Block, determine an allocation of money to each that fits your unique investing profile, and then leave these investments alone.

Because of the buy-and-hold nature of the Core Segment, we will search for investments that have the following characteristics:

- Each will represent an entire asset class by owning a basket of related securities

Figure 3.1   The Core Portfolio Segment

- Each will be extremely well diversified, and therefore less volatile
- Each will require little personal attention to monitor on an ongoing basis
- Emphasis will be placed on keeping expenses to a minimum for each investment selected

Remember, this is the ballast of your ship that will keep it steady in choppy waters. You will not trade these investments in response to temporary market events or economic cycles. Your portfolio time horizon should hopefully be many years so that even though the value of the Core investments may go up and down in the short term, the long-term trend for the entire Segment will be steadily upward. (Note that if your portfolio time horizon is relatively short, you will need to monitor these investments more closely. Doing so is a topic discussed in Chapters 11 and 12.)

The Core Segment Building Blocks

As discussed in Chapter 2, the investments that the PPM suggests you hold in the Core are:

- Cash
- Bonds
- U.S. Stocks
- Foreign Stocks

These are the traditional asset classes with a twist. Conventional portfolio construction theory does not define Foreign Stocks as a separate asset class. Times have changed and I believe that the characteristics of non-U.S. stocks along with recent performance history are sufficiently different to merit their classification as a unique type of asset. Therefore, for the purpose of the PPM portfolio design process, I am defining Foreign Stocks as a separate asset class and a separate portfolio Building Block.

Why did I define these asset types as Core Building Blocks? Because they enable you to place in your portfolio the entire stock market, the entire bond market, and a repository for cash. These building blocks combined represent the widest range of investments possible and each asset type is sufficiently different from the

Table 3.1   Core Building Block Correlations

Core Asset Type	U.S. Stocks	Foreign Stocks	Bonds
U.S. Stocks	1	.74	–.17
Foreign Stocks	.74	1	–.16
Bonds	–.17	–.16	1.

others to add valuable diversity to the portfolio. A key tenet of good portfolio design is to combine assets that have negative, or low, correlations. You will remember from Chapter 2 that correlation is a measure of how assets move in response to the same market events. Assets that move in the same direction are positively correlated and those that move in different directions are negatively correlated. Assets that move exactly the same have a correlation of 1.0 and those that move exactly opposite have a correlation of –1.0.

I have therefore selected these four Building Blocks to be in the Core Segment on the basis of their returns potential, their risk profile, and their correlation factors. Table 3.1 shows the correlations between each of the noncash assets in the Core Segment as of this writing.

You can see that the greatest diversity is added to the portfolio by the combination of stocks and bonds. These are totally different asset types and history has shown that when stocks move up, bonds tend to move down, and the reverse is also true. You can also see that by splitting the stock asset into U.S. and foreign components, additional diversity is achieved.

The Core Investing Vehicles

The PPM uses index vehicles for each Core Portfolio Building Block. As mentioned in Chapter 2, these will either be index mutual funds or Exchange Traded Funds (ETFs). I have selected these vehicles for several reasons. First, in the Core Segment we want low volatility and thus low risk investments. We can get the desired low volatility by selecting very broad-based funds. For example, instead of looking for a stock fund having a specific style such as large-cap value or small-cap growth, we want to own all stock styles in the market. Investors and most fund managers are just not smart enough to predict which stock or fund styles will perform better in the long term. So for U.S. stocks, we will look for an investment that buys a group of stocks that represents the entire stock market. We will apply the same logic to the Foreign Stock and Bond Building Blocks.

Another advantage of broad-based index funds or ETFs is that the expenses are low. As discussed in Chapter 2, index investments are passively managed and there is no need to pay a manager to make decisions. As a result, index fund expenses will be lower. Also, since the investments held by an index fund are infrequently traded, they produce very few taxable events. Low expenses and low exposure to capital gains taxes are key requirements of investments in the Core Segment that are intended to be held for years.

The Core Investment Selection Process

Enough with theory! It is now time to select investments for the Core Segment of a sample portfolio that I will build in this book. I discuss in this section the steps in the selection process. Then I illustrate each step in the process by selecting specific investments.

Steps for selecting Core Segment investments:

1. *Identify Investment Candidates:* We will identify for each of the four Core Segment Building Blocks multiple index fund or ETF candidates. Web resources that I specify will be used for this purpose.

2. *Collect Relevant Data:* We will then use Web resources to collect relevant data for each of the candidates. A worksheet will be used to record, analyze, and compare the following data:
   - *Returns.* We will collect and record historical returns data for each candidate for the periods of one year, three years, and five years. The numbers collected will be the average return per year for those time periods.
   - *Risk.* We will use Standard Deviation to measure the risk of an investment. This is a measure of how volatile the stock is; the higher this number, the riskier the investment. To learn more about Standard Deviation, go to the online supplement to this book, log in, click on *Links by Chapter* and then on *Chapter 3.*
   - *Expense Ratio.* For investments that you buy and hold, yearly management fees and related expenses can add up, so we must take them into consideration. This is the third and final data point we will collect for evaluating our investment candidates.

3. *Compare the Data and Select an Investment:* We will use a data collection worksheet to select one specific investment that best meets our requirements for each Core Building Block.
4. *Allocate Percentages:* After selecting specific investments, we will then assign a percentage allocation to each and determine an expected return for the Core Segment that we have designed.

The process is simple and effective. Building the Core Segment will not be as complex as building the Target Market Segment. This is why there is only one chapter devoted to the Core Segment and six devoted to the Target Market Segment. As mentioned earlier in the chapter, this does not mean that the Core is less important. It only means that the Core investments are easier to identify, analyze, and select. One of the reasons that the selection process is relatively simple is that we will use free Web resources to quickly and efficiently find investment candidates and collect the data required to analyze them. I discuss these resources next.

Core Segment Online Resources

I list in this section the Web sites and resources that we will use for finding and evaluating Core Segment Building Block investment candidates. These are not the only sites that can be used; they are simply ones that do the job simply, effectively, and with no charge. If any of these sites do not work exactly as described, go to the online supplement to this book, log in, and click on *Links by Chapter.* Then click on *Chapter 3* to find updated Web links and navigation descriptions. Here are the resources we will use:

- *The Core Building Block Data Collection Worksheet:* We will use this worksheet to record data for each Core Building Block candidate we identify for evaluation. To access it, go to the online supplement, log in, click *Links by Chapter,* and then on *Chapter 3* to find a link to this worksheet. It is presented in PDF format. Print at least four copies, one for each Core Building Block, or you can easily create this worksheet on your own.
- *Finding Index Funds Candidates:* We will use the site at finance .yahoo.com/funds to look for fund candidates in the Vanguard and Fidelity fund families. We only use these companies as

examples; their use is not meant as a recommendation by the author. There are dozens of other fund families that you may wish to consider. If you already work with a fund family, include an investment from it for each Core Building Block as one candidate for comparison purposes.

To find the index funds candidates on the finance.yahoo .com/funds site, first locate the menu on the left side of the page and look for *Funds by Family.* Click on this entry and you will be presented with an alphabetical list of fund families. To find fund candidates for our sample Core Segment, we will click on the Fidelity and Vanguard families and browse. Further details of the use of this site will be discussed as we look at each Building Block in the discussion that follows.

- *Finding Exchange Traded Fund Candidates:* For identifying ETF investment candidates, we will use Barclay's iShares and the site at ishares.com. We use this company because they offer ETFs for a full range of indexes. They also have an excellent Web site that allows us to search easily for ETFs that match our needs. There are also other companies that offer ETFs that you may wish to consider.

  On the iShares site, in the left column of the home page, you will find a menu labeled *iShares Quick Finder.* This is the resource we will use to find ETF candidates for our sample Core Segment Building Blocks. Its further use will be described when I discuss each Building Block in the following discussion.

- *The Data Collection Web Site:* We will use the site at finance .yahoo.com to collect the data needed to fill in the Core Building Block Data Collection Worksheet for each of our investment candidates. On the home page of this site, enter the fund or ETF symbol in the box labeled *Get Quote.* You will see a menu on the left side of the resulting page. Click on *Performance* to find returns data and then click on *Risk* to find the three-year Standard Deviation data. To find the *Total Expense Ratio* of the fund, click on *Profile* and scroll down the right side of the page to the *Expenses and Fees* box, where you will see the total expenses ratio at the top of the list. Remember, if this navigation changes, look in the online supplement for updates.

With these resources in place, I am now ready to illustrate the Core Segment Building Block selection process in the next four sections of this chapter, one for each asset type. Please note that the specific investments used in the following discussions are for illustration purposes only and do *not* constitute a recommendation of any fund company or investment by the author. Also be aware that the numbers displayed here are those that exist as of the time this chapter was written. They will be different by the time you read this. You are given the opportunity to collect current data and complete your own worksheets later in this chapter.

The Cash Building Block

A cash-based asset deserves a place in all portfolios. It is not a particularly good investment when measured by rate of return, and cash quite often actually loses value if the rate of inflation is higher than the rate of return on your cash deposits. But cash has its virtues. First, it is safe. It is highly unlikely that you will lose money on a cash investment regardless of the state of the market. Second, a cash component in the portfolio serves as a temporary holding area for money that is awaiting allocation to other investments.

Among the most popular choices for a cash investment include Money Market Funds, Money Market Accounts, and Certificates of Deposit. You can find a definition of each of these investment types along with current return rates on the excellent site bankrate.com. I suggest that you go there and browse the site to learn more about money deposits and accounts.

For our sample Core Segment, we will look for a Money Market Fund. These are funds that hold short-term (less than one year) securities representing high quality liquid debt and monetary instruments. The price of one share is always one dollar. Since all Money Market Funds are basically alike, it makes little sense to shop for the best. I suggest that you simply use as your Cash Building Block a money fund offered by the fund family you use to purchase your Bond and Stock Core Building Blocks. As we move through the process of selecting bond and stock index funds, a goal will be to try to find one fund family such as Fidelity, Vanguard, or another from which we can buy all of our Core funds. Selecting a Money Market Fund from the same family will then enable us to efficiently move money between Cash and Stock and Bond fund investments.

Table 3.2   Money Market Fund Worksheet

| Company | Symbol | Returns | | | Risk: Std. Dev. | Expense Ratio |
		1-year	3-year	5-year		
Vanguard	VMMXX	4.83%	4.48%	3.13%	N/A	.24%
Fidelity	SPRXX	4.60%	4.43%	3.11%	N/A	.42%

Note that a risk measure is not relevant for a Money Market Fund.

Table 3.2 shows the Core Building Block Worksheet for Money Market Funds offered by Vanguard and Fidelity. These are the fund families I am using in this sample selection process. The table shows the symbol for a fund offered by each family along with the relevant data. An Exchange Traded Fund is not a good candidate for the Cash component because you will incur a broker trading fee each time you add or withdraw money from this type of investment. You will not incur fees by buying or selling shares of a Money Market fund.

You can see that there is little difference in the returns of these funds, as they each hold only short-term government securities. The main difference is that the Fidelity fund has an expense fee that is almost double that of the Vanguard fund. We will not select the Money Market Fund, however, on the basis of these data. As mentioned before, we will strive to use one fund family to buy all of our Core Segment Building Blocks. We will then simply select the Money Market Fund offered by that family.

The Bond Building Block

The next task is to select a Bond Core Building Block. You have seen that Bonds offer valuable diversity to a portfolio by being negatively correlated with stocks. Bonds deserve a place in the Core Segment of all portfolios. The task currently at hand is finding and evaluating bond fund candidates. If you are working with an adviser or trying to find the best bond investment on your own, you will be faced with a dizzying array of choices. There are, in fact, nine bond fund styles, each related to a combination of bond maturity and credit rating. Thus, for example, there is a style related to long-term investment grade bonds, there is a style related to mid-term junk bonds, and so on. It is extremely difficult to predict which bond style will perform best. So, here we will forget about sorting through bond styles and just buy the entire bond market for our Core Bond Building Block.

To accomplish this task, we first go to the Web and look for *Total Bond* funds offered by our example families and also look for a total bond market ETF. The following are the investments I will use as candidates for my sample Core Segment. I found these investments using the Web resources discussed earlier in this chapter.

- *Vanguard Total Bond (VBMFX):* I found this fund by browsing the list of Vanguard funds on the finance.yahoo.com/funds site. This investment seeks to track the performance of a broad, market-weighted bond index. It invests at least 80 percent of its assets in bonds held in the index. The fund maintains a dollar-weighted average maturity consistent with that of the index, ranging between 5 and 10 years.
- *Fidelity Total Bond (FTBFX):* I found this fund by browsing the list of Fidelity funds found on the finance.yahoo.com/funds site. This investment seeks a high level of current income. The fund normally invests at least 80 percent of its assets in debt securities of all types and repurchase agreements for those securities. Fidelity allocates the fund's assets across investment-grade, high-yield, and emerging-market debt securities.
- *iShares Total Bond ETF (AGG):* To find a bond-related ETF, I used the iShares Web site described earlier. On this site, I placed my cursor over the *Fixed Income* menu item on the left side of the page. In the resulting dropdown menu, I placed the cursor over *Broad Market* and found this ETF. It seeks investment results that correspond to the price and yield performance, before fees and expenses, of the total United States investment grade bond market as defined by the Lehman Brothers U.S. Aggregate Index. The fund invests approximately 90 percent of its assets in the bonds represented in the underlying index and in securities that provide substantially similar exposure to securities in the underlying index.

Data Collection

Using the process and Web site previously defined in this chapter, I next collect relevant data for evaluation and comparison. Table 3.3 shows

Table 3.3   Bond Fund Worksheet

Company	Symbol	Returns			Risk: Std. Dev.	Expense Ratio
		1-year	3-year	5-year		
Vanguard Total Bond	VBMFX	7.70%	5.43%	4.53%	2.90%	.19%
Fidelity Total Bond	FTBFX	3.61%	4.49%	4.37%	2.41%	.45%
iShares ETF Total Bond	AGG	7.58%	5.34%	N/A	2.81%	.20%

Note that the ETF is too new to have a 5-year return.

returns, risk, and management fees for each of my bond candidates as of the middle of 2008.

Data Analysis and Investment Selection

The Vanguard fund seems to be better in all aspects with the exception that the Standard Deviation number tells us that it is a little riskier than either the Fidelity fund or the ETF. The Fidelity fund Expense Ratio is significantly higher than Vanguard's and this is a decidedly negative factor.

I will select the Vanguard Bond fund on the basis of this data. I will wait, however, until I review the stock funds before making a final decision. Again, my preference is to buy all of the Core Funds from the same fund company. If I find that Fidelity has better U.S. and Foreign Stock funds, then I may simply decide to buy the Bond fund from them as well. The difference in performance between bond funds is not sufficiently significant to cause me to open a separate brokerage account for just this one purchase.

The U.S. Stock Building Block

Next up is selecting the U.S. Stock Core Building Block. As with bonds, most advisers will give you choices of funds that relate to nine stock styles that relate to a combination of investment goal—value, blend, growth—and company size—small-cap, mid-cap, and large-cap. Thus, funds exist with styles such as small-cap growth, large-cap value, and so on. Sorting through stock fund styles to find the best is virtually impossible. So again, we will bypass this madness and simply look for a Total U.S. Stock Market fund.

Using our previously defined data collection process and the recommended Web sites, I find the following:

- *Vanguard Total U.S. Stock (VTSMX):* This investment seeks to track the performance of a benchmark index that measures the investment return of the overall stock market. The fund employs a passive management strategy designed to track the performance of the MSCI U.S. Broad Market Index, which consists of all the U.S. common stocks traded regularly on the NYSE, AMEX, and OTC markets. It typically invests substantially all of its assets in the 1,300 largest stocks in its target index, thus covering nearly 95 percent of the Index's total market capitalization.
- *Fidelity Total U.S. Stock (FSTMX):* This investment seeks to match the total return of the Wilshire 5000 Index. The fund normally invests at least 80 percent of assets in common stocks that are in this Index. It includes all of the stocks in the S&P 500 Index, excluding foreign securities. The adviser uses sampling techniques to replicate the returns of the Index while investing in a smaller number of securities.
- *iShares Russell 3000 Index ETF (IWV):* On the iShares Web site, I placed my cursor over *Market Cap* in the menu on the left side of the home page and then in the submenu, I placed it over *Broad U.S. Market.* I then scanned the resulting list to find this ETF. This investment seeks results that correspond generally to the price and yield performance of the Russell 3000 Index. The fund invests at least 90 percent of its assets in the securities of the underlying index. It uses a replication strategy to track the Russell 3000 Index, which measures the performance of the broad U.S. equity market. The fund invests in the largest capitalization-weighted public companies domiciled in the United States and its territories.

You can see from these investment choices that there are multiple ways of defining the total U.S. stock market. It will be interesting to see whether performance and risk differ according to how the fund type is defined. That is where we go to next.

Data Collection

Table 3.4 shows the comparison data for each of the fund candidates I have selected. The numbers are current as of the middle of

Table 3.4 U.S. Stock Worksheet

| Company | Symbol | Returns | | | Risk: Std. | Expense |
		1-year	3-year	5-year	Dev.	Ratio
Vanguard	VTSMX	–5.79%	6.19%	12.27%	9.10%	.15%
Fidelity	FSTMX	–5.78%	6.36%	12.33%	9.10%	.10%
iShares ETF	IWV	–6.25%	5.91%	11.85%	9.06%	.20%

2008. You will have the opportunity to collect current data later in this chapter.

Data Analysis and Fund Selection

With such broad market funds, each of which holds thousands of stocks, it is not surprising to see that returns and risk numbers are similar. The expense ratios are also very close. Based on these numbers, there is no obvious reason to choose one over another.

Only because I have previously seen that the Vanguard Bond Fund is a better choice will I tentatively select the Vanguard Total U.S. Stock fund. Again, I do this is in an effort to buy all of the Core funds from one family.

The Foreign Stock Building Block

I will look for a Total Foreign Stock Fund for the final Core Segment Building Block.

I have previously discussed that including a foreign stock component in a portfolio can provide important diversity as well as the potential for increased returns. This diversity has the potential to soften the impact of a downward movement of U.S. stocks and lessen portfolio volatility.

There exist a full range of international investment types. You can buy country funds such as a China Fund. You can buy regional funds such as a Europe Fund or a Pacific Fund. And you can buy Emerging Market Funds. All of these options are worth considering. But in the Core Segment as defined by the PPM approach, we want broad-based, extremely well-diversified investments. So for my sample Core Segment, I will concentrate on Total International Funds. We will look at more focused international funds in the Target Market Segment of the Perfect Portfolio when I discuss the Emerging Market Building Block in Chapter 9. The following are the fund candidates I discovered using the Web resources and the data collection process previously defined.

- *Vanguard Total International Stock (VGTSX):* This investment seeks to track the performance of a benchmark index that measures the investment return of stocks issued by companies located in Europe, the Pacific region, and emerging markets countries. The fund invests in three Vanguard funds—the European Stock Index Fund, the Pacific Stock Index, and the Emerging Markets Stock Index Fund. It allocates most of the assets based on the market capitalization of European, Pacific, and emerging markets stocks in the Total International Composite index.

- *Fidelity Total International Stock (FWWFX):* This investment seeks growth of capital. The fund usually invests in securities of issuers from anywhere in the world. It normally maintains investments in at least three countries, including the United States. The fund's equity investments may include established companies and new or small-capitalization companies. Although it may invest anywhere in the world, the fund mainly purchases securities of issuers in developed countries in North America, the Pacific Basin, and Europe.

- *iShares International Stock ETF (EFA):* To find this ETF on the iShares Web site, I placed my cursor over *International* in the menu at the left and then in the submenu over *Global* and scanned the resulting list to find EFA. The iShares MSCI EAFE Index Fund seeks to provide investment results that correspond generally to the price and yield performance, before fees and expenses, of publicly traded securities in the European, Australasian, and Far Eastern (EAFE) markets, as measured by the Morgan Stanley Capital International (MSCI) EAFE Index.

These are not the only selections possible in this varied field, of course. They are simply ones that I will use to illustrate the investment identification and analysis process. You may select others for your analysis.

Data Collection

Table 3.5 shows the data for each of the fund candidates I have selected. The numbers are current only as of the time this chapter

Table 3.5   International Stock Worksheet

Company	Symbol	Returns			Risk: Std. Dev.	Expense Ratio
		1-year	3-year	5-year		
Vanguard	VGTSX	1.34%	15.52%	23.18%	11.60%	.27%
Fidelity	FWWFX	2.02%	12.74%	18.46%	11.70%	1.02%
iShares ETF	EFA	–3.29%	13.15%	21.16%	10.86%	.34%

was written. You will have the opportunity to collect current data later in this chapter.

Data Analysis and Fund Selection

In this comparison, the Vanguard fund seems to have the slight advantage. We can see that for the three- and five-year periods, foreign stock returns have been spectacular with perhaps a cooling-off period setting in for the most recent year. Compare these numbers to the Total U.S. Stock Funds in Table 3.4 and you will see the value of including a foreign stock component in the Core Segment of the portfolio.

I will choose here the Vanguard fund because this fits our preferred model of buying all of our funds from the same family.

The Sample Core Portfolio Segment

I have selected the funds shown in Table 3.6 for my sample Core Segment as a result of the fund identification and analysis process described so far. I have used the Core Segment Design Worksheet that can be accessed in the online supplement and printed to record my selections as shown in Table 3.6.

The set of funds selected here is based primarily on my desire to buy all of the Core Segment funds from the same fund family, in this case Vanguard. Why is this important? Because with all of these funds in the same family, it is extremely easy to shift money among them and there are no transaction fees for doing so. If any one of the Vanguard funds had been seriously flawed in its performance, risk, or expenses, then I may have decided to buy funds from a different family or from multiple families. But when dealing with such broad market funds, returns and risks are likely to be virtually the same regardless of the family. So it just makes sense to stay within

Table 3.6   Core Segment Design Worksheet

Core Building Blocks	Fund Symbol	3-Year Avg. Returns	Risk Level	Allocation
Cash	VMMXX	4.48%	N/A	
Total Bond	VBMFX	5.43%	2.90%	
Total U.S Stocks	VTSMX	6.19%	9.10%	
Total Intl. Stocks	VGTSX	15.52%	11.60%	

one family. (This will not be the case with Target Market Funds, which we explore in Part II of this book.)

It must be repeated that the selections in Table 3.6 are not recommendations by the author. Also, the numbers shown are for illustration purposes only; they will not be valid by the time you read this. You may choose other funds and fund candidates for evaluation. The purpose here is to illustrate the process, the data to be collected, and the Web resources used. You will have the opportunity to complete your own worksheet using current data later in this chapter. I discuss filling in the Allocation column just below.

It is important to note that I could have selected Exchange Traded Funds (ETFs) for each of these Core Segment Building Blocks. I would favor ETFs if I wanted to monitor these investments and trade them. Why would I possibly want to do this? If my portfolio time horizon was relatively short—say less than three years—then I would not be able to take advantage of the up-trend that history tells me these Core investments would experience in the long term. Therefore, I would need to be more sensitive to short-term market conditions. Monitoring and trading Core Segment investments is an option discussed in Chapter 12.

Allocations

I now have a set of Core Segment Building Block investments. Each of these investments is very broad-based and diversified. Each is representative of a unique asset class (as defined by the PPM). Each has low expenses and they are all from the same fund family, allowing for easy money transfers among them. The question that remains is how much of the Core Fund investment money to allocate to each.

Keep in mind that this is a second-tier allocation. The first-tier allocation is between the Core Segment and the Target Market

Segment. But you will not be prepared to make the top-tier allocation until after reading Part II. Total portfolio allocations are discussed in detail in Chapter 10.

Allocation of money among the Core funds will depend on several factors. These include your risk tolerance, your time horizon, your target return goals, and your economic outlook. For instance, the more you allocate to Stocks, the higher will be the risk-reward profile of the Core Segment. The more bearish your view of the market, the more money you will want to allocate to Cash and Bonds.

A Sample Core Segment Design

Table 3.7 shows sample allocations of Core Segment money among the funds I have selected. The allocations shown in the table are for three investing styles that are listed along the top of the last three columns.

You can see that more aggressive allocations place a larger percentage in the stock categories. I have shown an *Expected Return* at the bottom of the table. This number results from the simple calculation of multiplying the allocation to a fund times its historical three-year return rate (as shown in the data collection worksheets for each Building Block discussed earlier) and adding the results for each investing style. This calculation is easy to perform using your own calculator, or you can use the Core Segment Expected Return Calculator found in the online supplement to this book. To access this calculator, log in to the supplement, click on *Links by Chapter,* and then on *Chapter 3* to find the link to this resource.

We will revisit these allocation numbers in Chapter 10, where we discuss the design of the total Perfect Portfolio. That process will include combining the Core Segment with the Target Market

Table 3.7   Sample Core Segment Allocations

Core Building Blocks	Fund Symbol	Conservative Allocation	Moderate Allocation	Aggressive Allocation
Cash	VMMXX	10%	5%	5%
Total Bond	VBMFX	40%	25%	15%
Total U.S Stocks	VTSMX	30%	40%	40%
Total Intl. Stocks	VGTSX	20%	30%	40%
Expected Return >>		7.58%	8.71%	9.72%

Segment and determining an overall expected return for the complete portfolio. I will not make my final allocation decisions for the sample Perfect Portfolio until we reach that point.

One factor missing in this table is a number showing how the risk level of the total Core Segment grows with the level of aggressiveness and expected return. This is not an easy calculation, and I will not burden you with the details of it here. Simply realize that higher returns are associated with higher risk. This is a topic that I discuss in more detail in Chapter 10, where we complete the design of the sample Perfect Portfolio.

Building *Your* Perfect Portfolio!

Reading how to build a portfolio and actually doing it are two different things. I have always found that education is more effective when students actively participate in the learning process. You are prepared at this point to identify, evaluate, and select specific investments for the Core Segment of your very own, unique Perfect Portfolio and I suggest that you do so.

To make this process more convenient, I provide tools found in the online supplement to this book. They are accessed by logging in to the supplement, clicking on *Links by Chapter* and then on *Chapter 3*. Or, optionally, you can create worksheets and do calculations on your own as described in this chapter. Here are your action items:

- *Print the Core Building Block Data Collection Worksheets.* Start your building process by clicking on this link in the online supplement. It will display a worksheet in PDF format that will enable you to document the data you collect as you work through the PPM evaluation process for each Core Building Block. Print at least four blank copies, one for each asset type in the Core Segment.
- *Work through the Investment Selection Process.* Now follow the four-step process presented in this chapter for each Building Block. Use the Web resources presented in this chapter to identify mutual fund and ETF candidates and collect current data for each. Then analyze these data and select specific investments for your Core Building Blocks.
- *Print the Core Segment Design Worksheet.* After selecting four Core investments, print this worksheet from the online supplement. It enables you to document your selections along

with related data and design your Core Segment by assigning test allocations to each.

- *Access the Core Segment Expected Return Calculator.* When you have filled in the data on your Design Worksheet, access this calculator in the online supplement to derive an expected return for your test allocation sets. Now you can complete your Core Segment Design Worksheet.

At this point, building a Core Segment of your own is an exercise meant to enable you to participate in the learning process so that you may understand it more fully. The sample investments you select here may or may not be the ones you end up buying should you decide to go live with your own Perfect Portfolio. For now, I suggest that you follow the earlier-described steps just to get your feet wet!

You will have an opportunity to find investments for each of the Target Market Segment Building Blocks in Chapters 5 through 9. You will then be shown in Chapter 10 how to combine your Segments to produce a total Perfect Portfolio. It is obviously not a requirement that you perform these tasks. But if you do, when you complete this book, you will have more than knowledge, you will also have a detailed action plan for implementing a powerful portfolio that meets your unique needs.

Chapter Summary

I have shown in this chapter how to put into place the ballast of your portfolio sailing ship in the form of the Core Segment. It establishes a firm foundation for stabilizing your investment vessel in stormy seas.

If you have done the work suggested, then you have selected four funds or ETFs, each representing a Core Segment Building Block. You have identified, evaluated, and chosen a fund or an ETF for Cash, Bonds, U.S. Stocks, and Foreign Stocks. Through these investments, you will have an ownership interest in thousands of different stocks and bonds of all styles. This will give your Core Segment maximum diversity and stability while also giving you the potential for returns that can, in the long-term, exceed portfolios designed by experts.

The funds selected here are buy-and-hold investments. The PPM approach recommends that while you will monitor their performance periodically, a topic discussed in Chapter 11, you will not trade these investments on a regular basis. If your portfolio holding time is measured in multiple years, then history tells us that your Core Segment will trend upward in the long term. If your portfolio holding time is shorter, then you may consider monitoring these investments more closely. This topic is discussed in Chapter 12.

I have shown you sample Core Segment allocations and the expected returns of each allocation set. You may have been disappointed that these returns were in the single digits. You obviously want higher returns. Don't despair. The Core Segment is not where we look for high returns. We will seek returns in the 20 percent-plus range in the Target Market Segment that I discuss in Part II, which starts with the next chapter.

We have made a good start by defining our Core Segment. Many advisers and individuals stop here. Using traditional portfolio-building techniques, a portfolio containing Cash, Stocks, and Bonds is all that is needed. I disagree. You are reading this book because you are skeptical of conventional investing wisdom. And you are not satisfied with average market returns.

You want more and are willing to work for it. So, the Perfect Portfolio Methodology does not stop with just a portfolio consisting of three (or in our case four) asset classes. There is an entire other world of investment opportunities out there beyond the Core. This is the world of Target Markets, and the PPM defines a Portfolio Segment dedicated to these investments.

The Core Segment is the ballast of your portfolio ship that keeps it stable in the long term. The Building Blocks that the PPM defines for the Target Market Segment are the sails of your portfolio ship that will allow it to cruise at full speed ahead! Learning what these sails are and how and when to hoist them is the subject of Part II of this book. That is where we go to next.

SUPERCHARGING YOUR PORTFOLIO WITH TARGET MARKET INVESTING

I show you in this part of the book how to implement the second segment of the Perfect Portfolio. This is the Target Market Segment and here is where the fun begins! Here is where we will invest in asset classes and Portfolio Building Blocks that have the potential for annual returns that can reach 20 percent, 30 percent, 40 percent, and even higher.

But to achieve returns of this magnitude, you will need to study each asset type and become more involved in the investing process. I give you the knowledge and resources you need to do so in the following six chapters that make up Part II.

Don't worry! Completing these chapters will take time and some work, but there is nothing in these chapters that you will not be able to understand and implement using free Web sites. Remember, a requirement of the PPM approach is that it be easy to understand and simple to work with. Also, don't be overly concerned at this point about these more volatile assets exposing you to excessive risk or requiring too much of your time to watch over. I show you how to implement a Web-based trading plan that automatically monitors your investments and manages the risks of owning them.

Let's face facts: the Core Segment that you learned about in Chapter 3 was just plain boring. It consisted of a scoop of bonds, a splash of foreign and domestic stocks, and a dollop of cash. The Core is not an area where a lot of analysis will produce earth-shaking returns. So we just bought entire markets for each asset type. It is unfortunate that most people stop building their portfolios with just the Core Segment assets. Many cookie-cutter portfolio designs doled out by advisers simply allocate money among the three traditional asset classes of Cash, Stocks, and Bonds and are done with it. In my opinion, this is totally inadequate for taking advantage of the opportunities that exist in today's market.

A full range of investment types exists beyond the Core that offer the potential for extraordinary annual returns. Among these investments are Gold, Energy, Agricultural Commodities, Real Estate, and Emerging Markets. These are the five Portfolio Building Blocks that we will discuss, analyze, and select for the Target Market Segment. This is where things start to get interesting.

Building Your Portfolio's Target Market Segment

FIVE ASSET BUILDING BLOCKS THAT WILL SUPERCHARGE YOUR PORTFOLIO

I introduce in this chapter the Target Market Segment of the Perfect Portfolio. The purpose of the Core Segment created in Chapter 3 was to build a solid foundation for the portfolio that should produce steady, if not spectacular, returns in the long run. The goal of the Target Market Segment is to add assets that are capable of producing spectacular returns in both the short and the long term.

I give you in the pages that follow an overview and a fundamental understanding of what the Target Market Segment is, its purpose in the total Perfect Portfolio, and how it is built. Then, in Chapters 6 through 9, I discuss each Target Market Building Block in detail.

The Building Blocks in the Target Market Segment are Gold, Energy, Agricultural Commodities, Real Estate, and Emerging Markets.

The Purpose and Characteristics of the Target Market Segment

The main purpose of the Target Market Segment is to add more returns potential to the portfolio. It contains five asset Building Blocks that were introduced in Chapter 2 and listed earlier. These are investments that are more narrowly focused than those in the

Core Segment. Because they have a higher risk-reward profile, it is important that you understand each in detail. I have therefore dedicated a separate chapter to each Target Market Building Block. These are Chapters 5 through 9. This chapter sets the stage for how we will build the entire Target Market Segment.

The securities in the Target Market Segment will not be buy-and-hold investments. They will instead be buy-and-sell investments. You will see as you move through the upcoming chapters that these investments are more volatile than Core investments, so they will require more upfront analysis before buying and closer monitoring once purchased.

For each investment placed in the Target Market Segment, we will define a trading plan that will automatically alert us to when we should consider selling a position to either take profits or to limit losses. The trading plan will significantly reduce the higher risks that are associated with assets that have higher returns potential. I discuss the elements of the trading plan in more detail later in this chapter.

Benefits of the Target Market Segment

The following is a list of reasons that explains why the Perfect Portfolio Methodology (PPM) includes a Target Market Segment.

- *To Add Returns Potential:* The Core Segment is not designed to provide extraordinary returns. The Target Market Segment is. This segment includes investments in Gold, Energy, Agricultural Commodities, Real Estate, and Emerging Markets. These asset types are defined as Target Market Building Blocks because history has shown that each has the potential of providing annual returns of 20 percent and higher. Our goal will be to find a mix of these assets that thrives in current market conditions so as to provide a significant boost to the returns of the entire portfolio. Too many portfolios ignore these assets or include them indirectly through diverse mutual funds. The PPM structure enables you to plug directly into their power to create wealth.
- *To Reduce Portfolio Risk:* The Core Segment consists of Stocks, Bonds, and Cash. The Core is diversified within itself because Stocks and Bonds are negatively correlated. Yet, there exist other categories of assets that are not closely correlated with

either Stocks or Bonds. These are asset types that the PPM includes in the Target Market Segment. For example, Gold has a low correlation with both Stocks and Bonds. Each Target Market asset provides valuable diversity to the total portfolio, and this, of course, reduces risk.

- *To Take Advantage of Market Conditions:* An effective portfolio must be sufficiently flexible to respond to current market conditions and world events. The Core Segment contains investments that you buy and hold. You will not trade these in response to short-term market events. Yet, to realize returns that significantly exceed market averages, you must be aware of, and take advantage of, market dynamics. The assets included in the Target Market Segment enable you to do so.

  Within the Target Market Segment will be assets that thrive in down markets and those that thrive in up markets. There will be assets within this Segment that respond well when the economy is in turmoil and there will be assets that excel when bad things happen in the world. The Target Market Segment enables you to easily and rapidly make adjustments to your portfolio in response to changes in the market, the economy, and world events. Understanding when and how to make these adjustments is key to profiting from them, and you will gain this understanding in this chapter and those that follow.

  The ability to make a rapid response to changing market conditions is missing in most portfolios, and they suffer for it. The Target Market Segment gives you this ability and it enables a portfolio designed using the PPM approach to excel in all market conditions.

- *To Enable Effective Personal Participation:* In the personal investing classes I teach at the college level, I see many students who want to take more personal control of their portfolios. They are willing and eager to exchange time and effort for additional returns. Yet they hit a wall when dealing with conventional portfolios provided to them by advisers. A portfolio filled with a random assortment of stocks and fund styles does not encourage personal participation. There exists no structure that enables individuals to channel effort into higher returns. The PPM does provide such a structure with the Target Market Segment, and you will learn in this and following chapters how this Segment enables you to translate personal involvement in the investing process directly into increased wealth.

The Target Market Segment Building Blocks

The Perfect Portfolio Methodology defines five Asset Building Blocks for inclusion in the Target Market Segment. When added to the four Core Segment Building Blocks, which were defined in Chapter 2, we have a total of nine portfolio Building Blocks to work with. No longer inhibited by the three-asset-class straitjacket, the PPM portfolio design process is more flexible, more profitable, more exciting, and just plain more fun.

The Target Market Building Blocks are illustrated in Figure 4.1.

An Overview of the Target Market Building Blocks

Now let's take a quick look at the Target Market Building Blocks. Each is an investment type with unique characteristics. All deserve a place in your portfolio and a separate chapter is dedicated to learning about each in this Part of the book. The following is a short overview of each Building Block.

Gold: This asset is the ultimate "safe haven" for investors. Unlike stocks and bonds, Gold has intrinsic value. Its value will never go to zero. So, when the stock market is diving or disruptive events are occurring in the world, such as terrorist attacks or natural disasters, investors flee to the safety of gold. Gold is explored in more detail in Chapter 5.

Energy: While Gold has intrinsic value, Energy has intrinsic demand. The world simply cannot do without it. The main player in this asset category is oil and until something better comes along, demand for it simply has to grow for a variety

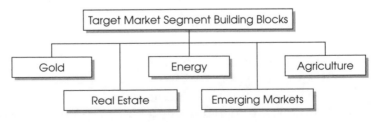

Figure 4.1   The Target Market Building Blocks

of reasons that are discussed in Chapter 6. A portfolio without a focused Energy component is not taking advantage of the state of the world as we currently know it.

Agricultural Commodities: This Building Block contains assets such as sugar, wheat, orange juice, rice, livestock, cocoa, and the famous pork bellies. These are the foodstuffs that people need every day to live. Regardless of market and world events, people need to eat, so the demand for Agricultural Commodities will always be strong and it will grow stronger as the world population increases and becomes more affluent. I discuss the fascinating field of Agricultural Commodities in Chapter 7.

Real Estate: This Asset Building Block contains income producing commercial properties such as hotels, apartment complexes, office buildings, and retail space. As I write this book, this asset type has hit a rough patch partly due to a crisis in the credit markets. But all asset types go through cycles. For the person who understands market dynamics the current dip in Real Estate prices may be a tremendous buying opportunity. I give you the knowledge and tools you need to make informed decisions in the area of Real Estate investments in Chapter 8.

Emerging Markets: This category of assets includes stocks from companies in developing countries such as China, Russia, India, Brazil, and others. Each has tremendous potential for growth. Yet, each is also subject to unique risks, such as political upheaval and natural disasters. To diversify away single country risk, investments exist that combine multiple developing economies into individual securities. These are called Emerging Market investments. I show you how to find, analyze, select, and monitor Emerging Market investments in Chapter 9.

Now that I have introduced to you the five Asset Building Blocks in the Target Market Segment, let's look at the characteristics that are common to all.

Characteristics of the Target Market Building Blocks

The Perfect Portfolio Methodology designates only five asset types as Building Blocks in the Target Market Segment, so they must be special. In fact, they are. Each has the following unique characteristics that you will learn more about in the five chapters to come.

- *High Demand Potential:* The five Target Market Building Blocks represent asset types that have the potential for high demand now and in the future. Gold, Energy, and Agricultural Commodities are in high demand now, as of the time this book was written. Real Estate has been in high demand throughout most of recorded history and, while currently experiencing a slump, will inevitably rebound. Emerging Markets, the fifth Building Block, does not represent a specific tangible asset, but rather equities from a specific area of the world. For this Building Block, we look for areas of the world where demand for their stocks is high.
- *High Returns Potential:* High demand translates into the potential for high returns. To be accorded the status of a Target Market Building Block, annual returns of 20 percent, 30 percent, 40 percent, and higher must be possible. We would not expect this of the broad-market Building Blocks of the Core Segment. We will expect this potential from Target Market Building Blocks. Will we get such returns every year? No. There will be times when each Target Market Building Block asset experiences a downturn. You will see as you study the PPM approach in upcoming chapters that we will only include in our portfolio those Building Blocks that are *currently* thriving.
- *Portfolio Diversity:* To qualify as a Target Market Building Block, the price of the underlying asset must react differently to market conditions and catalysts than do Core Building Blocks and other Target Market Building Blocks. Thus, when stocks are moving down, there should be at least one Target Market Building Block that is moving up. In other words, Target Market Building Blocks each add a valuable component of diversity to the total portfolio. Rarely will all PPM Building Blocks be moving in the same direction at the same time. This diversity is a key reason why the PPM approach is so powerful.
- *Ease of Investment:* You must be able to buy and sell a Target Market Building Block with ease. Fortunately we have seen that this is possible using either a traditional mutual fund or

an Exchange Traded Fund (ETF). These single investments hold a basket of stocks or equities that represent entire Building Block asset types. Thus, for the Gold Building Block, we can buy just the ETF with the symbol GLD. For Emerging Markets, we can buy just the ETF with the symbol EEM. The Target Market Segment has a total of five Building Blocks, and buying them all requires no more than five investments.

Why These Five Building Blocks?   You may be asking yourself at this point, "With all of the asset types available in the market, why did I choose Gold, Energy, Agricultural Commodities, Real Estate, and Emerging Markets as Target Market Building Blocks?"

Throughout my many years of research and teaching personal investing, I recognized that these asset types each have a unique and distinct profile in terms of their returns potential, risk profile, correlation with other asset types, and how their prices move in response to various market, economic, and world events. They also represent a wide swath of the market. My research shows that, in combination with the four Core Building Blocks, they are really all you need to build a powerful portfolio that can give you extraordinary returns while at the same time giving you the diversification to effectively manage the risk associated with these higher returns. You will understand these benefits more fully as you move through the chapters in this Part of *The Perfect Portfolio*.

Table 4.1 shows historical data related to each Target Market Building Block and compares it to the same data for U.S. Stocks, which is a Core Segment Building Block. The data, collected for the year 2007, illustrate the returns potential, the risk, the volatility, and the amount of diversity (as shown by correlation to U.S. Stocks) that each Building Block brings to the Perfect Portfolio. For purposes of collecting these data, I have used an Exchange Traded Fund (ETF) as a proxy (that is, a single investment) for each asset class. I show you how to find other investment candidates for each Building Block in the chapters that follow.

Note the incredible 2007 returns from these asset classes as compared to the Core Building Block of U.S. Stocks, except for Real Estate, which took an equally incredible dive. Look at the risk of each of these Target Market Segment Building Blocks in comparison to the risk of buying the entire U.S. stock market. (Remember, the higher the Standard Deviation for an investment, the higher

Table 4.1   Target Market Building Block Data

Building Block	Sample ETF	2007 Return	2007 Risk / Std. Deviation	Correlation with Stocks
U.S. Stocks	IWV	4.57%	9.26%	1.0
Gold	IAU	30.36%	17.03%	.63
Energy	IYE	35.75%	19.41%	.49
Agriculture	DBC	31.60%	Insufficient Data	-.70
Real Estate	ICF	-18.21%	18.04%	.69
Emerging Mkts.	EEM	33.08%	19.84%	.68

its risk.) Also note the relatively low correlations between our new Target Market asset classes and the Core asset of Stocks. You can see that each adds significant diversity to the entire portfolio.

The table data show that in working with these assets, we essentially have a tiger by the tail. Our goal is to realize the incredible returns potential provided by Target Market assets while protecting ourselves from the volatility of each. We achieve this goal by implementing a trading plan for each, as explained later in this chapter.

Are other Building Blocks possible within the Perfect Portfolio Methodology? Yes, and I show you how to add them in Chapter 12. But I suggest that you only add Building Blocks if you would describe yourself as an involved investor who is willing to devote significant time and effort to the investing process. For most investors, the five Target Market Building Blocks described here are sufficient.

Extra Credit

Learning More

I suggest that you now go to the Web and get data for the investments in Table 4.1 for the most recently completed full year, 2008, for example. You can use the site at finance.yahoo.com for this purpose. Simply enter the investment symbols from Table 4.1 on the home page of this site to find the data. A comparison of yearly returns will provide very valuable insight into the movement and behavior of each asset class. Take this opportunity to get involved in the learning process!

Note: Throughout the upcoming chapters you will see Extra Credit opportunities such as this. These suggestions will direct you to the Web to find information that will expand your understanding of the topic currently being discussed.

The Target Market Investment Selection Process

Now that you have an understanding of the Target Market Building Blocks, we turn to the topic of how to select the best specific investment for including each in our portfolio.

I walk you through a logical process for this purpose for each Building Block in Chapters 5 through 9. As with the Core Segment, I will not subject you to the agony of searching through hundreds of stocks or fund styles. I show you instead how to buy each entire asset class or market segment with only one investment. For example, we will add a diversified Gold component to the portfolio with the purchase of one Exchange Traded Fund.

The following is an overview of the five-step PPM Target Market investment selection process.

Step 1. *Learn about the asset:* Because the PPM concentrates on only five asset types in the Target Market Segment, you have the luxury of learning about each in great detail. I discuss the characteristics of each Building Block in the five chapters that follow, the factors that influence its price, and how it can be purchased. I also present for your consideration Web site references that enable you to learn more. You can't be an "expert" in large-cap value funds. But you can be an expert in tangible assets such as Gold, Energy, and Real Estate.

Step 2. *Identify at least three investment candidates:* For each Building Block the PPM dictates that instead of buying individual stocks, you buy a basket of equities that are representative of the entire asset class. This could be an ETF or a focused mutual fund. I provide Web resources and a structured process for finding at least three investment candidates for each Building Block in upcoming chapters.

Step 3. *Collect and analyze data:* I next provide a worksheet and Web resources for collecting relevant data for each investment candidate you identify. Then I discuss the process of comparing and analyzing these data to select the one investment candidate that has the most promising profile.

Step 4. *Display and analyze the price chart:* Having selected an investment, the next step is to view and analyze its price chart. The goal is to buy only those Target Market assets that are *currently* experiencing a positive price trend. A price chart gives you this information. I provide Web resources that you can use to display charts along with a checklist of factors to look for and analyze.

Step 5. *Define a trading plan:* Finally, using information from the price chart, I show you how to define and implement a trading plan for any investment that you decide to place in the Target Market Segment of your portfolio. This plan will put into place *sell* points to either stop losses or to take profits. This step significantly reduces the risk of what can be a very profitable but very volatile investment.

The goal of these five steps is to give you the knowledge, tools, and structured process you need to effectively invest in Target Market assets.

Target Market Segment Online Resources

With an investment selection process in place, let's now look for Web sites that enable us to implement it. The following is a list of Web sites and resources that I will use in upcoming chapters for finding, evaluating, selecting, and monitoring Target Market Building Block investments. These are not the only sites that can be used; they are simply ones that do the job required simply, effectively, and with no charge. If any of these sites do not work exactly as described, go to the online supplement to this book, log in and click on *Links by Chapter*. Then click on *Chapter 4* to find updated links and navigation descriptions.

- *The Data Collection Worksheet:* We will use the Target Market Building Block Worksheet in the process of finding and evaluating specific investments. To access it, go to the online supplement, log in and click on *Links by Segment,* then on *Chapter 4,* and look for a link to this worksheet. It is presented in PDF format for ease of printing. You will use this worksheet to record data for your Target Market investment candidates.
- *Finding Index Fund Candidates by Family:* We will use the site at finance.yahoo.com/funds to look for investment candidates in the Vanguard and Fidelity fund families. I use these companies as examples only and their use is not meant as a

recommendation. There are dozens of other fund families that you may wish to consider. If you already work with a fund family, include an investment from it as one candidate for comparison purposes.

To find the index funds candidates on the finance.yahoo.com/funds Web site, first locate the menu on the left side of the page and look for *Funds by Family.* Click on this entry and you will be presented with an alphabetical list of fund families. Click on the family of interest and you will see a list of the funds they offer. Browse this list to find a fund for the asset type you are investigating. Further details of the use of this site are discussed as we look at each Target Market Building Block in upcoming chapters.

- *Finding Index Fund Candidates by Performance:* As a second investment candidate for each Target Market Building Block, we will use the site at finance.yahoo.com/funds to look for the best performing funds in each asset category.

  To find these funds, look in the left menu and click on *Top Performers.* You will see a list of categories. Click on the one for the asset type you are evaluating and you will see the top-performing funds for multiple time periods. We will look for a fund that is in more than one of these lists.

- *Finding Exchange Traded Fund Candidates:* An ETF will be our third investment candidate for each Building Block. To find one, we will use the site at finance.yahoo.com/etf. On this site click "View ETFs" in the left menu. You will see a drop-down menu for "category" that will be used to list ETF candidates for the Building Block of interest. We will also be using the site at iShares.com for finding ETF candidates.

- *The Data Collection Web Site:* We will use the site at finance.yahoo.com to collect the data needed to complete the worksheet for each of our investment candidates. Enter the mutual fund or ETF symbol in the box labeled *Get Quote* on the home page of this site. You will see a menu on the left side of the resulting page. Click on *Performance* to find returns data and then on *Risk* to find the three-year Standard Deviation data. To find the Total Expense Ratio of the fund, click on *Profile* and scroll down the right side of the page to the *Expenses and Fees* box, where you will see the Total Expenses Ratio at the top of the list.

- *The Price Charting Web Site:* Again, we will use the site at finance .yahoo.com to get the price charts needed to analyze Target Market investment candidates and create a trading plan for any we select to purchase. Enter the investment symbol on the home page of this site and in the left column click on *Basic Technical Analysis*. We want a one-year chart, so click *1y* in the menu above the chart. We also want to see Bollinger Bands, so click on that item in the menu above the chart as well. I explain how to analyze the chart later in this chapter.

These are the sites that I will use as we go through the process of selecting a specific investment for each of the Target Market Building Blocks presented in Chapters 5 through 9. If these sites or the navigation of them change, you can get updates in the online supplement to this book as previously described.

Target Market Allocations

The Perfect Portfolio Methodology requires you to make two basic decisions. The first is to find the best investment for each Portfolio Building Block. The second is how much of your investment money to allocate to each Building Block you decide to buy. This decision will define the risk-reward profile of your total portfolio. Let's now discuss the factors that will influence your allocation decisions in the Target Market Segment.

The amount of money you decided to allocate to each asset in the Core Segment was determined largely by your risk tolerance and time horizon. For example, the higher your risk tolerance or the longer you plan to hold the portfolio, the more you allocated to stocks, because in the long term this asset class has a higher returns potential than cash or bonds. The factors influencing your Target Market allocation decisions are different. In looking at the data for the five asset classes in the Target Market Segment shown in Table 4.1, you see that they all have essentially the same risk level, as measured by Standard Deviation. So, you will not affect this Segment's risk level by allocating more money to any one Target Market Building Block.

In the Target Market Segment, your money allocation will mainly depend on short-term price trends for the asset along with your current view of the market, the economy, world events, and your knowledge of how each asset class reacts to these factors.

The following factors will influence the allocations you give to each Building Block in the Target Market Segment.

- *Asset Price Trend:* As a part of the investment selection process discussed in this chapter, you will view the price trend of each Building Block you are considering using a Web-based price chart. You may decide to allocate more money to those that are currently experiencing a significant uptrend and less to those that are showing less positive price trends. You may in fact decide to allocate zero percent to any Building Block currently experiencing a downtrend.
- *Your View of the Economy:* You will learn in the next five chapters about each Target Market asset class and the economic factors and market conditions that influence its price. You may decide to allocate more money to those assets that respond well in current market conditions.
- *Your Involvement Level:* This factor is a measure of how much time and effort you are willing to devote to the investing process. If you are an involved investor, then this may influence the allocations you give to specific assets. In the Emerging Markets class of assets, for example, there are many options and variables to consider. I discuss them in Chapter 9. If you are willing to spend significant time studying these factors and perhaps even subscribe to an Emerging Markets newsletter, you will have greater confidence in your investment selection and perhaps be willing to allocate a greater percentage of your money to this Building Block. Other opportunities for greater involvement are discussed in Chapter 12.

Allocation Dials

You will understand as you move through this book that the PPM approach has three dials that determine the overall risk-return profile of the portfolio you are creating. The first is an allocation between the Core Segment and the Target Market Segment. The more money you allocate to the Target Market Segment, the higher will be the risk-return profile of the portfolio.

Then, within each Segment, you can fine-tune the risk-return profile by choosing how to allocate money among the various

Building Blocks. In the Core Segment, you increase the risk-return profile by allocating more money to Stocks. In the Target Market Segment, you adjust the risk-return profile by allocating more money to the Building Blocks that *currently* have the higher return potential, and these will constantly change.

Allocations play a key role in the design of your Perfect Portfolio; the PPM is designed to enable you to easily adjust them. I discuss the topic of allocations and portfolio design in much greater detail in Chapter 10, where we design a total Perfect Portfolio and the revolutionary nature of this approach to investing becomes obvious.

Risk Management for the Target Market Segment

As mentioned earlier, the purpose of the Target Market Segment is to produce returns that are significantly higher than market averages. This Segment has the potential for returns of 20 percent, 30 percent, 40 percent, and higher.

But in the world of investing, higher returns are always associated with higher risks. To realize returns on the order of 20 percent plus, you must invest in assets that can be very volatile. A portfolio containing an entire segment dedicated to these investment types can easily exceed your risk tolerance level. So, the risk of the Target Market Segment must be managed and controlled. This leads to yet another revolutionary element of the PPM: the concept and implementation of a *trading plan* for each investment in the Segment.

Remember that the investments you place in the Target Market Segment are not intended to be buy-and-hold securities. They are buy-and-sell securities. You cannot simply buy the Asset Building Blocks defined for this Segment and forget about them. They must be sold to either stop losses, to take profits, or to reallocate money to more promising investments. These investments must therefore be continuously monitored. A trading plan for this purpose is needed for each investment you buy in this Segment. You cannot eliminate risk, but with a trading plan you can control it.

Fortunately, the Web provides tools that make the implementation of the required trading plan simple and automatic. A requirement of the PPM approach as defined in Chapter 2 is that the portfolio not require you to spend hours in front of a computer to monitor. The trading plan methodology that I discuss next frees you from this task.

Elements and Tools for Implementing a Trading Plan

The trading plan concept is simple. When you buy a security for the Target Market Segment, you should immediately define price points at which you will sell it to either limit your losses or to take profits. For example, if you buy an ETF for the Gold component of your portfolio for $50 per share, you may want to sell if the price goes down to $45, to limit losses, or you may want to sell if the price goes up to $60 to take profits. Determining these sell price points and putting in place tools that trigger actions when they are reached is central to the PPM trading plan.

I next discuss tools for implementing the PPM trading plan for each Target Market investment you buy. Then I discuss how to set the target prices for selling. Once you have set these price points, you obviously don't want to have to continuously check your computer to see when or if they have been hit. You don't have to. The Web offers a variety of tools that automatically trigger actions when your preset price points are met. Let's look at a few.

Automated Action Triggers

The hard part of creating an effective trading plan is defining sell price points. The easy part is automating actions based on them. A relatively recent Web-based trading capability offered by most major online brokers is called a *trigger*. In general terms, triggers allow you to specify an investment, define a condition, and then tell the system the action to take when the condition is met. Here is the anatomy of a trigger followed by an example using an ETF for the Gold asset class with the symbol GLD.

Trigger Format: Symbol—Condition—Operator—Price—Action

Example: If GLD's per share market price is less than $85, then sell my 100 shares.

You may want to set a trigger like the one shown in this example if you had bought GLD at $90 per share and wanted to limit your losses by having your broker's system automatically sell your shares if the price moved down to $85 or lower.

Most trigger capabilities also allow you to use percentages rather than specific dollar amounts. So, in this example, you could have entered "If percent change is greater than –10 percent, then sell 100 shares." This is a simple illustration of the powerful concept of automated triggers.

Trailing Stop Triggers

Triggers will be at the center of the trading plan advocated by the PPM for use with every investment you place in the Target Market Segment of your portfolio. A special type of trigger that we will employ is the *trailing stop trigger* that almost all online brokers offer.

A trailing stop trigger is one that enables you to enter a stop-loss sell price that moves up with the market price of the ETF. The stop parameter can be entered as a dollar value or a percentage value below the current bid price. A trailing stop could look something like this:

"If GLD price is down $5 or more from the highest price of GLD since I have owned it, then sell my 100 shares at market price."

So, let's say that you bought 100 shares of GLD for $90 per share and set the above described trailing stop trigger at the time of purchase. If the ETF were to immediately drop to $85 or below without first going up, then your position will be automatically sold.

Now, instead of dropping, let's suppose the price goes up $2 to $92. Your stop-loss price *moves up $2 to $87.* Your stop-loss amount of $5 is moving up with the market price. But once the stop-loss price starts to move up, it never goes down again! Thus, if the ETF price then moves back down to $90 (after first advancing to $92) your stop price remains at $87.

The fact that a trailing stop price moves up but not down is very powerful. It allows you to stop losses *and* let profits run. This is exactly what we are looking for to manage risk and maximize return in the Target Market Segment. I illustrate how to set stop-loss triggers for each Building Block in upcoming chapters.

Trigger Action Types

In the previous example, the action was to sell the ETF. A well-designed trigger alert capability will also allow for the action to be "Send me an e-mail." Such an e-mail would alert you to the fact that one of your predefined sell points has been hit. But your position will not be automatically sold, rather you will get an e-mail. When you get the e-mail, you can then research the situation and decide whether you want to sell or not. This is called a *soft stop,* whereas an automated sell action is called a *hard stop.*

Soft stops allow you more flexibility to make your own decision as to whether to sell or not. But by using them, you also run the risk of the investment's price falling further during the time it takes you to react to the e-mail.

As stated previously, all major online brokers should offer a *trigger* capability. The aforementioned example is taken from TD Ameritrade's implementation of triggers at the time this chapter was written. Implementations of triggers by other brokers may be different, but the capability should be essentially the same. Refer to the online supplement to this book for updates in this area as they become available.

Take-Profit Alerts

The PPM trading plan is designed not only to enable you to stop losses due to share price decreases but also to alert you to increases in the price of the investments in your Target Market Segment. I refer to these as *take-profit alerts.* They will be set at prices *above* your purchase price.

When you purchase an investment, in addition to setting a stop-loss price level, you should also set a price at which you would be happy to sell to take profits. A trailing stop can be used to lock in profits as the market price of your investment goes higher. But if this is the only trigger you set, you will take profits only after your investment's price has dropped from its high during the time you own it by the amount you defined. A take-profit alert can enable you to sell when your return goal has been achieved without a specific price drop occurring.

Let me make this clear with an example. Assume that you buy GLD at $90 per share and put a trailing stop that automatically sells your position if GLD shares drop $5 or more from the highest price reached while you own it. Now say the price goes up to $98 and your trailing stop follows it up to $93. If this is your only stop, you will sell only after you have lost $5! This is good for protecting against losses, but you may want to try to keep more of this profit by setting a take-profit alert. In this example, if you had also set a profit alert for GLD at $98 at the time of purchase, you then have the potential for keeping a larger share of the profit than if you had simply let the stop-loss trigger sell it.

The PPM suggests that take-profit alerts be in the form of e-mails sent to you, not in the form of an automatic selling of your position. A take-profit e-mail will prompt you to research what is happening with the stock.

If you get a take-profit e-mail, look at the investment's price chart and see that the trend is solidly up, then you may simply wish to raise your take-profit alert price. If the upward price trend is flattening out, however, or if you have other investments where the money has more potential to grow, you may wish to sell the position and take your profits. Selling to take profits is almost never a bad move.

In addition to moving up your take-profit alert price when you get a take-profit email, you may also wish to tighten your stop-loss trigger. For example, you may want to change a $5 drop sell-trigger to a $3 drop sell-trigger, thus locking in more profits.

In Chapter 12, I discuss other actions you can take when you get a take-profit alert. It is just as important as a stop-loss trigger. One of the biggest problems I have seen from students in my investing classes is that they don't sell to take profits. The PPM encourages you to do so.

Fund Alerts

Triggers work with ETFs because they trade like stocks. Conventional mutual fund shares do not trade like stocks. Their prices change only once per day, at the end of the trading session. So, another type of Web alert resource is required for any focused mutual funds that you place in your Target Market Segment. You will see in the chapters that follow that for some Target Market Building Blocks a traditional focused mutual fund may be a better investment than an ETF, so we must discuss how to deal with alerts for these investments.

Fund price alerts are available on many Web sites. The site at finance.yahoo.com is one example. Using this site, you can set a price alert for a fund that will send you an e-mail when a predefined price is hit.

On this site and others that offer fund alerts, you will not be able to automatically trigger the sale of your fund position. Your only option is to be alerted by an e-mail or perhaps a text message to your cell phone when your stop-loss or take-profit sell price is hit. When you receive an alert for a fund, you can research the situation and take appropriate action. Immediate action is not as critical for funds because their price changes only once a day, at the end of each trading session.

The Protective Put Option

The third risk control tool that you can use is the Protective Put Option. This alternative for controlling risk requires you to dip ever so lightly into the world of options trading. This is a field that is wide and varied and an in-depth discussion of options trading is beyond the scope of this book. There exists, however, a very simple type of options trade that may, at times, be the best tool for protecting an investment in your portfolio from serious loss. This is the Protective Put Option.

Very simply, buying a Protective Put Option is a transaction that protects the downside risk of a stock or ETF that you own. When you buy such an option, you specify the stock or ETF symbol, a number of shares, a price, and an expiration date. You then own the right to sell the stock or ETF that you have purchased for the price specified in the Put Option contract. You own this right until the expiration date of the contract.

Here is an example. Suppose you buy 100 shares of GLD at $90 per share. To protect yourself from a falling price, you might buy one Put Contract with a Strike Price of $85, expiring in December 2009. You may pay, for example, $1.20 per share for this contract. And since one options contract relates to 100 shares of GLD, you would pay $120 for a contract that covers all of your shares. You have essentially paid $120 for insurance on the 100 shares of GLD that you own. Regardless of how far the price of GLD falls, you own the right, but not the obligation, to sell it for $85 per share at any time before the December 2009 expiration date, even if its price falls to $30!

More information on Put Options can be found in the online supplement to this book. To find it, log in to the supplement, click on *Links by Chapter,* and then on *Chapter 4.*

I concentrate on triggers and alerts as the elements of the trading plan that control the risk of Target Market trading in the chapters that follow. But you should be aware of the Put Option alternative.

Using A Watch List

The goal of the PPM trading plan is to exit a position in order to either limit losses or to take profits. But when this occurs, what happens to the Portfolio Building Block that is sold? Is it no longer a PPM Building Block? Certainly not. The reason it was sold was because its price was declining. It will, at some point in the future, be on the rise and we will want to buy it again. Our goal once we sell an investment is to continue to automatically monitor its price and be alerted to when its price is coming back. To do this, we will immediately place each Building Block that we sell in a Watch List.

A Watch List is a Web-based tool that we will use to monitor any of the Portfolio Building Blocks that are currently not in our portfolio. Using Watch List capabilities, we can place alerts on the price of the investments we don't currently own in the same manner as described previously for assets we do own. The difference is that there is no need to place an automated sell trigger, since we don't own these investments, and I don't advise that you place an automated buy on them either without first analyzing their price charts.

The inclusion of a Watch List capability as a part of the total PPM trading strategy is discussed in Chapter 11 and its use is illustrated in detail in the Appendix, where we follow a Real Estate investment as it moves between our Perfect Portfolio and a Watch List.

How to Determine Trading Plan Target Prices

You now have an understanding of the tools for implementing an automated trading plan for the Target Market Segment of the portfolio. But these tools are worthless without knowing how to set stop-loss and take-profit sell prices for your Target Market investments.

To determine these price targets, we will use investment Price Charts along with some very simple analysis tools that are available for free on many Web sites.

Using Price Charts

The Perfect Portfolio Methodology uses simple price charts to enable you to determine sell prices for your trading plans. The study of price charts and indicators is called *Technical Analysis* (TA) and is a field of study that is very extensive and can be quite complicated. We will use only the simplest TA tools for our purposes here.

A simple price chart is illustrated in Figure 4.2. It shows the price for a Gold ETF with the symbol GLD. The price line is the middle of the three lines on the chart. The chart shows the ETF price on the left axis and the date on the bottom axis. The price line then shows the market price of one share of GLD on a given date.

Figure 4.2   One Year Gold ETF Price Chart
Reproduced with permission of Yahoo! Inc. ® 2008 by Yahoo! Inc. YAHOO! and the YAHOO! logo are trademarks of Yahoo! Inc.

Please note that this chart is shown for illustration purposes only and will obviously have changed by the time you read this.

The following is a discussion of what you should consider as you view and analyze this chart.

The Trend.   The first thing to look for on the chart is the price trend. This will be fairly obvious as you scan the price line from left to right. It will either be going up, down, or sideways. If the trend line is moving down, this is a red flag and you may consider not buying this asset at the current time. A trend line moving up is a positive factor and a sideways trend is neutral, leaving you to base your purchase decision on other factors.

Price Support and Resistance.   If you decide to include the asset being investigated in your portfolio, then you need to set sell prices for your trading plan. The simplest way to do this is to look at the chart and note the price levels at which the price line tends to bounce up or down. Price levels at which the line tends to go up are called *support levels*. Prices at which the line tends to bounce down are called *resistance levels*. The most recent area of the chart is the area in which to look for these levels.

In our sample chart, a resistance level seems to exist at a little below $100. We can estimate it to be at $99. For a support level, one seems to be forming at about $85. These estimates are the basis for a trading plan sell strategy.

Let's assume that GLD is currently selling for $93. We might set our stop loss price at $85, our estimated support level. If GLD falls this far, it may be a good time to get out to stop our losses. We might set our take-profit alert at $99, just below the resistance level. This would give us a nice profit and enable us to avoid any bounce down if the resistance level holds. The price chart has given us a solid basis for setting our sell points and implementing a simple but effective exit strategy. But we want to make sure that we do not exit our position based on normal, everyday price fluctuations. This is where the factor of volatility comes into play.

Volatility: Using Bollinger Bands.   A technical indicator that can assist in the process of setting sell points is called *Bollinger Bands.* These are the lines on the example chart that appear above and below the price line. They form a channel within which the price has traded in the recent past. The bottom band can be used to determine a support level and the top band to determine a resistance level. The uniquely valuable information provided by this indicator is that the more volatile the investment is, the wider the bands.

The event you are trying to avoid when setting exit pricing is automatically selling when the price is simply experiencing normal daily ups and downs. Even in an uptrend, there will be days when the price goes down. And in downtrends, a daily price may go up. So, you need to be aware of the amount of price swing that is normal, and you must take this into account when setting exit prices. You may otherwise get "whipsawed" out of a position that is still moving up. The width of the Bollinger Bands shows you the recent normal volatility of the investment and gives you information you need to avoid prematurely exiting your position. So we will use Bollinger Bands in upcoming chapters as one input factor when setting price exit points.

A Sample Trading Plan

Setting trading plan target prices is as much an art as a science. You need to take the information you have before you and make reasonable choices. For our example, it would be reasonable to set up the following trading plan.

- Buy GLD at current market price of $93.
- Place a take-profit e-mail alert trigger at $99.

- Set a trailing stop trigger as follows: "If the market price of GLD goes down by $8 or more from the highest price it has reached since I have owned it, then sell the GLD position." (Note that this could also be a percentage drop as opposed to a dollar drop.)

Here are various scenarios that can occur with this plan in place:

- If GLD immediately goes down to $85, the GLD position will be automatically sold.
- If GLD goes up to $95, then the stop-loss price automatically increases to $87 ($8 below the current market price).
- If GLD goes to $98, the stop-loss price automatically increases to $90.
- If GLD then goes back down to $90 from a high of $98, the GLD position will be automatically sold.
- If GLD goes to $99, I will get an e-mail informing me of this fact at which point I may wish to sell with a $6 per share profit or I may wish to simply raise my take-profit alert to $105, for example. If I see that the price trend is still strong and do not wish to sell now, I might also tighten my stop-loss trigger to sell with any drop of $3 or more, for example, to lock in more profit.

You can see the beauty and power of an automated trading plan in this example. It immediately protects me from a loss of more than $8 on GLD. As GLD moves up, the stop-loss price moves up with it. *But* the stop-loss price *never* moves down. The $8 drop from the highest price GLD has reached during the time I have owned it is always in place regardless of how high the price of GLD goes. The stop-loss trigger lets profits run. When I get a take-profit alert e-mail, I can either sell and walk away happy or increase the take-profit price while at the same time decreasing the stop-loss sell price, thus locking in more profits.

Note that your trailing-stop trigger can also be set to send you e-mails as opposed to automatically selling your position.

Risk Management Summary

As mentioned earlier, your Target Market Portfolio Segment will include five Asset Building Blocks that hold the potential for significant gains. Yet they are also volatile, and thus risky. The above discussion shows you how you will manage and control this risk using the PPM trading plan methodology. You decide how much risk you are willing to take simply by where you set the sell points both below and above the purchase price for each asset that you purchase.

There is certainly work involved in setting up a trading plan for your Target Market Segment purchases. But the process is simple, the Web tools for implementing it are free, and you are dealing with only five investments.

The trading plan is also completely automated after you have put it in place. You do not have to constantly monitor your portfolio or spend hours in front of your computer on a regular basis to guard against dramatic losses or to take your profits when they become available. Your trading plan Web resources are doing this for you automatically and around the clock. Not requiring a lot of your time to monitor and manage a very powerful portfolio is one of the main goals of the PPM methodology set forth in Chapter 1.

I constantly monitor the Web for the best resources for implementing automated trading plans. Those I believe to be particularly effective will be listed in the online supplement. To view them, log in to the supplement, click on *Links by Chapter* and then on *Chapter 4*. Look for the appropriately titled link.

Betting Against an Asset Type

An additional element of the Perfect Portfolio Methodology that makes it extremely powerful is one that actually enables you to make money when markets are performing badly. You do this by using a specialized category of ETFs that *short* the market or asset represented by each PPM Building Block. A short investment is one that increases in value in direct proportion to the decrease in value of the underlying asset. Thus, for example, there is a *short-oil ETF* that increases in value when the price of oil goes down. There is a *short-gold ETF* that increases in value when gold prices fall. There are short-ETFs for virtually all of the PPM Building Blocks, and they are referenced in Chapter 12.

With short-ETFs in your toolkit, you now have three choices when analyzing the price chart for a PPM Building Block investment. If its price trend is up, you will buy. If its price trend is down, you may decide not to buy at this time and monitor the investment in a Watch List. Or, if its price line is moving down and your research tells you that this trend is likely to continue, you can buy a short-ETF for the Building Block you are working with and actually make money as the value of that PPM asset class falls. Of course all short-ETFs must be placed under the watchful eye of a PPM trading plan as previously discussed.

You can readily see that the use of short-ETFs can enable your Perfect Portfolio to thrive in *any* market condition. Adding these unique investments to your portfolio is discussed further in Chapter 12 under the heading Adding Doomsday Building Blocks. You can also learn more about this topic now by logging into the online supplement, clicking *Links by Chapter, Chapter 4* and then *The Shorting Option* link.

Chapter Summary

I discussed in this chapter one of the key components that makes the Perfect Portfolio Methodology uniquely powerful. This is the Target Market Portfolio Segment.

We strive for returns in this Segment that significantly exceed market averages. The potential exists here for returns on the order of 20 percent, 30 percent, 40 percent, and higher. Higher returns are associated with higher risks, of course. The PPM approach enables us to manage and control this additional risk with the simple but powerful trading plan described in this chapter. The Target Market Segment of the Perfect Portfolio consequently gives us the potential of significantly higher returns without significantly higher risk.

The five asset types that I have chosen to define as Target Market Building Blocks make superior returns a real possibility. These assets are Gold, Energy, Agricultural Commodities, Real Estate, and Emerging Markets. For the purpose of building a Perfect Portfolio, I have defined these as separate asset classes. Why? Because each has the potential for extremely high returns and each can respond differently to the same market conditions. Thus, when combined, these asset types provide extensive diversity, resulting in lower portfolio risk.

After completing this chapter, I hope you understand how the Perfect Portfolio is designed to give you exceptional returns while enabling you to limit its risk. I give you in the next five chapters the knowledge, structure, and tools you need to invest with confidence in each of the five Target Market Segment Building Blocks. I show you in Chapter 10 how to combine the Core and Target Segments together to design a total Perfect Portfolio.

Let's get to work starting with the Gold Building Block in the next chapter.

CHAPTER 5

Adding Gold to Your Portfolio

AN INVESTMENT WITH INTRINSIC VALUE

This is the first of five chapters that will teach you how to build the Target Market Segment of the Perfect Portfolio. Each chapter provides the knowledge, structure, and resources you need to effectively invest in one of the five Target Market Portfolio Building Blocks discussed in Chapter 4.

The first building block of the Target Market Segment I discuss in detail is Gold. To find, analyze, select, and monitor this investment, I will use the five-step process described in Chapter 4. The process starts with understanding the Gold asset in more detail. I will then discuss how to add it to the portfolio and monitor and trade it so as to maximize the returns of this Building Block.

I also begin building a Target Market Segment for a sample Perfect Portfolio using data current at the time this chapter was written. While the numbers used in the example will have changed by the time you read this, the process will not have. When you have learned the process, you can then go to the Web and find the best investments for your own Target Market Segment using current data.

Step 1: Understanding Gold

Gold has been treasured since ancient times for its beauty, warmth, sensuality, and spiritual qualities. It is the metal of choice for millions of consumers for the jewelry they wear. Governments and financial institutions view it as the top commodity for storing, supporting, and retaining wealth. A growing number of industrial applications also depend on this rare metal.

About 90 percent of the gold supplied to the market each year worldwide goes into manufactured products while the remainder goes to private investors and to financial institutions as monetary reserves. The manufacture of jewelry is by far the most common use of gold. This application consumes about 75 percent of the gold that comes to market each year.

The Demand for Gold

One of the major reasons I designate the Gold asset as a PPM Building Block is that the demand for it can only continue to grow far into the future. Following are the main uses of gold that support this contention.

- *Consumer Jewelry:* The manufacture of jewelry makes up most of the demand for gold today by far. As stated earlier, jewelry consistently accounts for around three-quarters of gold usage on an annual basis. This demand will grow. As developing countries climb toward economic prosperity, large middle and upper class consumer markets will emerge in countries such as China, India, Russia, and others. Millions of new customers for jewelry will sustain a high demand for gold far into the future.
- *Financial Institution Reserves:* Another significant use of gold is by financial institutions such as banks. Gold is considered an important reserve asset by the central banks of most nations, even though it is no longer at the center of the international financial system as it once was. Gone are the days when the value of a currency was measured by how much gold it could buy. Still, gold is commonly used as a store of a nation's wealth. Why? Because its value is determined by global trading markets and cannot be affected by a single country's economic policies or undermined by its inflation rate. The same

cannot be said of a nation's currency. While this use for gold is not growing significantly, and in many cases is being reduced, a substantial amount of gold is kept off the market for the purpose of serving as financial reserves.

- *Electronics Use:* Gold has valuable properties as a metal that will also cause demand to grow dramatically. It is used widely in the manufacture of electronics because it is one of the most efficient conductors of electricity known to humankind. It is far more reliable than most metal conductors such as copper because it is also an excellent conductor of heat. Gold is also inert, which means that it does not react when it comes into contact with other substances, eliminating corrosion and tarnishing. It is the perfect material for making reliable electronic components. This use of gold can only increase with time.

- *Medical Use:* You may be surprised to learn that gold is biocompatible. This means that it does little to no harm when coming into contact with the human organism. Thus, medical devices such as pacemakers and insulin pumps use gold because of both its biocompatibility and its reliability in electronic devices. Gold also has a high degree of resistance to bacterial colonization, which makes it the perfect choice for implants where the risk of infection is high. Gold is also being increasingly used in pharmaceutical applications to deliver biologically active materials directly into target tissues in the body. The use of gold in medical applications is yet another factor that ensures continued demand growth.

- *Environmental Usage:* A final example that supports the contention that the demand for gold will increase for the foreseeable future is its relatively new application in environmentally friendly applications. Research has revealed that gold catalysts can clean up chemical processes that are used every day to produce pharmaceuticals, detergents, and food additives. Gold nanoparticles have been shown to have the ability to split oxygen atoms and facilitate oxidation reactions. This has a powerful cleansing affect on many chemical processes. Environmental use represents a major path for the growth of demand for gold.

These are only a few of the many uses of gold that point to increased demand far into the future. And since supplies are finite and becoming increasingly expensive to find, access, and process, the laws of supply and demand portend a bright future for the price of gold in the long term.

But the price of gold will not simply go up in a straight line. It will have its ups and downs like all assets. Let's now look at the various factors that can influence its price.

Factors that Influence the Price of Gold

The price of gold is influenced by a number of factors that you must understand so you can take maximum advantage of having this Building Block in your portfolio. These factors will inform your decisions related to when, or if, you will invest in gold, and if you do, how much money you allocate to it.

The following are factors that have historically influenced the price of gold. Note that several Web sites are mentioned in the list presented here. If they change, go to the online supplement to this book, log in, click on *Links by Chapter* and then on *Chapter 5* for updates.

- *Safe Haven Investing:* In general, gold is seen by investors as a safe place to put money when the value of other major assets is diving or uncertain. The fact that gold has intrinsic value gives people confidence that it will retain its value in the face of disaster and turmoil. When fear and uncertainty in the markets are high, the price of gold typically goes up.
- *World and Market Instability:* Gold has historically been used as a protection against disaster—financial, political, social, and natural. Significant negative events of almost any sort can cause economic markets to falter. Terrorist attacks in the United States and Europe have proven to have severely negative impacts on equity markets. Political upheaval in countries that control vital natural resources such as oil can affect economies worldwide. Hurricanes in the Gulf of Mexico can shut down oil rigs and drive the price of energy higher, causing stock prices to move lower. Major instability and turmoil anywhere in the world tend to increase the price of gold.
- *Inflation:* Less spectacular, but often more insidious than disasters, are the creeping effects of inflation. Inflation is caused by the expansion of money and credit in a market

without a corresponding increase in productivity. Inflation causes money to lose purchasing power. Investors use gold as a protection against inflation. It has consistently retained its purchasing power for decades. For example, in 1900, the gold price was $20.67 per ounce, which is about $520 per ounce in today's dollars. The price of one ounce of gold was over $800 when this chapter was written! So the real price of gold has more than beat the cost of inflation while the purchasing power of most currencies has generally declined. High or rising inflation typically causes the price of gold to increase. You can view the current rate of inflation by going to the Web site inflationdata.com/inflation/ (note that the trend is more important than the current number).

- *The Value of the Dollar:* Research shows that gold prices are negatively correlated with the U.S. dollar. When the dollar weakens against other major currencies, gold prices tend to climb. When the dollar is strong, gold prices have historically stagnated. Thus, gold is a good hedge against the dollar. The value of the dollar against, for example, the euro is another input in your decision related to investing in gold. You can view the current dollar exchange rate information by going to the Web site finance.yahoo.com/currency. Again, look at the trend.

- *Supply and Demand:* I discussed earlier in this chapter that the demand for gold will continue to rise as more people worldwide are able to afford it and as new manufacturing and industrial applications are found for its use. When demand increases at a rate at which supply cannot keep up, then the price of gold goes up.

- *Exchange Trading Forces:* Gold is a commodity that is traded on stock exchanges and on commodity exchanges. You can buy or sell gold-based securities on U.S. stock exchanges in the form of ETFs, which I discuss later in this chapter. Gold is also actively traded on commodity exchanges in the form of futures. A gold futures contract is a legally binding agreement for delivery of gold bullion in the future at an agreed-upon price. In a free market of exchange, the price of gold can be, and is, influenced by speculators and hedge funds that are trading for short-term gains. As individual investors, we have very little access to the inner workings of these market forces and thus no fundamental way of analyzing the effect of speculators on gold prices. Our only tool for recognizing and predicting the effects of these hidden forces is the price chart. Fortunately, analyzing price charts is part of the PPM approach, and is discussed later in this chapter.

These are among the major forces and factors that affect the price of gold. There are others. Before deciding to include a Gold Building Block in your portfolio you must consider each of these influences and whether it is currently showing a negative or positive signal for gold price movement. Also, after investing in gold, you must continue to be aware of each factor and stay alert for any factor that may turn negative for the price of gold. The trading plan that is part of the PPM methodology will assist you in this effort. It is discussed later in this chapter as Step 4 of the process.

Extra Credit

Learning More About Gold

There is just no two ways about it, the more you know about an asset, the more successful you will be investing in it. The discussion here about gold is sufficient to show why I have defined it as a Target Market Building Block and to enable you to make informed gold investing decisions. But I would like to see you become an expert in this asset type!

I provide for this purpose links in the online supplement to Web sites where you can learn more about gold. To find them, go to the online supplement site, log in, click on *Links by Chapter* and then on *Chapter 5*. You will find an entry here for *Learning More About Gold.*

You will see this same opportunity in the following chapters for extra credit by going to the Web and learning more about each of the Target Market assets discussed. It is not required that you do this. But since there are only five well-defined asset classes to deal with and since I give you excellent resources for learning more about each, why not become an expert in them all? A little extra time devoted to understanding the assets in your portfolio can result in your having a lot more confidence in your investing decisions.

How to Invest in Gold

The next thing you need to understand about gold is how to include it in your portfolio. What follows are the investment vehicles available for this purpose. At the end of this list, I identify those that best fit the PPM model.

- *Buy the Metal:* The most conservative of investors will simply buy gold metal in the form of gold coins. Bullion coins come in one-twentieth, one-tenth, one-quarter, one-half, and one-ounce weights. Among the coins available are the American Eagle, the Australian Kangaroo Nugget, the Austrian Philharmonic, the Canadian Maple Leaf, and the South African Krugerrand. If you want to buy and hold gold in your portfolio, then purchasing the metal is a viable option. Just be very careful because there are a lot of gold-selling scams in the market today. Buying the metal is not a good option for the PPM approach. The PPM requires that the gold component be sufficiently liquid to be bought and sold quickly, easily, and automatically via a Web-based trading plan. Coins do not fit this criterion.

- *Buy Gold Jewelry:* This is also not a good way to make a pure gold investment. Much of the price of jewelry is related to the value added in the form of design and workmanship, not to the value of the gold itself. Jewelry also does not have the liquidity required by the PPM investing approach.

- *Buy Commodity Contracts:* Another way to invest in the gold market is to buy and sell gold commodity futures as discussed briefly in the previous section of this chapter. To do this, you would open a futures trading account at a major commodities trading firm. I do not suggest this form of gold investing for the average investor because it can be extremely risky and it requires a great deal of time and specialized knowledge.

- *Buy Gold Mining Stocks:* Instead of buying the metal or futures contracts tied to the metal, you could buy stocks in companies that mine gold. But you must keep in mind that when doing so you are not just buying mineral rights, you are also buying in to a company with overhead (energy costs, labor costs, seismic data costs, and so on) that will eat into the value of whatever gold it manages to bring out of the ground. Buying these stocks also exposes you to company risks such as bad management decisions, lawsuits, and other factors unique to the company's operations.

- *Buy Mutual Funds:* A multitude of mutual funds exists that focus on gold. Such funds may invest in mining company

stocks, gold bullion, and even other precious metals and minerals.
- *Buy Exchange Traded Funds:* And finally, you can buy shares of gold-based ETFs. For example, the World Gold Council has launched the streetTRACKS Gold Shares investment vehicle, an ETF in which investors own shares backed by actual gold bullion. Each share, listed on the New York Stock Exchange under the symbol GLD, represents one-tenth of an ounce of bullion. I used this ETF to illustrate the process of implementing a trading plan in Chapter 4. There also exist ETFs that track an index of gold mining company stocks. GDX is an example.

You can see that there are many ways to buy gold. But there are only two that fit the PPM approach. These are buying a gold-related mutual fund and buying a gold-related ETF. Both types of investments can be easily bought and sold. Both can also be automatically monitored by the PPM trading plan that I discuss in Step 5 of the investing process later in this chapter.

Having identified the appropriate investing vehicles for a Gold Building Block, the next task is to find multiple mutual fund and ETF candidates for evaluation.

Step 2: Identifying Gold Investment Candidates

We are now prepared for Step 2 of the PPM process. Here the goal is to find at least three gold investment candidates for evaluation. I will look for either gold-related mutual funds or for gold-related Exchange Traded Funds to add a gold component to the sample portfolio I am building.

For finding mutual fund candidates, I will use the site at finance.yahoo.com/funds as discussed in Chapter 4. I will illustrate how to use this site to find a gold investment candidate from my Core Fund Family and to find a top performing gold-related fund.

For finding a gold-related ETF, I will use the site at finance .yahoo.com/etf. If any of these sites don't work as described in this section, log in to the online supplement, click on *Links by Chapter* and then on *Lesson 5* to find updated link descriptions.

You can also get gold investment candidates from other sources such as your adviser, a newsletter, and even from the financial media. Evaluate as many funds or ETFs as you like, but I strongly recommend that you consider no fewer than three.

The following are the candidates I will evaluate for my gold investment.

- *Gold Candidate 1: From My Core Fund Family.* I first go to the site at finance.yahoo.com/funds. In the left column of this page I locate a menu item labeled *Funds by Family* and click on it. I am presented with an alphabetical list of fund families. I used this site in Chapter 3 when choosing funds for my example Core Segment. For the sake of convenience, I tried to find mutual funds for all four Core Building Blocks from one fund family. I decided to use Vanguard as my Core Fund Family in my sample portfolio. Since the logical first place to look for a gold investment is in this fund family, I click on Vanguard in the list of fund families.

  Looking at the list of funds available from Vanguard at the time this chapter was written, I found a very promising fund called Vanguard Precious Metals and Mining (VGPMX), which specializes in gold. But further examination of this fund shows that it is closed to new investors. So I need to look in another fund family. You are certainly free to choose any family, but for my example, I will look at Fidelity's list. I find here Fidelity Select Gold (FSAGX).

  Clicking the fund symbol in the list brings up a Web page for the fund with a menu on the left. Clicking on the *profile* selection in the menu gives me information that tells me the fund owns both gold bullion and stocks of companies that mine and process gold. This is a good, diversified mix. So FSAGX will be my first gold investment candidate.

- *Gold Candidate 2: A Top Performing Fund.* For my next candidate, I will look for a gold-related fund that has been one of the top performers over the past several years. How do I find these funds? The finance.yahoo.com/funds Web page has an interesting entry in the menu at the left of the page titled *Top Performers*. Clicking on this item gives me a list of fund categories. I click on the category titled *Specialty-Precious Metals*. I then see a list of the top-performing precious metal funds for various time periods.

  I will look for a fund that appears in more than one of these lists. At the time this chapter was written, a fund that appeared on the top performer lists for one, three, and five years was USAA Precious Metals and Minerals (USAGX). I see from looking at its profile that its holdings are 80 percent dedicated to stocks of companies at all stages of the gold mining process. The other 20 percent can include stocks related to other metals, oil, coal, and forestry products. This should make for an interesting comparison with my first candidate, so I will make USAGX my second fund candidate selection.

- *Candidate 3: An Exchange Traded Fund.* As my third and final gold investment candidate, I will select an ETF that tracks a gold index or one that represents actual ownership in gold bullion. A good place to look is the Web site at finance.yahoo.com/etf. I click "View ETFs" in the left menu and on the resulting page use the category dropdown menu to select "Specialty-Precious Metals." Then I click "View" to see and browse for gold ETFs.

  Here I find IAU, an ETF that is based on actual ownership of gold bullion. I also find GDX, an ETF that tracks the AMEX Gold Miners Index, which consists of stocks in gold mining companies. Since IAU is the more pure gold play and does not include elements of company risk as does GDX, I will choose IAU as my third gold investment candidate. (Note that I could have also selected GLD, which I used as an example in Chapter 4. For sake of diversity, I will use IAU in this example.)

Having identified three gold investment candidates, I am prepared to evaluate and compare each. That is where we go to next.

Step 3: Collecting and Analyzing the Data

I am now ready to gather and compare relevant data for each of my investment candidates. The goal is to identify the one that has the best overall profile in terms of return, risk, and management fees. I will use the worksheet template shown in Table 5.1 to collect the data needed for my analysis. You can access and print a copy of this worksheet in PDF format in the online supplement to this book. To do so, log in, click on *Links by Chapter,* and then on *Chapter 5* to find the Target Market Building Block Worksheet.

There are many sites on the Web that you can use to collect the data required here. I suggest that you simply continue to use the site at finance.yahoo.com as discussed in Chapter 4. When you

Table 5.1   Gold Building Block Data Collection Worksheet

Company/ Fund	Symbol	Annualized Returns			Risk: Std. Dev.	Expense Ratio
		1-year	3-year	5-year		
Fidelity Select Gold	FSAGX	31.47%	33.27%	26.36%	29.50%	.87%
USAA Precious Metals	USAGX	34.25%	42.03%	36.40%	28.65%	1.52%
IShares Gold Trust ETF	IAU	37.73%	28.35%	No Data	16.38%	.40%

Note that IAU has not been in existence long enough to have 5-year data.

browsed fund families and fund top performers in the candidate identification process using the funds area of this site, you could have simply clicked on the symbol of the fund you selected to get the data needed to fill in the worksheet. Or you can go to the finance.yahoo.com home page and enter the fund or ETF symbol in the area labeled *Get Quote* to display the same information page for each investment.

On the information page for the investment you are evaluating, you will see a menu on the left side. Click on *Performance* to find returns data and then click on *Risk* to find the three-year Standard Deviation data. To find the Total Expense Ratio of a fund or ETF, click on *Profile* and scroll down the right side of the page to the *Expenses and Fees* box. You will see here the total expenses ratio at the top. Note that for some ETFs, this box on the Yahoo! site will display *N/A*. If this is the case, go to morningstar.com, enter the ETF symbol where the site asks for *Quote,* and click on the *Expenses and Fees* menu item. Here you will find ETF management fees.

Table 5.1 shows the completed data worksheet for my gold investment candidates. Please note that the specific investments used in this table are for illustration purposes only and do *not* constitute a recommendation of any investment. Also be aware that the numbers displayed are those that exist at the time this chapter was written. They will be different at the time when you read this.

Comparison and Selection

I note in reviewing the worksheet data that the Returns figures are virtually the same, which is not surprising, because each of these investments is closely related to the price of gold. All of the returns are extraordinary. When you perform your own analysis, of course, the picture is likely to be different.

The factor that stands out in this analysis is the risk measure for the ETF candidate. It is almost half the risk of the mutual funds. The ETF also has a very low expense ratio. I will select IAU as the Gold Building Block of my Target Market Segment on the basis of this analysis. Your analysis may bring a different conclusion.

All other factors being relatively equal, I will always pick an ETF over a fund for one major reason. An ETF can be traded like a stock, which makes implementing a trading plan for this investment simple. I discuss the value of placing triggers on an investment to limit losses and to take profits in Step 5 of this process. I can use automated trailing stops for an ETF but not for a mutual fund. If for any of my Target Market Building Blocks a traditional mutual fund is a significantly better choice than an ETF, the trading plan will need to be implemented using e-mail alerts as opposed to the more convenient trailing stops.

Step 4: Price Chart Analysis

Now that I have selected an investment to represent the Gold Building Block in my sample portfolio, I need to decide if this is a good time to buy it. Remember, the Target Market Segment of the portfolio is for buying and selling, not for buying and holding. So, I don't want to buy an investment that is currently experiencing a significant downtrend. I therefore need to view a price chart for my selection. This is Step 4 of the PPM Target Market Segment analysis process.

There are many Web sites that enable you to display a price chart. For the sake of simplicity, I will continue to use the site at finance.yahoo.com. I go to the site and enter the symbol IAU in the *Get Quote* input box. I see a menu on the left on the resulting investment information page. I click on *Basic Technical Analysis,* and a price chart appears.

I want a price chart for at least one year, so I click on the *1y* menu item above the chart. I also want to plot the Bollinger Bands as discussed in Chapter 4 for the purpose of creating a trading plan. So I click on that item in the menu above the chart. I get the chart shown in Figure 5.1.

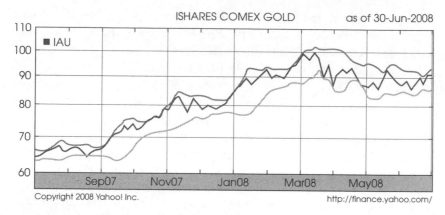

Copyright 2008 Yahoo! Inc.   http://finance.yahoo.com/

Figure 5.1   One-Year Price Chart for IAU

Reproduced with permission of Yahoo! Inc. ® 2008 by Yahoo! Inc. YAHOO! and the YAHOO! logo are trademarks of Yahoo! Inc.

The line in the middle on the chart is the price line. The lines above and below are the Bollinger Bands. Price level is shown on the left of the chart, and the bottom of the chart shows time. Always keep in mind that this chart shows pricing as of the time this chapter was written. Your chart will look different.

Here are factors to look for on the chart and my observations.

- *Current Price:* The current price is $93 per share.
- *Price Trend:* Looking at the price line, I see that for the last year the price has been moving up sharply. A dip began in April 2008 but the uptrend seems recently to have continued.
- *Support:* I discussed in Chapter 4 the factors that need to be put in place for a trading plan related to any investment I buy. Part of this plan is finding points of price support and resistance. Identifying a price support level is simply a matter of eyeballing the chart and looking for a price level where the stock seems to bounce up. I can estimate that a support level on this chart exists at about $85. The bottom line of the Bollinger Bands can also help in defining this point.
- *Resistance:* The resistance level is the price at which the stock seems to bounce down. Again, looking at the chart, I can estimate this to be at a level of about $100.
- *Volatility:* This is a measure of how widely the investment's price has varied in the recent past. The more volatile the

price is, the riskier the stock is. The Bollinger Bands provide an indication of volatility. The farther the bands are apart, the more volatile the investment. As discussed in Chapter 4, this factor will help decide how far from the current price to set a trailing stop. Higher volatility tells me to set the trailing stop price further from the current price. Looking at the chart, I would feel comfortable placing a trailing stop at the support price of $85.

Additional Analysis

At this point, the process of understanding, identifying, and analyzing a gold component for my Target Market Portfolio Segment is complete. Now I must decide if I want to buy this investment at this time. Here is my current analysis of the external factors that I mentioned earlier in this chapter.

I believe that it has been convincingly illustrated that a strong demand for gold currently exists and will continue to grow in the future. This is one reason why it is defined as one of the five Target Market Building Blocks in the first place. The question is whether now is a good time to buy. For this purpose, I will look at the following indicators.

> *The Price Trend:* I can reasonably conclude from looking at the price chart that the long-term uptrend still has legs. While a dip has recently occurred, it did not significantly penetrate any support level. The chart therefore gives me a positive buy signal.

> *Strength of the Dollar:* Gold prices have a negative correlation with the strength of the dollar. To check the trend of the exchange rate between the dollar and the euro, I go to a Web resource mentioned earlier that shows this information. The site is finance.yahoo.com/currency. At the time this chapter was written, the dollar was still weak against the euro and showed little sign of improving. This factor also supports a buy decision.

> *Inflation Trend:* Gold prices tend to rise when inflation is rising. So I next check the trend of inflation. As mentioned earlier in this chapter, there are many Web sites that show this information. One site I can use is inflationdata.com/inflation/.

Or I could simply search for "U.S. inflation chart" using a search engine. I saw a flat-to-moderately increasing inflation rate at the time this chapter was written. This is a slightly positive signal for the price of gold.

Stock Market Trend: Gold prices tend to rise when the stock market is heading down. When I last looked at a chart of the S&P 500 while writing this chapter, I saw a major downdraft in the market. This is a yet another positive sign for the current purchase of a gold investment.

All of these external factors support a decision to buy the gold investment now. I will buy a gold component at this time even though I am somewhat concerned about how sharply the price of gold has risen in the past year. A speculative bubble may be occurring and the price of gold may be due for a correction in the near future. But since I am putting this investment in my Target Market Portfolio Segment where its price is constantly monitored and where I will limit my risk of a price drop by using trailing stops, I can move forward with my purchase decision with confidence. If this is a bubble, I will take advantage of it as long as it continues and I will limit my losses if it bursts.

Step 5: Defining a Gold Investment Trading Plan

I have collected the data needed to make an informed decision related to including a gold investment in my portfolio. My decision based on this information is to buy IAU at this point. Now I need to define a trading plan as illustrated in Chapter 4.

For IAU, using current data, it would be reasonable to set up the following sample trading plan.

- Place a market order to buy IAU at the current share price of $93.
- Set a trailing stop trigger as follows: "If the market price of IAU goes down by $8 or more from the highest price it reaches during my ownership, then sell my IAU position." (Note that this could also be a percentage drop as opposed to a dollar drop.)
- Place a take-profit e-mail alert trigger at $100.

Here are various scenarios that can occur with this plan in place:

- If IAU goes immediately down to $85, the position will be automatically sold.
- If IAU goes up to $97, my stop loss price automatically increases to $89 ($8 below the current price).
- If IAU then goes to down from $97 to $89 with no further rise above $97, my shares will automatically be sold.
- IF IAU goes to $100 without first getting stopped out, I will get a take-profit e-mail alert. This will prompt me to investigate what is happening with IAU to decide whether I want to sell to take profits. If I believe the uptrend will continue, I may decide to tighten the stop loss trigger to sell if IAU drops $3 instead of $8, thus locking in more profit. I will increase my take-profit alert price to perhaps $105 at the same time.

You can see the absolute beauty of a well-thought-out trading plan and the power of an automated trailing stop trigger. It immediately protects me from a loss of more than $8 on IAU. As IAU moves up, the stop loss price moves up with it. *But,* the stop loss price *never* moves down. With this parameter, the $8 maximum drop limit is always in place regardless of how high the price of IAU goes.

Note that my trailing stops can also be set to send me e-mails as opposed to automatically selling the investment.

It is also important to note that stop loss protection has some risk involved. If the IAU price drops dramatically, there may be no buyers available at the stop loss price I have set. The IAU sell order simply becomes a market order when the stop price is hit and my shares will be sold at the price available when my order finally gets executed. Stop loss prices are therefore not guaranteed. Such prices are only guaranteed if you buy Put Options, which were discussed briefly in Chapter 4.

Building *Your* Perfect Portfolio!

You began building your own Perfect Portfolio in Chapter 3, when you identified specific investments for the Core Segment. You are now prepared to put into place a Gold investment as the first Building Block of your Target Market Segment and I suggest that you do so.

Your first step is to go to the online supplement and print one or more Target Market Building Block Worksheets. To do this, log in to the site, click on *Links by Chapter,* and then on *Chapter 5.* Look for the link to this worksheet, which is presented in PDF format, and print it.

Now use the Web sites referenced in this chapter to identify Gold investment candidates. Collect and compare current data for each using the steps described in this chapter and then view the price chart for the most promising specific investment. Based on your analysis of the price chart and other market factors discussed in this chapter, decide whether this is a good time to include gold in your portfolio. If so, develop a trading plan for it. Record all of your work on the Target Market Building Block Worksheet.

You will see this same opportunity to build your Perfect Portfolio in the next four chapters for each Target Market Building Block. It is obviously not a requirement that you do this. But your involvement in the learning process enables you to transform concepts into actions, which is an essential part of true education. Also, when you finish this book, you will have more than knowledge, you will have a concrete action plan for implementing and monitoring a powerful portfolio.

Chapter Summary

I discussed Gold in this chapter as one Building Block of the Perfect Portfolio's Target Market Segment. I worked through the PPM Target Market Building Block investment process to illustrate the data and analysis needed to make an informed decision when selecting a Gold component for my sample portfolio.

I also suggested that you use the same process along with related Web sites and worksheets to collect and analyze current data for a Gold investment. Your data and analysis may support a completely different conclusion than the one formed here. Remember, the actual data presented in this chapter are not important. Understanding the process for collecting and evaluating the data is.

I now have a Gold component for my sample Target Market Segment. Finding an Energy component is next.

CHAPTER 6

Adding an Energy Component to Your Portfolio

AN ASSET THAT RUNS THE WORLD'S ECONOMY

Energy is much on our mind these days. As the price of a barrel of oil has pin-balled from $60 to $140 and back to even below $60, it has become very apparent how great an influence the cost of energy has on just about everything we buy. We feel the effects of energy costs most directly at the gas pump. But we also see the effects of the price of energy creep into other areas such as the cost of food, consumer goods, and the price of airline tickets, among others.

While alternative sources of energy are being aggressively explored, for now and the foreseeable future the health of our economy is dangerously dependent on oil and its price. The inevitability of the growth in demand for oil-based energy assets means that this asset class must be considered as a component for any well designed portfolio. For this reason and others I have defined Energy as one of the five Target Market Building Blocks.

Energy fits the profile of all of the Target Market Building Blocks. The demand for energy related assets will increase exponentially for the foreseeable future, investments in energy have the potential for high annual returns, and its price is affected by a host of influences unique to this asset type, thus adding valuable diversity to the portfolio. Also, investments that enable you to buy the entire Energy sector are easy to identify, analyze, trade, and monitor.

In this chapter, to find an Energy investment I again use the five-step Target Market asset evaluation and selection process introduced in Chapter 4 and used in Chapter 5 for the Gold Building Block. I begin by discussing a few facts about energy and its growing demand and point to resources where you can learn more. I next list factors that influence the price of energy, and oil in particular. I then go through the steps required to find, analyze, select, and monitor an investment for my sample portfolio.

Let's get started by learning a little more about Energy.

Step 1: Understanding Energy

Oil and the energy it produces are the lifeblood of the American economy and most economies around the world. Almost every product we buy depends on the availability of this resource—if not to make it, then most certainly to transport it. The U.S. economy runs on oil.

There are certainly alternative energy sources being explored and developed, but at present they are a long way from replacing oil. Finding oil substitutes must be a national priority, but at the current time we must face reality. The world will be dependent on oil for many years to come regardless of what the politicians say. So while it may feel good to invest in alternative energies, oil is still the investment of choice for the Perfect Portfolio Building Block.

The Demand for Energy

I define assets as PPM Building Blocks only if there is virtually no doubt about the strength of their long-term demand and their potential for investment returns that can significantly exceed market averages. Energy fits these criteria perfectly.

According to the U.S. Department of Energy's Annual Energy Outlook 2007, market trends suggest that the demand for energy resources will rise dramatically over the next 25 years. Here are a few relevant statistics produced by the DOE.

- Global demand for all energy sources is forecast to grow by 57 percent over the next 25 years.
- U.S. demand for all types of energy is expected to increase by 31 percent within 25 years.
- By 2030, 56 percent of the world's energy use will be in Asia.

- Electricity demand in the United States will grow by at least 40 percent by 2032.
- New power generation equal to nearly 300 (1,000MW) power plants will be needed to meet electricity demand by 2030.

Based on these statistics, it is obvious that demand for energy is high and it will continue to grow at an incredible rate far into the future. This is the type of asset that belongs in my, and your, portfolio.

Factors that Influence the Price of Energy

In the wake of extremely volatile gasoline prices, devastating hurricanes, instability in the Persian Gulf, and increasing demand from China and India, tough questions are being asked about the United States' continuing dependence on oil and our need to develop long-term, sustainable energy alternatives. Alternative energy must certainly be considered and developed. But for the foreseeable future, the United States and most of the world will depend on oil as the major source of energy. This being the case, it is important to understand the factors that influence the price of this commodity. Among these are the following:

- *Demand:* In today's world, energy is provided mainly by oil and natural gas, both resources that have a finite supply. Global energy consumption is soaring. The demand for oil has already been discussed. Energy demands will increase exponentially as China, India, and other developing countries continue to build thousands of factories and their massive populations become more affluent consumers.
- *Supply:* The world has enough oil for the foreseeable future. A major problem, at least in the United States, is that in many areas we are not allowed to drill for it. Environmental groups have pressured Congress into placing vast oil sources in the United States off-limits to drillers and thereby increasing our dependency on foreign supplies. It is also virtually impossible to get the permits needed to build an oil refinery today. As a result, only about 4 percent of U.S. needs are supplied by domestic drilling. This leaves us dependent on a host of external forces such as OPEC, an oil cartel consisting of 13 of the world's top oil-producing countries. This group can

decide how much oil to release to the market and is a major determinant of world supply and its price.

- *Political Instability and World Tensions:* A major disruption in the production of oil in any of a number of countries can cause the price of oil to spike everywhere in the world, dramatically affecting the U.S. economy. While Canada and Mexico are the main suppliers of U.S. oil, other countries more prone to political instability are also major suppliers. These include Saudi Arabia, Venezuela, Kazakhstan, Nigeria, and others. A terrorist attack or internal revolt in any of these countries can cause oil prices to skyrocket.

- *Weather Events:* Natural disasters such as earthquakes and hurricanes can temporarily disrupt oil supplies and cause prices to spike. A good example was Hurricane Katrina in the Gulf of Mexico that shut down oil drilling rigs for an extended period of time and decreased supply. Oil prices typically move up at the beginning of hurricane season as oil users hedge their risk by purchasing oil futures contracts to protect against the risk of weather events.

- *Lack of Viable Near-Term Alternatives:* We will eventually have to find alternatives to oil. Alternate energy resources include solar power, wind power, biofuels, and hydrogen fuel to name a few. But none is a near-term solution, because much research is needed to bring the cost per unit of energy down to that of the price of oil.

- *Hedging and Speculation:* Oil is like any other commodity—the last unit sold determines its price. Trading market dynamics are the greatest driver of oil prices in the short term. Oil futures contracts are traded on commodity exchanges. They are purchased by users of oil to hedge against the risk of future oil prices. Thus, sentiment and expectations are important factors. If oil futures traders believe there will be a shortage of oil supplies in the future, they will raise prices *now,* before the shortage actually occurs. Even the threat of political instability or bad weather will raise the price of oil. In addition to hedgers, there are also speculators in the market, who can artificially drive up the price of oil so they can realize short-term gains.

You can see that there exist a variety of factors that investors need to be aware of when investing in an oil-based energy asset.

Many of these factors cannot be analyzed using traditional fundamental analysis methods. Fortunately, much of this information is factored into current price trends and we can study these trends on a price chart. We do so in Step 4 of the process that is discussed later in this chapter.

Extra Credit

Learning More About Energy

There is a lot more to learn about the field of energy. I provide Web links in the online supplement of this book that you can access to obtain further education and a more complete understanding of energy resources. To access them simply go to the online supplement, log in, click on *Links by Chapter,* and then on *Chapter 6* to find these links.

How to Invest in Energy

There are a number of types of energy in which you can invest. And for each type of energy, there are multiple investment vehicles that can be used. Let's first address the question of what type of energy to invest in.

As I mentioned earlier in this chapter, among the choices for energy investments are oil, natural gas, nuclear energy, coal, and alternative energy sources such as wind and solar. My personal opinion, based on significant research into each of these investments, is that oil is currently the most profitable form of energy in which to invest. Why? Because it is the cheapest and most reliable source of energy available today and will be for the foreseeable future.

Alternative energy sources are promising, but they are a long way from being commercially viable. Most such technologies depend on government subsidies, and these are fickle in the extreme and hard to analyze and predict. Investing in alternative energy sources, therefore, is a risky business right now. I include a section at the end of this chapter, however, that shows how to invest in various alternative energy assets if you wish. But for now, I will stick with an investment having oil as its primary focus for my sample portfolio.

Having made this decision, the next goal is to decide on the type of investment vehicle to use to add an energy component to the portfolio. The following are the options. You will note that they are the same investing vehicles as for Gold, described in Chapter 5, the exception being that you will not want to own the actual commodity. Buying a barrel of oil is not as appealing as buying a gold coin or a gold bracelet.

- *Buy Commodity Contracts:* One way to invest in energy assets is to buy or sell crude oil futures on a commodities exchange. To do this, you would open a futures trading account at a major commodity trading firm. Trading commodity futures, however, is risky and requires a great deal of specialized knowledge.
- *Buy Individual Oil-Related Stocks:* There are plenty of companies in the oil business, doing everything from drilling to refining to manufacturing equipment. But buying individual stocks exposes you to company risks such as bad management decisions, lawsuits, and other factors unique to the company's operations. The PPM advocates buying groups of stocks to eliminate specific company risks.
- *Buy Mutual Funds:* A multitude of mutual funds exist that focus on energy. Such funds may concentrate on oil stocks or be more diverse by including other forms of energy such as coal and natural gas. I will use mutual funds as one option when searching for an energy component for my sample portfolio later in this chapter.
- *Buy Exchange Traded Funds:* You can choose to buy an ETF that holds a basket of energy-related stocks. I will use ETFs as one investment candidate in the selection and evaluation process presented further on.

Of the various ways to invest in energy, only two fit the PPM approach. They are mutual funds and ETFs, both of which can be automatically monitored by the PPM trading plan that I discuss in Step 5 of the investment identification and evaluation process. The next task is to find mutual fund and ETF candidates for further study.

Step 2: Identifying Oil-Related Energy Investment Candidates

Now the goal is to find at least three energy-related investment candidates for evaluation. I will look for either energy-related mutual funds or for energy-related Exchange Traded Funds. In the process discussed here, I point to Web sites for finding possible investment candidates. These sites are suggestions only and if I feel the need to update these references, I will do so in the online supplement. You can also get investment candidates from other sources such as your adviser, a newsletter, and even from the financial media. You can evaluate as many funds as you like, but I would strongly recommend that you consider no fewer than three.

I discussed in Chapter 5 how to use the finance.yahoo.com/ funds site for finding investment candidates for Gold. The same menu clicks apply for the processes discussed here. Review the process presented in Chapter 5 if you need to refresh your memory.

The following are the investment candidates I found for the Energy Building Block.

- *Candidate 1: From a Specific Fund Family.* For Gold, I used Fidelity as an example fund family and will do so again. You can use any fund family that you like. So my first step is to look for an energy-related mutual fund in that family. I can browse a list of Fidelity energy-related offerings by using the Yahoo! Funds by Families capability. I find FSENX—Fidelity Select Energy. By clicking on the symbol and then on the *Profile* menu item on the resulting page, I find that the fund normally invests at least 80 percent of its assets in the securities of companies principally engaged in the energy field, including the conventional areas of oil, gas, electricity, and coal, and newer sources of energy such as nuclear, geothermal, oil shale, and solar power. This is not a pure oil play but most energy funds are not. So I will use it as one candidate for comparison.
- *Candidate 2: A Top-Performing Fund.* I next look for a top-performing energy fund. Using the Yahoo! Top Performers capability, I click on the *Natural Resources* category and browse the lists related to various time periods looking for a fund that appears multiple times. I find PSPFX—U.S. Global Investors Global Resources fund. This fund normally invests at least 80 percent of its assets in the equity securities of companies within the natural resources sector. The fund profile tells me that it may invest in oil, gas, and other basic materials. Again, this is not a pure oil investment, but its price is significantly driven by energy demand. So this will be my second candidate.

- *Candidate 3: An Exchange Traded Fund.* As my last candidate, I will go to ishares.com and look for an energy-related ETF. On this site, I place the cursor over the *Sector* menu item on the home page and then select the *Energy* Sector. Here I see multiple choices and will select IYE—an ETF that tracks the Dow Jones U.S. Energy Index. This Index includes companies in the following sectors: oil and gas producers and oil equipment, services, and distribution.

These are my candidates for further evaluation. The energy-related investments you find for your own portfolio can, and probably will, be different. Also feel free to consider more than three candidates.

Step 3: Collecting and Analyzing the Data

I am now prepared to gather and compare relevant data for each of my energy investment candidates. The goal is to identify the investment having the best overall profile in regard to return, risk, and management fees. I will use the same Yahoo! Finance site and data collection worksheet as explained in Chapter 5 for Gold.

Table 6.1 shows the data I collected at the time this chapter was written for each of my Energy investment candidates. To record this data, I used the Target Market Building Block Worksheet found in the online supplement.

Comparison and Selection

The return figures are virtually the same; this should not be surprising because each of these investments is related closely to the price

Table 6.1 Energy Building Block Data Collection Worksheet

Company/ Fund	Symbol	Annualized Returns			Risk: Std. Dev.	Expense Ratio
		1-year	3-year	5-year		
Fidelity Select Energy	FSENX	28.29%	26.35%	30.91%	21.65%	.89%
U.S. Global Resources	PSPFX	28.38%	26.40%	43.18%	23.80%	.94%
Dow Jones Energy ETF	IYE	24.39%	20.79%	28.05%	19.44%	.48%

of oil. All of the returns are extraordinary. When you perform your own analysis, of course, the picture may have changed.

While PSPFX has an exceptional five-year annualized return, it also has a higher risk profile. FSENX is a good choice with a lower risk profile than PSPFX and lower expenses, yet none of these differences is striking. The ETF has a very low expense ratio, lower risk, and since it trades like a stock, it will be easier to fit into the PPM trading plan.

Based on all of the factors considered, I will pick IYE as the Energy Building Block of my Target Market Segment. Your analysis may bring a different conclusion.

Step 4: Price Chart Analysis

I have selected an investment to represent the Energy component of my sample portfolio. Now I need to decide whether this is the time to buy it. Remember, the Target Market Segment of the portfolio is for buying and selling, not buying and holding. I don't want to buy an investment that is in a significant downtrend. I need to view its price chart, and this is Step 4 of the PPM process.

As in Chapter 5 where we analyzed a Gold asset, I will continue to use the site at finance.yahoo.com. Here I enter the symbol IYE in the *Get Quote* input box. I see a menu on the left of the resulting investment information page and click on *Basic Technical Analysis*. A chart will appear.

I want a price chart for at least a year, so I click on *1y* in the menu above the chart. For the purpose of creating a trading plan, I will also want to plot the Bollinger Bands as discussed in Chapter 4. So I click on that item in the menu above the chart. I get a chart that looks something like Figure 6.1.

The line in the middle on the chart is the price line. The lines on either side are the Bollinger Bands. Price is shown on the left of the chart, and the bottom of the chart shows time. Always keep in mind that this chart shows pricing as of the time this chapter was written. Your chart will look different.

Here are factors to look for on the chart.

- *Current Price:* The current price is $150 per share.
- *Price Trend:* Looking at the price line, I see that for the last year the price has been moving up sharply. Recently, however, there has been a sideways movement, but since IYE is a volatile

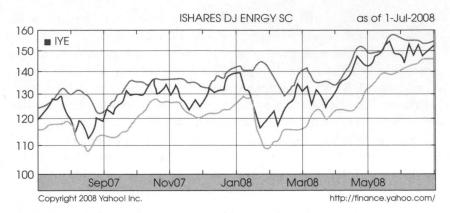

Figure 6.1 **One Year Price Chart for IYE**

investment, I am not overly concerned by this. I would not be hesitant to buy at this time based on the current price trend.

- *Support:* Simply from viewing the chart, I would put a support price at $140. For most of the past year, this price seems to have been a level of resistance where the price has bounced down. But around April of 2008 when this price was penetrated, $140 seems to have transformed to a level of support where the price tends to bounce up.

- *Resistance:* A short-term price resistance level seems to be forming at around a price of around $155, but this is much too close to the current price to serve as a reasonable price point at which I want to consider taking profits. I would consider taking profits, however, if the $160 level were reached. This is a price level that has been tested in the not too distant past. So I will set my take-profit alert at $160.

- *Volatility:* This is a measure of how widely the investment's price varies over short periods of time. The more volatile the price, the riskier the stock. The Bollinger Bands give us an indication of volatility. The farther the bands are apart, the more volatile the investment. As discussed in Chapter 4, this factor will help me to decide how far from the current price to set a trailing stop so that I will not get whipsawed out of my position based on normal daily fluctuations. Higher volatility tells us to set the trailing stop price further from the current price.

The current Bollinger Bands are showing a spread of about $10 from $145 to approximately $155. But they seem to have narrowed only recently. The spread was $20 just two months ago. Being conservative, I will use my own judgment and consider a normal price swing to be less than $8 on either side of the current price. So I determine that my initial support price of $140 will not whipsaw me out of my position if I place a stop trigger there.

This completes my analysis of the current price chart. All factors tell me to buy IYE at this point. Having made this decision, I do have concerns that energy prices have climbed so steeply over the past six months. I don't believe that fundamental factors can explain this sudden price increase and it may be the result of a speculative bubble. But, as with Gold, Energy is a Target Market investment that will be monitored constantly by the PPM trading plan I implement. This plan limits losses and lets profits run. So if this is a "bubble" I can ride it up and should it burst, my losses will be limited. The bottom line is that I would not buy this investment for a buy-and-hold strategy. I will buy it for a buy-and-trade strategy.

I am now prepared to define a trading plan for my selected investment.

Step 5: Defining an Energy Investment Trading Plan

Setting up the following sample trading plan for IYE using current data looks to be reasonable.

- Place a market order for IYE at the current purchase price of $150.
- Set a trailing stop trigger as follows: "If the share market price of IYE goes down by $8 or more from the highest point it reaches during the time I own it, then sell my IYE position." (Note that this could also be a percentage drop as opposed to a dollar drop.)
- Place a take-profit e-mail alert at $160.

This trading plan definition is based on both subjective and objective analyses. There can be little argument that the demand for oil-based energy will continue to grow far into the future. But it is a very volatile investment that will have ups and downs along the way, some of which may be severe.

The trading plan I put into place for this, and all Target Market investments, protects me from extreme down-side volatility. If the price starts to deteriorate significantly as would happen in a bursting bubble scenario, the trading plan described here automatically sells to limit my losses to a maximum of $8 dollars per share. Yet, even bubbles can continue to expand, and the trading plan allows me to take advantage of price increases with the assurance that the stop loss triggers are moving up with the price. If the share price moves up to a point where my take-profit alert is triggered I can either take profits or tighten my stop-loss parameter to, say, $2 and in this manner continually lock in profits as the price rises—even if we are currently experiencing a price bubble.

Therefore, even though oil has had a significant run-up in recent months, my decision to buy at this time seems justified. The upside is significant and the downside is limited by my trading plan.

Considering Alternative Energy

Many of my students ask me about investing in alternative energy. It is a subject touted by both the media and politicians, and as a result, people get excited about investing in it. This is certainly an area where tremendous growth potential is possible. But in my opinion the time has not yet arrived to consider an alternative energy investment in my sample Perfect Portfolio. Your assessment, at the time you read this, may be different. If so, you have several options to consider.

There are multiple ETFs and funds that hold the stocks of companies focused on alternative energy. To find them go to the site at finance.yahoo.com/etf. Click "View ETFs" in the left menu and on the next page select "Specialty-Natural Resources" from the "Category" menu. You will see the following ETF investments available for alternative energies, among others.

- KWT—Solar Energy
- NLR—Nuclear Energy
- PBD—Clean Energy

Each owns a basket of stocks of companies involved with alternative energy. Yet, there are several problems with these ETFs and investments like them. Here are a few that should raise a red flag.

- *Difficult to Analyze:* These ETFs are too new to have a significant amount of data to analyze. It is difficult to get a handle on their performance and risk profile based on what is typically less than a year's worth of data. I recognize that by the time you read this, however, more data will be available.
- *Low Trading Volume:* Many of the new ETFs in the area of alternative energy have very low daily trading volumes. Any security with an average trading volume of fewer than 500,000 shares per day is a questionable investment. Low volume results in a large difference between the Bid and Ask prices for each share, which costs you money the instant you buy. More than one ETF has been simply discontinued for lack of trading volume.
- *High Degree of Uncertainty:* The operations of many companies in the alternative energy field are currently financed either by government grants or venture capital, not by earnings. Much of the technology involved is not yet commercially feasible. This makes for a very risky and unpredictable investment.

I tell my students to feel free to monitor these investments and be prepared to invest as technologies mature. But the Target Market Segment of the sample Perfect Portfolio I am building here is meant to produce significant returns in the short term. So, the Energy component of choice now should be primarily focused primarily on oil.

Building *Your* Perfect Portfolio!

Now it is your turn to find an energy investment for your PPM Target Market Segment. Follow the steps illustrated in this chapter and use the Target Market Building Block Worksheet, which you can print from the online supplement. To find the worksheet in PDF format, log in to this book's Web site, click on *Links by Chapter,* and then on *Chapter 6.* Print one or more copies.

Use the Web sites referred to in this and previous chapters to collect data and display a price chart. Analyze the data you have collected

(Continued)

and the external factors discussed. Then select a candidate and, by viewing the price chart, decide whether now is the time to buy it. If the price trend is positive and you decide now is a good time to buy, develop a trading plan as illustrated in this chapter.

Always keep in mind that if any of the Web references used in this chapter do not work as described, go to the online supplement to get updated information.

Chapter Summary

You have learned in this chapter about the Energy asset type and how to select an Energy Building Block for the portfolio's Target Market Segment.

Energy deserves a place in the Perfect Portfolio because demand for it will only increase in the future, and supplies are limited. This will predictably result in higher prices in the long term.

But the price will experience ups and downs in the short term. That is why it is placed in the Target Market Segment under the constant monitoring of a PPM trading plan. You may buy and sell your Energy investment multiple times during the year on the basis of this plan. It limits your losses and lets your profits run. This is the beauty and the power of the PPM approach. And this is why you can reasonably expect returns that are significantly higher than market averages from this, and all, investments that you place in your Target Market Segment.

We next consider Agricultural Commodities as a key Building Block of the Perfect Portfolio.

CHAPTER 7

Adding Agricultural Commodities to Your Portfolio

THE STAPLES OF LIFE AS A STAPLE OF YOUR PORTFOLIO

When most people think about commodities, the assets that immediately come to mind are gold and oil. These are the commodities, after all, that grab the headlines on a daily basis. Yet there is also a commodities market in agricultural products that is massive in scale. It includes the trading of assets such as corn, soybeans, coffee, orange juice, livestock, and other foodstuffs necessary for the very existence of life. Current world events and trends make it absolutely essential that you consider an agriculture-related investment for your Perfect Portfolio.

Agriculture Commodities are the third Building Block that I have defined for the Perfect Portfolio Target Market Segment. It is one of only five such Building Blocks for the same reasons that the others are. The demand for agricultural commodities is currently high and growing at a tremendous rate. Returns of investments in this area have been astounding in the recent past. And the price of these assets is influenced by different catalysts from those that affect the other PPM Building Blocks. It is truly a unique asset class.

I first help you understand in this chapter what agricultural commodities are and the factors that influence their price. I then walk you through the five-step process of identifying, analyzing, and selecting an investment to fill this spot in the sample Target Market Segment I am building. The information presented will enable you to do the same for your portfolio.

The process starts with understanding what agricultural commodities are.

Step 1: Understanding Agricultural Commodities

The field of agricultural commodities is broad and diverse, ranging from wheat to livestock and from pork bellies to coffee. So, before exploring how to invest in this class of commodities it is essential that you understand what they are. The three major agricultural commodity categories are as follows:

Grains/Soy Beans: These are essential food and feed supplies for both people and livestock. Prices of these commodities are especially sensitive to weather conditions in growing areas at key times during a crop's development and to economic conditions that affect demand. The major futures contracts in this category are corn, soybeans, soybean oil, soybean meal, and wheat. These products are traded in the United States at the Chicago Board of Trade (cmegroup .com), the Kansas City Board of Trade (kcbot.com), and the Minneapolis Grain Exchange (mgex.com).

Livestock: This category includes live cattle, feeder cattle, lean hogs, and pork bellies. They are all traded at the Chicago Mercantile Exchange (cmegroup.com). Their prices are affected by consumer demand, competing protein sources, the price of feed, and factors that influence the number of animals born and sent to market, such as disease and weather.

Food and Fiber: The food and fiber category includes cocoa, coffee, cotton, frozen concentrated orange juice, and sugar. In addition to global consumer demand, the usual growing factors such as disease, insects, and drought affect prices for all of these commodities. Futures contracts for these commodities are traded at the New York Mercantile Exchange (cmegroup .com) and the Intercontinental Exchange (theice.com).

You can see that the agricultural commodities market is wide and varied. And prices for these assets are affected by a unique set of factors. This adds important diversity to the Perfect Portfolio model.

Why Demand Will Grow

The demand for food and foodstuffs can only continue to grow at an exponential rate. Buying agricultural commodity investments is the means by which you can take advantage of this trend. The following are several reasons why the demand for this asset type will grow in both the short and the long terms.

Population Growth: According to the United States Census Bureau, there are over six billion people on the planet now. And in continents like Africa, there are already millions of people starving. Forecasts show that there will be three billion more people in the world by 2020. This means we are going to have to figure out how to boost global agriculture production by approximately 50 percent over the next decade just to meet the demands presented by world population growth.

Shifting Global Consumer Patterns: The world is experiencing dramatic shifts in consumer classes and patterns of consumption. Countries with developing economies such as China, India, Russia, Brazil, and others are becoming more prosperous because of globalization of their economies. As these countries emerge onto the world economic stage, they will attract investment to take advantage of relatively cheap labor and to develop the natural resources many of these countries own.

With an inflow of money into developing countries, a new middle class of people will arise who will be able to buy new and better things. A more affluent population will demand a higher quality diet. Instead of subsisting on grains such as rice, wheat, and corn, they will demand better, more protein-rich food such as meat and dairy products. This does not reduce the demand for grains because they must continue to be fed to livestock. Billions of people in the near future will enter the market for higher quality food products, and this will dramatically increase the demand for all agricultural commodities.

Alternative Uses of Agricultural Products: Politicians worldwide and producers in the grain industry continue to promote ethanol as a way to decrease U.S. dependence on foreign oil. Ethanol is made from corn (and to a lesser extent sugar). The United States and other countries have set aggressive goals for ethanol production and this results directly in higher demand for the raw material from which it is made, especially corn. At the time this chapter was written, global prices for staples such as corn and sugar had spiked to the point where in some countries consumers with diets based on wheat, corn, and rice had taken to the streets in protest. Using foodstuffs to produce energy is creating a significant new area of demand for agricultural commodities.

These demand factors and others lead experts to predict a sustained uptrend in agricultural commodity pricing stretching far into the future. This is why we, as individual investors, should place this asset type in our portfolios. This is why I have defined Agricultural Commodities as a separate Building Block for the Target Market Segment of the Perfect Portfolio.

Factors that Influence the Price of Agricultural Commodities

The cost of food was soaring at the time this chapter was written. Some of this price increase was due to the rising cost of energy used to grow it and transport it. Other factors were, and still are, the following:

- *Demand:* I have previously discussed the growing worldwide demand for agricultural commodities. The demand is not being met now. But the demand will grow even stronger as world population continues to increase and as billions of people in developing countries demand more and better food and as the use of grains to produce energy siphons off supply. Higher demand translates into higher commodity prices and this will cause agricultural investment returns to rise as well.
- *Supply:* Unlike gold and oil, food is a renewable resource. But the land on which it is grown and the energy it takes to produce it are not. So while demand grows, supplies will have a difficult time keeping up. There are areas of hope, however. Today much of the world's grain supplies are lost to crop diseases and weather-related problems. Genetically altered crops have been developed that are much more robust and

can ward off diseases and survive harsher conditions. Use of such altered grains can increase yield from existing land. Yet, many political and environmental groups are opposed to the use of these designer crops. The bottom line is that supply is dynamic. Prices will fluctuate on the basis of such politically charged factors as the amount of grain used to produce energy and the acceptance of genetically altered crop seeds.

- *Weather and Natural Events:* In the short term, a major factor that influences food commodity prices is weather. Hurricanes, earthquakes, droughts, and insect swarms can have a devastating effect on crops and food production. We hear on a regular basis of freezes in the southern United States spiking the price of orange juice. Monsoons and floods can wipe out thousands of acres of rice paddies in Asia. To protect against price swings related to weather and natural events, grains and other foodstuffs are traded on commodities markets where future prices can be locked in. Thus, perhaps the greatest mover of agricultural commodities prices in the short term is related to futures contracts trading, which is discussed next.

- *Hedging and Speculation:* Agricultural commodities are traded on exchanges in the same manner as gold and oil. They are traded in the form of futures contracts. These contracts are the basic unit of trade for agricultural commodities and specify the type of commodity, the amount of the commodity, a future delivery date, and a price. The price of a commodity is set by the last contract sold. This is called the *spot price.*

    There are two types of players that trade commodity futures. There are hedgers and speculators. Hedgers are companies that buy futures contracts so they can lock in a future price for whatever commodity is covered by the contract. For example, Starbucks will buy coffee bean futures to eliminate risk related to the uncertainty of future bean prices. As mentioned earlier, these prices can be influenced by such unpredictable factors as weather events and crop failures. Hedging against risk is the original intent of commodities exchanges.

    Then there are speculators, who are looking for short-term gains. They have no intention of ever taking delivery of the commodity for which they buy futures. Nor do they intend to make delivery of the commodities related to the futures that they sell. Speculators such as hedge funds can drive prices up for reasons that have nothing to do with the fundamentals of supply and demand. There is always, therefore, a degree of uncertainty in commodities prices because the fundamentals will never tell you the full story. The only tool that allows us, as individual investors, to predict prices in the short term is the study of price charts and trends. The PPM approach fortunately includes this activity in the investment analysis process described later in this chapter.

You need to be aware of the factors that influence the price of these assets to make informed investing decisions in the area of agricultural commodities. The PPM suggests that you buy-and-sell this asset type as opposed to buying and holding. The factors discussed in this section will inform your trading decisions.

Extra Credit

Learning More About Agriculture

The more you know about agricultural commodities, the more effective your trading decisions will be. The online supplement of this book provides Web links that enable you to learn more about this asset type and the factors that affect its pricing. Simply go to the supplement site, log in, click on *Links by Chapter,* and then on *Chapter 7* to access these educational links.

How to Invest in Agricultural Commodities

It has been only recently that we, as individual investors, have been able to conveniently invest in agricultural commodities. You learned in Chapters 5 and 6 that Gold and Energy investments are numerous and have been around for a long time, giving us a good historical record for performance and risk. Agriculture related investments are not as numerous and the ones that exist do not have a long historical track record. This will affect the analysis of the candidates we consider for the sample portfolio as presented later in this chapter.

Here are the current alternatives for investing in agricultural commodities and a short description of each.

- *Buy Commodity Futures Contracts:* One way to invest in agricultural commodities is to trade futures contracts for specific commodity types such as sugar, coffee, orange juice, and others. Futures contracts are traded on various commodity exchanges as mentioned previously in this chapter. You would need to open a trading account at a major commodities trading firm to trade futures. I do not recommend this investing vehicle for the average investor because it is very risky and requires considerable knowledge and time.

- *Buy Agriculture-Related Stocks:* There are plenty of companies that are in the agriculture business. Examples are Monsanto, which provides products to farmers around the world; Archer-Daniels-Midland is a prominent agriculture-related company; Deere & Company supplies equipment to farmers. Buying stocks in individual companies, however, exposes you to company risk, and this is an element that the entire PPM approach is designed to avoid.

- *Buy Mutual Funds:* At the time this chapter was written, it was very difficult to find a mutual fund that concentrated on agricultural commodities. Unlike for Gold and Energy, good funds that focus on holding agriculture stocks do not, in my opinion, currently exist. By the time you read this, such funds may have emerged and you can include them as candidates in your investment selection analysis. To look for agriculture-focused mutual funds, ask your adviser, search your fund family, or perform a Web search to try to find one or more. But for now, I cannot include any in my sample analysis.

- *Buy Exchange Traded Funds:* The best hope for finding an agricultural commodity investment today lies in Exchange Traded Funds. Several such ETFs have recently been introduced into the market in response to the growing awareness by the public of the value of including this asset type in their portfolios. There should be more available by the time you read this.

- *Exchange Traded Notes:* A significant number of agriculture-related Exchange Traded Notes (ETNs) were emerging at the time this chapter was written. ETNs are a relatively new development. The value of an ETN depends on the movements of a stock index, and they trade on stock exchanges. In these respects, ETNs are similar to ETFs.

But ETNs have a big difference: They are debt securities, not equity securities. When you buy an ETF, you are buying a piece of a diversified portfolio of stocks or bonds. When you buy an ETN, you are buying a promise that the issuer will pay the note according to the terms laid out in the ETN's prospectus. This introduces into the mix the credit risk of the issuer, typically a major financial institution. While most issuers are solid members of the financial community, so were Bear Stearns and Lehman Brothers before those companies imploded. Also, at the time this chapter was written, the IRS had not yet determined the appropriate tax treatment of these investment vehicles.

For the reasons of credit risk, uncertainty of tax status, and the relative newness of this type of investment resulting in the lack of historical data to analyze, I cannot at this time include ETNs as an agricultural investment candidate. Perhaps by the time you read this, ETNs will deserve your consideration. To find them, simply go to the site at finance. yahoo.com/etf, click "View ETFs" in the left column and select the "Natural Resources" category. Then scan the list for ETNs related to Agricultural Commodities.

Step 2: Identifying Agricultural Commodity Investment Candidates

Having learned about agricultural commodities and how they can be purchased for inclusion in a portfolio, it is now time to search for and identify investment candidates for evaluation. This is Step 2 of the Target Market Building Block selection process.

I mentioned earlier that it was virtually impossible at the time I wrote this chapter to find a traditional mutual fund focused on agriculture stocks or commodities. I have therefore limited the universe of candidates for the Agricultural Commodity Building Block of my sample portfolio to Exchange Traded Funds. After searching the list of available ETFs on the finance.yahoo.com/etf Web site, I have found only two that I believe to be worthy of consideration. They are as follows.

- *Powershares DB Agricultural Fund (DBA)*—Issued by Invesco, this is one of the first pure agriculture ETFs available to the market. It seeks to track the price and yield performance, before fees and expenses, of the Deutsche Bank Liquid Commodity Index—Optimum Yield Agriculture Excess Return. The index is a rules-based index composed of futures contracts on some of the most liquid and widely traded agricultural commodities—corn, wheat, soy beans, and sugar. Make note of the fact that its holdings are futures contracts, not stocks in companies doing business in agriculture. This is a pure commodities play, and no company risk factor is involved.

• *Market Vectors Global Agribusiness ETF (MOO)*—This investment seeks to replicate as closely as possible, before fees and expenses, the price and yield performance of the DAX Global Agribusiness Index. The Fund normally invests at least 80 percent of total assets in equity securities of U.S. and foreign companies primarily engaged in the business of agriculture, which derive at least 50 percent of their total revenues from agribusiness. This ETF holds stocks in agribusiness companies. Among its top holdings are companies such as Deere, Monsanto, and Archer-Daniels-Midland. You can find a list of the companies owned by going to the site at finance.yahoo. com and entering MOO in the quote box. Then in the left menu click on *holdings*.

I have identified two ETFs that are based on entirely different asset types, futures and company stocks. Both should reflect the price of agricultural commodities but in different ways. The next step is to collect data and compare them.

Step 3: Collecting and Analyzing Data

I have identified two investment candidates for evaluation. Step 3 in the PPM evaluation process is to gather data for each and compare. I will use the site at finance.yahoo.com to collect the relevant data using the same navigation methods as described in previous chapters. I will also use the Target Market Building Block Worksheet to record the data. Review the data collection process in Chapter 5 if you need to.

The first thing I notice is that these are both relatively new investments and the historical data are slim indeed. DBA started trading in January 2007 and MOO started in August 2007. By the

Table 7.1   Agricultural Commodity Data Collection Worksheet

Company/ Fund	Symbol	Annualized Returns			Risk: Std. Dev.	Expense Ratio
		1-year	3-year	5-year		
Powershares Ag. Fund ETF	DBA	46.68%	N/A	N/A	N/A	.75
Market Vectors Agribusiness ETF	MOO	Year to Date as of 07/2008 −6.68%	N/A	N/A	N/A	.65

time you read this, much more data will be available. The data I collected is shown in Table 7.1

Comparison and Selection

I am virtually flying blind here. Both investments are too new to have significant historical data to analyze. I have no risk number because Standard Deviation is typically calculated on the basis of three years of performance data. But returns for the short period of the existence of DBA are impressive. The aptly named MOO seems to be struggling, but this was not particularly surprising because at the time this chapter was written in the middle of 2008, the S&P 500 index was down significantly. And MOO is, after all, a collection of stocks, whereas DBA is a collection of commodity futures contracts.

When looking at fairly new ETFs, one of the most important factors to consider is not in the table. This factor is volume. Many new ETFs have incredibly low volume and you should avoid them. Using the finance.yahoo.com site, I see that the volume for MOO is over one million shares per day, and the volume for DBA is close to two million. This is an acceptable volume for both. A daily volume of less than 500,000 shares per day is a red flag. More than a few new ETFs have been discontinued because of the lack of trading volume.

The choice here is clear. DBA holds futures contracts and is the more pure way to participate in the increase of agricultural commodity prices. Its daily trading volume is higher and returns for its one year of existence are spectacular.

I will select DBA for my sample portfolio. The decision you make may be different after viewing the data you collect at the time you read this. You will also most likely have more choices to select from.

Step 4: Price Chart Analysis

I have selected an investment to represent the Agricultural Commodities Building Block of my Target Market Segment. Now I proceed to Step 4 of the evaluation and selection process: viewing and analyzing my investment's price chart.

I want a price chart for at least a year, so I go to finance.yahoo.com, enter the DBA symbol, and click on the menu item titled *Basic Tech Analysis.* Up will come a chart. I want one that shows me a price line for one year, so I click on the *1y* menu item above the chart. For the purpose of creating a trading plan, I also want to plot the Bollinger Bands, as discussed in Chapter 4. So I click on that item in the menu above the chart. I get the chart shown in Figure 7.1.

The line on the chart in the middle is the price line. The lines on either side are the Bollinger Bands. Price is shown on the left of the chart and the bottom of the chart shows time. Always keep in mind that this chart shows pricing as of the time of this writing. Your chart will look different.

Here are factors to look for on the chart.

- *Current Price:* The current price is $42 per share.
- *Price Trend:* Looking at the price line, I see that for the last year the price moved up sharply and then took a breather in March 2008 and traded sideways for a couple of months. Recently, however, the traces of another uptrend are beginning to appear. The chart shows a positive buy signal.

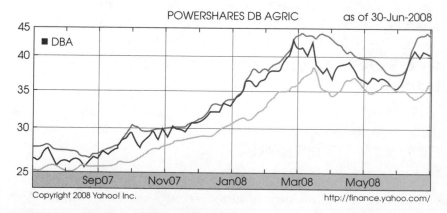

Figure 7.1   One Year DBA Price Chart

- *Support:* Simply viewing the chart, I would put a support price at $35. This is a level at which the price has seemed to bounce up in the recent past.
- *Resistance:* Price resistance seems to be forming at about $45. This doesn't really matter for my stop loss strategy because the PPM trading plan uses trailing stops to sell. In other words an automated *sell* will not be triggered when a certain price level is hit. A sell is triggered when the investment drops by a certain amount from its highest point during the time I have owned it. I will determine this amount by the investment's volatility. I do want to set, however, a take-profit e-mail alert that is above the current price. The $45 resistance price is too low because I will not be satisfied with a $3 profit. I will therefore set my take-profit e-mail alert at $48. Your goals may be different and thus your take-profit alert price may be different.
- *Volatility:* The current Bollinger Bands are showing a widening channel, indicating that volatility of this investment is increasing. This tells me to set a stop price that is not too close to the current price. Using my judgment, I will set a stop at $7 below the current price, right on the support price of $35. As discussed in Chapter 4, I could set this trigger to send me an e-mail instead of automatically selling. This would give me an opportunity to investigate why the price is falling before selling.

My analysis of the price chart is complete. I am now ready for Step 5 of the process. I am ready to define my trading plan for this ETF.

Step 5: Defining an Agricultural Commodities Trading Plan

My decision, based on the data collected and my analysis of these data, is to buy DBA. I will proceed with my purchase decision using the following simple trading plan:

- Place a Market Order at $42 per share.
- Place a trailing stop to automatically sell my position when the price falls $7 or more from its highest price during the time I own it. This action will initially be triggered if the ETF price falls to $35. As the price of the ETF rises above $42, the

stop-loss price will rise with it. But after the stop-loss has risen, it will never fall. For example, if the ETF rises to $45, the stop-loss price rises with it to $38. If the ETF price then drops to $40, the stop-loss price remains at $38.

- Place a take-profit alert at $48. This alert will send me an e-mail, it will not sell my position. Thus, should DBA rise to $48, I will get an e-mail alerting me to consider taking profits. I will then use the site at finance.yahoo.com to research what is currently happening. If all factors are still positive, then I may simply move up my take-profit alert to, say $52, and tighten my stop loss price from a $7 drop to a $3 drop. I lock in more profit in this way and still allow profits to run.

My trading plan is based on both subjective and objective analyses. There can be little argument that the demand for commodities will continue to grow far into the future. The main decision revolves around the timing of the purchase.

At the time this chapter was written, the price of commodities had risen sharply over the previous year. Is this a price bubble that is about to burst? Is this a price driven by supply and demand, or by speculation? These are questions that we, as individual investors, cannot answer with certainty. Fortunately, the PPM trading plan I have decided to implement protects me from speculative bubbles. The trailing stop-loss allows me to participate in stock price movements on the upside and sells my position should the price start to significantly deteriorate. I am thus protected from catastrophic loss resulting from a bursting agricultural commodities bubble.

The decision of how much money to allocate to this investment in the portfolio is discussed in Chapter 10.

Chapter Summary

The ability for us as individuals to invest in agricultural commodities is relatively new. As you saw in this chapter, in the middle of 2008 my options for investing in these assets were limited to a few ETFs. Fortunately for my sample portfolio, I found one that has a reasonably long performance history and an excellent track record. Still, I would have preferred to have more data to analyze.

You will have more investments from which to choose when you read this book. There should be more mutual funds and ETFs

Building *Your* Perfect Portfolio!

You are now prepared to complete a Target Market Building Block Worksheet for your own Agricultural Commodity Building Block. You have an advantage. You will almost certainly be able to find more investment vehicles than were available to me in the middle of 2008. You will also have more performance data for those you identify.

Go to the online supplement, log in, click on *Links by Chapter,* and then on *Chapter 7* to find and print the Target Market Building Block Worksheet in PDF format. You can also simply create a worksheet on your own. You will list the agricultural investment candidates you find for evaluation on this worksheet along with the data collected for each, your selection, and your trading plan.

It will be interesting for you to see by using current data if the uptrend for agricultural commodities has continued or if a bubble in this market has burst. In either case, the trading plan discussed here allows me to take whatever profits occur from this point forward and protects my downside risk by limiting losses to $7 per share from my original purchase price at the maximum.

available in this market and the new ETNs may be a more established investment type. You will also have the advantage of more data to analyze for the investments that exist.

Agricultural commodities deserve a place in the Perfect Portfolio. This asset type has sufficiently unique characteristics to be defined as a separate and distinct asset class. But it is a volatile investment, which is why it is placed in the Target Market Segment under the constant supervision of an automated trading plan.

As you finish this chapter, you should have the knowledge and resources needed to find an agricultural commodity investment for your Perfect Portfolio.

A Real Estate investment is the next Portfolio Building Block we will consider.

CHAPTER 8

Adding A Real Estate Component to Your Portfolio

CONSIDERING A TRULY UNIQUE ASSET

Recently, when I mention the words *real estate* in the classes I teach, a collective groan rises from my students. The housing market has been in a slump since before this chapter was written. Many of my students are homeowners who have lost a lot of net worth because of the declining value of their property. So they don't want to hear about real estate investing. Fortunately, the type of real estate investment that goes into the Perfect Portfolio does not deal with residential housing. Rather, it deals with income-producing commercial properties, as you will learn as you work through this chapter. Still, the current housing problems cannot be ignored.

At the mid-point of 2008 when this book was being written, the economy was working through what is referred to as the subprime mortgage crisis. This crisis was brought on by banks and mortgage companies lending money to home buyers with questionable (that is, subprime) credit ratings.

Most of these loans carried a variable interest rate that started low and increased after a contractually specified length of time, typically three to five years. Many people could afford the monthly payments during the initial rate period but when the rates adjusted upward they could not. Most thought that the value of their homes would increase sufficiently during the initial period to enable them to use this additional equity to afford the higher payments. Well, home prices have not appreciated as expected, and home loan defaults have skyrocketed. The problem has snowballed as bank foreclosures increased and the market became flooded with homes for sale. This drove home prices down even more, and suddenly a lot of people were not as wealthy as they thought.

The subprime mortgage crisis has had far-reaching effects. It has sent the prices of stocks in the financial services sector into a tailspin. Banks and companies in this sector are holding massive asset values on their books that are based on mortgages that cannot be properly valued. No one can be sure of the quality of the loans that make up these assets.

The U.S. government has already intervened in this mess by orchestrating the takeover of Bear Stearns by JPMorgan Chase; saved American International Group (AIG), the largest insurance company in the world, from bankruptcy; allowed Lehman Brothers to go bankrupt; and passed a bill that would allow the government to invest $700 billion in the financial markets to ease a credit crisis that is rippling throughout the entire economy. And this may just be the start of the problems that equity markets will face. In my opinion, any time the government starts to interfere with free markets, bad situations tend to become rapidly worse.

So, in the face of this mess, why is Real Estate the fourth PPM Target Market Building Block? The answer is because PPM Building Blocks are not defined on the basis of transitory or cyclical events. They are defined on the basis of inherent long-term demand for an asset, the potential for high returns based on this demand, and the uniqueness of the factors that influence the asset's price. Real estate has always met these long-term criteria. It is an asset that has produced incredible returns in the past and will again. Like almost all other assets, the value of real estate is cyclical, and will again rise at some point in the future. In fact, current conditions could be a tremendous buying opportunity.

I illustrated in Chapters 5 through 7 how the PPM approach handles Target Market Building Blocks that are currently in an uptrend. This chapter devoted to the Real Estate Building Block gives me the opportunity to show you how the PPM approach handles assets that are currently moving down.

The process of considering a real estate component for your portfolio starts with understanding this asset type and how to invest in it. We thus begin the normal five-step Target Market Building Block analysis and selection process.

Step 1: Understanding Real Estate Investing

You may understand how to buy a house and, yes, a house is certainly a real estate investment. But in the Perfect Portfolio model, real estate investing will be about investing in stocks of companies that own and operate various types of commercial real estate. This will include such property types as hotels, shopping malls, casinos, warehouses, office buildings, apartment complexes, and others that produce income for the owners. So you need to understand real estate from a point of view that is significantly different from that of a homeowner. Giving you this understanding is the purpose of this first step of the real estate investing process.

Let's start with a quick overview of the real estate asset that we will consider and then discuss how to conveniently place it in a portfolio.

Real estate has been one of the greatest creators of wealth in history. After all, land is in limited supply and demand for it can only grow with the expansion of the world's population and the increasing demands of commerce. But until recently, it has not been easy for individuals to invest in commercial real estate. Buying and selling actual commercial properties takes money, time, and expertise that most people don't have.

Fortunately, these barriers have been removed with the introduction of a relatively new type of investment vehicle called a Real Estate Investment Trust, or REIT for short. REITs enable you to add ownership of a diverse set of commercial properties to your portfolio as easily as buying stocks. The advent of REITs has enabled the average investor to add major real estate assets to their portfolios, and so for the Perfect Portfolio, we will consider *only* REIT-based investments. Let's take a closer look at this unique investing vehicle.

Understanding REITs

In 1960, Congress, and of course, lobbyists, saw that small, individual investors were essentially barred from investing in large-scale, commercial real estate ventures. Only the very wealthy or corporations had the resources needed to take advantage of the wealth creation potential of commercial properties. No investing vehicle existed that allowed people of average means to participate. Congress looked at the mutual fund model that year and decided to create a similar investment type dedicated to commercial real estate. These were called Real Estate Investment Trusts, or REITs.

As defined by Congress, a REIT is a public company having as its primary business owning and operating income-producing properties. Examples of such properties are apartment buildings, warehouses, shopping centers, hotels, casinos, and office buildings, to name a few. The key requirement for being classified as a REIT is that the company must pay at least 90 percent of its taxable income to shareholders in the form of dividends every year. In exchange for meeting this requirement, and others as established by the IRS, a REIT does not pay corporate taxes.

Thus, corporations had a tremendous incentive to organize as REITs because they could avoid taxes. The public had a tremendous incentive to buy shares of REITs because the REITs would enable them to, with just the cost of a REIT share, participate in the wealth appreciation of major commercial real estate assets not previously accessible to individuals. REIT shares also gave individual investors an income-producing investment because at least 90 percent of the income generated by the REIT had to be distributed to shareholders on a yearly basis.

As a result of these mutual benefits, REITs have become the main vehicle used by the public to invest in commercial real estate. And through REITs, a vast new source of capital has become available to companies in the commercial real estate industry.

REITs will be the investment vehicle of choice as we look to add a Real Estate component to the Perfect Portfolio.

The Top Benefits of Including REITs in a Portfolio

Real Estate Investment Trusts add these benefits to a portfolio:

- *The Potential for High Returns:* As stated earlier, at the time this chapter was written, real estate prices have plummeted because of credit problems in the overall market. But all major asset classes go through cycles. In the data collection phase of the real estate investment selection process discussed later in this chapter, you will see that investments in this asset class have produced incredible returns in the past three-year and five-year periods. They have slumped only recently. We can predict with a fair amount of certainty that returns will rise again in the future. The unknown factor is when.

- *The Benefits of Both Capital Appreciation and Income:* Because REITs annually pay out almost all of their taxable income in the form of dividends, this adds significantly to the returns performance of this type of investment. REIT investments provide returns both in the form of share price appreciation *and* in the form of dividends.

- *Portfolio Diversification:* The value of commercial real estate properties is influenced by a number of factors that do not influence other PPM Building Block assets, particularly those in the Target Market Segment. Thus, adding REITs to the Perfect Portfolio mix can significantly lower its overall risk.

- *Instant Diversity with One Purchase:* Using REITs, investors with a minimal amount of money can buy a diverse group of properties with one purchase. By purchasing only one REIT fund or ETF, you can own a full range of property types located in widespread geographic areas. This diversity is important, as real estate values are heavily influenced by localized factors.

- *Ease of Buying and Selling:* Unlike real estate directly held by the investor, REITs are a liquid asset that can be sold quickly on stock exchanges to take profits, stop losses, or to take advantage of other investment opportunities. Real property such as houses and land can take days, months, or years to sell.

- *The Advantages of Professional Management:* Investing by yourself in commercial properties takes a significant amount of time, money, and specialized expertise. Real estate professionals manage REITs. They provide the know-how needed to navigate the very complex world of commercial real estate investing.

- *Limitation of Personal Risk:* REITs significantly limit your personal liabilities when investing in real estate. If you want to acquire property on your own, it is likely you will take on debt by borrowing money and you will probably have to personally guarantee this debt. Purchasing a REIT investment leaves you with no personal liability for such debts or other risks such as lawsuits. Your only risk is the potential of losing the price of the REIT stock or fund share.

Based on these benefits, Real Estate in the form of REITs deserves a place in the very select group of assets that I have chosen to be PPM Building Blocks.

REIT Categories

Now let's dig a little deeper into the types of REITs that exist. The universe of REITs can be divided into categories and distinguished by property type. Let's look at REIT categories first. They are as follows:

- *Equity REITs:* These are corporations that purchase, own, and manage real estate properties. They do not own or originate real estate loans. They may also develop properties.
- *Mortgage REITs:* These are corporations that purchase, own, and manage real estate loans. They do not own real estate properties. They typically originate commercial or residential loans. Mortgage REITs are essentially loan portfolios as opposed to ownership of the properties, as is the case with their equity counterparts.
- *Hybrid REITs:* These are corporations that purchase, own, and manage both real estate loans and real estate properties. They have the characteristics of both equity and mortgage REITs, which is why they are referred to as hybrids.

For the purpose of our PPM approach, *only* Equity REITs will be considered for our Real Estate investment, not Mortgage or Hybrid REITs. Why? Because Equity REITs represent true ownership in commercial real estate properties. They are less vulnerable to interest rates and credit problems. They have also historically provided better long-term return, more stable performance, lower risk, and greater liquidity than Mortgage REITs. We want direct ownership in property for the PPM Real Estate Building Block.

Equity REIT Property Types.   Equity REITs can be further classified by the types of property they own and operate. While different sources will use slightly different terms, the property types (also referred to as Sectors) are generally labeled as follows:

- Apartment REITs
- Retail REITs

- Office REITs
- Healthcare REITs
- Industrial REITs
- Hotel and Resort REITs
- Diverse/Specialty REITs

Properties in each of these sectors have unique characteristics and are thus treated as different types of investments.

Property Type Diversity Is Important.   Why is this Sector structure important? Because the value of different property types is influenced by a unique set of economic factors and conditions. For example, Hotel REITs performed poorly during the subprime mortgage crisis as investors worried about the state of the economy and curtailed travel plans. Yet the same set of factors was favorable for Apartment REITS, which thrived as people forced out of houses moved to apartment living. Not all REITs move in lockstep in response to the same market conditions. Therefore, when looking for a real estate investment for our sample portfolio, we will look for a REIT that owns a wide and diverse range of property types.

Property Location Diversity Is Important.   REITs can also be diversified by location, and this presents an additional opportunity for risk reduction. Why? Because economic conditions can vary for different parts of the country. A Hotel REIT that owns properties in Las Vegas, for example, may be thriving, while a Hotel REIT that concentrates in Florida properties may be stagnant. In the PPM portfolio, we can diversify away location risk by making sure our REIT investment choice holds properties in different geographical areas.

Diversity Is Key To REIT Investing.   Understanding the diversity inherent in commercial properties is critical to effective investing in the real estate market using REITs. There are too many factors that affect real estate prices to risk our investment money in a narrowly focused geographic area or in a specific property type. So as we look for a REIT investment later in this chapter, we will make sure that it is diversified both in terms of property type and in location. This will be a key factor for consideration during the analysis and selection process.

Factors that Influence REIT Returns

As discussed earlier, narrowly focused REITs in regard to property type and geography are affected by more narrowly focused factors. A REIT that owns properties in only one geographic area can be influenced by local politics, local weather, local business conditions, and other factors that are unique to the property location. In the same vein, REITs that are focused on a single type of property can be influenced by factors unique to the property type. For example, a REIT focused only on hotels will be influenced by factors such as gas prices and the public's ability to travel to vacation destinations.

In the Perfect Portfolio, we don't have the time, energy, or need to deal with localized factors, so when I search for REIT candidates for my sample portfolio in Step 2, I will look only for mutual funds or ETFs that hold a basket of REIT companies owning properties of all types and located in all geographic areas. This diversifies away localized influences that are virtually impossible to predict and allows me to concentrate on more general market factors that can be analyzed with some degree of accuracy. The following are the macro factors that can influence the Real Estate component of the Perfect Portfolio.

- *Interest Rates:* The price of real estate is closely tied to interest rates. Virtually all real estate transactions involve the buyer taking out a loan. Higher bank interest rates obviously make such loans more expensive. When interest rates are high or climbing, there are fewer purchasers for existing properties, and REIT returns tend to stagnate or retreat. When interest rates are low, or falling, more money becomes available to the real estate market, and REIT returns should increase. Thus, current interest rates and their trend is a factor to consider when investing in REITs. A great place to check on this factor is the Web site bankrate.com.
- *The State of the Economy:* When the overall economy is suffering, Real Estate assets suffer with it. In hard times, businesses have less money to expand and office space vacancy rates increase. In hard times, people travel less and spend less. This has a negative effect nationwide on properties such as hotels, casinos, and resorts. A drop in consumer spending also has a negative effect on retail properties because owners

are limited as to how high they can increase lease rates. All of these traits of a slumping economy tend to hurt the returns of REIT investments.

- *The Trend of the Stock Market:* You will note that the factors that affect REIT returns are much the same as those that affect the stock market in general. This is in contrast to "safe-haven" investments such as Gold and Commodities, which have price lines that tend to move in an opposite direction to the stock market. REIT prices move roughly in tandem with stocks, and this makes them a great diversifying element in the Target Market Segment we are building. A chart for the past year, as of mid-2008, illustrates the correlation between the movement of the overall stock market and REIT prices. Figure 8.1 shows a comparison chart between an ETF that tracks the S&P 500 and an ETF that tracks a REIT index. It will be interesting for you to create the same chart and see how it has changed as of the time you are ready to do your own research.

This is a chart created using the Web site finance.yahoo.com. It is created by first entering the symbol for an ETF that tracks a diversified REIT index. I have used VNQ, which is a Vanguard ETF focused on REITs and is discussed later in this chapter. After entering the VNQ symbol and seeing a summary page for this

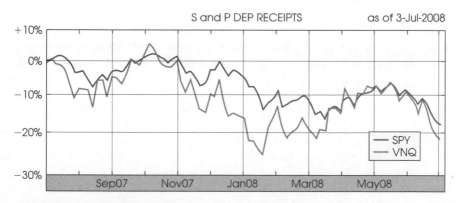

Figure 8.1   One-Year Performance Comparison: Real Estate versus Stocks

investment, I click on *basic chart* in the left menu When the chart appears, I select a one-year (1y) chart from the menu above the chart. Then in the area above the chart that prompts for a comparison investment I enter SPY, an ETF that tracks the S&P 500. I get a chart that compares the two investments and by proxy the two asset classes of Real Estate and Stocks. This is not a chart of prices. It is a chart that compares performance. The chart assumes that I have invested the same amount of money in each investment at the beginning of the chart and then plots the growth (or in this case the decline) of each investment in a manner that allows for easy comparison. Both the stock market and the REIT market have lost money in the past year. Of interest here is that the performance lines seem to move in approximately the same manner. This means that the two asset types have a positive correlation and they tend to react in the same manner to the same market catalysts.

Understanding the factors that influence REIT prices and the correlation of these prices with the overall economy and stock market will be an important input factor when deciding if now is a good time to include REITs in a portfolio or whether it is more prudent to wait. I walk you through this decision process later in the chapter.

How to Invest in REITs

As explained earlier in this chapter, REITs are companies, and stock in most of these companies can be bought on a stock exchange.

Extra Credit

Learning More about REITs

I have given you a solid foundation of knowledge related to Real Estate investments and REIT investing. This should be sufficient to enable you to make informed choices when considering the addition of a Real Estate Building Block to your portfolio.

There is a lot more that you can learn. To enhance your knowledge, go to the online supplement to this book, log in, click on *Links by Chapter,* and then on *Chapter 8.* You will see an area where I list Web links to sites that you can use to further your Real Estate investment education.

However, as with all PPM investments, we do not want to be bothered with company risk. We also want a very diversified investment in regard to property type and location. We will therefore seek out a basket of REIT stocks for our Perfect Portfolio Real Estate component. Here are the various investment vehicles that enable us to buy such a basket.

- *Actively Managed Funds:* For actively managed REIT mutual funds, professional managers analyze the market and select the best REIT stocks based on a host of factors. The advantage of actively managed funds is that managers can buy winners and sell losers. The disadvantage of using mutual funds in the PPM approach is that they are not as easy to trade as stocks and a trading plan set up for them is less responsive. For example, an early redemption fee is often charged for selling a fund within the first several months.
- *Index Funds:* There are mutual funds that hold only REIT stocks identified by a Real Estate index. There is no active management here. The REITs in the fund change only when the index is tracking changes. Advantages include lower expenses and less buying and selling, which results in fewer taxable events. Disadvantages include that these funds cannot buy winners that are not in the index or sell losers that are in the index. Also, as mentioned before, funds are not as easy to trade as stocks.
- *Exchange Traded Funds (ETFs):* A third way to invest in a basket of REITs is by purchasing an ETF that tracks a Real Estate index. Following is a list of several Real Estate indexes and a sample ETF that tracks each.
  - *Dow Jones U.S. Real Estate Index:* This Index seeks to provide a broad measure of the U.S. real-estate securities market. The Index consists of components that make up the real estate portion of the Dow Jones U.S. Total Market Index. An ETF that follows this Index is IYR from iShares.
  - *Dow Jones Wilshire REIT Index:* The Dow Jones Wilshire REIT Index is a subset of the Dow Jones Real Estate Securities Index and includes only REITs. Its objective is to provide a broad measure of publicly traded REITs. An ETF that follows this index is RWR from streetTRACKS.

◆ *Cohen & Steers Realty Majors Index:* This Index tracks the performance of large, actively traded U.S. real estate investment trusts. An example ETF based on this index is ICF from iShares.

◆ *Morgan Stanley U.S. REIT Index:* The Morgan Stanley U.S. REIT Index consists of REITs included in the MSCI U.S. Investable Market 2500 Index, excluding specialty equity REITs that do not generate a majority of their revenue and income from real estate rental and leasing operations. The MSCI U.S. REIT Index excludes mortgage and hybrid REITs. Unlike the Wilshire real estate index, however, this Index includes health-care REITs. VNQ is a Vanguard ETF based on this index.

With a full array of REIT investing vehicles to choose from, I am prepared to move to Step 2 of the PPM analysis process and identify candidates for further research.

Step 2: Identifying Real Estate Investment Candidates

Now the goal is to search for specific REIT-related investments to evaluate. Remember, we are looking for a basket of REITs, not single REIT company stock. Unlike Agricultural Commodities, where we had very few investing options, for Real Estate, we have many. I will use in the following discussion the same Yahoo! Web site and navigation steps as used in Chapters 5 through 7 to find investment candidates. You should be familiar with the process by now.

There are obviously more sources for finding candidates than are discussed here. You may, for example, get a recommendation from your adviser. You may read about a good Real Estate fund in the newspaper or in a newsletter or you may use a service like Morningstar, which analyzes and rates such funds. The more candidates you evaluate, the better, but I suggest that you never analyze fewer than three.

Here are the candidates I will use for the sample Target Market Segment I am building.

• *From a Specific Fund Family:* In the sample portfolio being created, I have used Vanguard as my sample Core fund family.

So I will use the Funds by Family resource of the site at finance
.yahoo.com/funds to look for their REIT-based mutual fund
offerings. The methods for doing this have been detailed in
previous chapters. I find VGSIX, the Vanguard REIT Index
Fund. I read from its profile that this fund invests at least 98
percent of its assets in the stocks of real estate investment trusts
(REITs), which are included in the Morgan Stanley REIT
index. This will be my first candidate for further evaluation.

- *Top-Performing Managed Fund:* I then look for a top performer,
using the finance.yahoo.com/funds site as described in previous chapters. I find a company called CGM Realty, symbol CGMRX, to be at the top of the list for virtually all time
periods. This is an interesting instance that deserves further
examination and illustrates an important point. I see that
while most real estate funds lost between 15 percent and 20
percent in 2007, this one actually gained 26 percent! Something must be different with this fund.

To discover this difference, my next step is to click
on the *Holdings* menu item on the Yahoo! page dedicated
to this fund. I find something very interesting. At the
time this chapter was written, it owned stock in two companies that had nothing to do with real estate but rather
with commodities; one sells agricultural chemicals and the
other sells potash. This ownership represented over 25 percent of the funds' assets! Since our goal here is to invest
in Real Estate, I must disqualify this fund from the candidate list, and even though it seems like a very nice fund,
I already have an Agricultural Commodities component in
the portfolio.

This brings to light an important point. Always check
the fund's holdings when comparing funds in the same
category and seeing one that shows returns that are significantly out of line with the majority of funds in the same
category. Many actively managed funds give the manager
around 20 to 25 percent leeway to invest in stocks that are
not related to the fund's prime objective. Here is where
managers have a free hand to pump up returns by investing in virtually anything. You don't want these types of sur-
prises, so always check the holdings for actively managed
Real Estate funds.

I don't see anything else interesting in the Top Performers list, so I move on without selecting a candidate from this source.

- *Third-Party Recommendation:* Since I don't have a top performer candidate, let's assume that I have asked an adviser for a Real Estate fund recommendation or I have read about one in the news. Perhaps the fund I identify by these means is the T. Rowe Price Real Estate Fund, with the symbol TRREX. I go to the finance.yahoo.com site and enter this symbol and find its profile described as follows: "The fund normally invests at least 80 percent of assets in the equity securities of real estate companies. It may invest up to 20 percent of assets in companies deriving a substantial portion of revenues or profits from servicing real estate firms, as well as in companies unrelated to the real estate business." Because this fund has come to my attention on the basis of a recommendation from a third party, I will make this my second Real Estate fund candidate.

- *An Exchange Traded Fund:* I now need at least one Real Estate-related ETF as a candidate for evaluation and comparison. I listed earlier in this chapter various Real Estate indexes, and for each one I identified an ETF that tracks the index. These are four potential evaluation candidates. I could investigate each but here is a tip that will make this unnecessary. The charting capability at finance.yahoo.com allows you to compare the price charts of two investments very easily. When you have the chart displayed for one, you can simply enter a second symbol in the *Compare* area and the chart of the second will be displayed on the same graph.

  I displayed in this instance the price chart for IYR and then consecutively compared it to each of the other ETFs in the list presented earlier. The price performance for all were virtually identical. This tells me that I don't need to use all four as candidates in my analysis. But I would like to see the difference in expenses for a couple of them, so I will choose IYR from iShares and VNQ from Vanguard as evaluation candidates.

I have chosen four real estate investment candidates for comparison purposes. You can probably find others when you perform this step for your own portfolio.

Step 3: Collecting and Analyzing Data

With four real estate investment candidates, I am ready to move forward to the data collection and analysis phase. This is Step 3 of the evaluation process. I will use the site at finance.yahoo.com to collect the data presented in Table 8.1. As described in previous chapters, I simply enter the investment symbol where designated on the site and use these menu items for the related data: *Returns, Risk,* and *Profile* to find the Expense Ratio. If the Web site or how it is navigated to find the required evaluation data changes, this information will be updated in the supplement to this book. Also, always keep in mind that the data shown are valid only as of the time this chapter was written. You will have the opportunity to collect current data later in this chapter.

Comparison and Selection

The subprime mortgage problem and resultant tightening of credit in 2007 and 2008 is evident in the numbers presented in Table 8.1. All of my investment candidates lost a significant amount of their value during this period. Returns were excellent, however, in the three-year, and particularly the five-year, period. In Step 4 that follows, I will look at the price chart of my selected candidate to determine the current trend. For now, the task is to select one of these candidates as being the most promising investment.

I see no reason to select TRREX over VGSIX. It has virtually the same performance history as VGSIX but with almost four times

Table 8.1   Real Estate Building Block Data Collection Worksheet

Company/Fund	Symbol	Annualized Returns			Risk: Std. Dev.	Expense Ratio
		1-year	3-year	5-year		
Vanguard REIT Index	VGSIX	−12.37%	10.54%	16.94%	16.54%	.20%
T. Rowe Price Real Estate	TRREX	−15.03%	10.61%	18.03%	16.65%	.73%
iShares DJ Real Estate ETF	IYR	−20.28%	9.44%	N/A	16.10%	.48%
Vanguard REIT Index ETF	VNQ	−17.60%	11.74%	N/A	16.58%	.12%

Note: N/A Means *Not Available*—the investments are too new as of the current date.

the expense ratio. Plus, I am already working with Vanguard as my Core Fund Family.

Looking at the ETFs, I will select VNQ over IYR. Even though both were relatively new investments at the time this chapter was written, and I didn't have three-year data, the more recent returns favor VNQ. VNQ also has a significantly lower expense ratio.

My choice then, is between VGSIX and VNQ. Both have the same risk profile. Expense ratios are extremely low on both. VGSIX has a slight advantage in that it lost less value in the past year, but the three-year performance data favor VNQ.

I will select VNQ for my portfolio Real Estate component. I make this decision based on my preference to buy ETFs over traditional mutual funds when all else is equal. Why? Because an ETF trades like a stock and fits better into the PPM trading plan methodology. Also, further investigation into VGSIX on the Vanguard site shows me that this fund has a 1 percent early redemption penalty if I sell it within a year of buying it. Many mutual funds have this same penalty clause. This is not to say that I would never choose a mutual fund. There will be times when a mutual fund is significantly superior to an ETF for a specific investment type. When this occurs I will not be deterred from buying it because it has an early redemption penalty or because of the minor inconveniences inherent in setting up a trading plan for a fund as opposed to an ETF (remember the discussion from Chapter 4; I cannot use trailing stops on a fund, I must use e-mail alerts).

I have made my selection based on the data collected. But is now the time to buy? This question can be answered only by looking at the price chart for VNQ. This is where we go next.

Step 4: Price Chart Analysis

The next step of the evaluation process is to look at a price chart. Figure 8.2 shows a one-year price line with Bollinger Bands on either side of it. You learned the steps for creating this chart in previous chapters and should be familiar with it by now. These data are not current as of the time you read this, and your chart will look different.

Here are factors to look for on the chart.

- *Current Price:* The current price is $58 per share.
- *Price Trend:* The price of VNQ in the past year has had its ups and downs. But the most recent price movement has been decidedly negative.

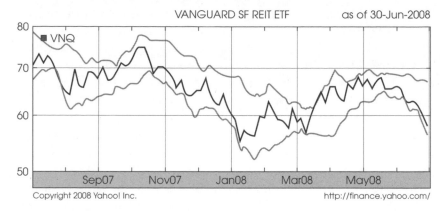

Figure 8.2   One Year Price Chart for VNQ
Reproduced with permission of Yahoo! Inc. ® 2008 by Yahoo! Inc. YAHOO! and the YAHOO!
logo are trademarks of Yahoo! Inc.

- *Support:* A quick scan of this chart tells me that a support price seems to exist at about $56. The price line has bounced upward from that level twice in the last six months.
- *Resistance:* There is no obvious resistance price level on this chart. A recent top went as high as $68, but there is not much evidence that this is a level of resistance, which needs at least two bounce-downs to qualify as a tentative resistance line.
- *Volatility:* The Bollinger Bands are currently widening. This means that uncertainty and volatility are increasing at the time this chart was created. Also, the price line is approaching the bottom Bollinger Band. This is an indication that the price may be on the verge of rebounding.

The price chart for VNQ, and for the entire REIT market, is currently negative.

Step 5: Making A Decision

I have identified a viable investment for my Real Estate investment. I now need to look closely at the market environment to determine whether conditions are favorable for a move up in real estate prices. Interest rates were extremely low at the time this chapter was written. This is a positive. Also, I am reading in some of the financial press that many industry analysts are suggesting that the REIT downturn may be in the process of bottoming out. This is a relatively positive sign, but one that I will not rely on too heavily.

On the other side of the coin, I am also reading that signs of inflation are creeping up and this may eventually force the Federal Reserve to raise interest rates. I am also concerned about the health of the overall economy as the credit markets show no signs of loosening and consumer spending is being significantly affected. I also believe that the mortgage credit crisis that I discussed at the beginning of this chapter is not totally resolved. More financial institutions may be in danger of insolvency as the quality of their mortgage holdings is revealed.

Since I know that Real Estate prices are closely tied to the health of the economy that I have deemed to be not good at this point, and because my analysis of the price chart is not positive in the short term, I must decide that I will *not* buy VNQ or any Real Estate investment at this time.

Using A Watch List

This is the first PPM Building Block that I have decided not to buy for my sample portfolio at this time. This does not mean that Real Estate no longer deserves its designation as a PPM Building Block. It simply means that now is not the time to allocate money to it.

This instance calls for the implementation of another element of the PPM approach that I discussed briefly in Chapter 4, namely setting up a Watch List and a related monitoring plan.

I do not want to simply forget about Real Estate. My goal is to monitor it and set up an alert plan that will tell me when conditions for buying are more favorable.

There are two types of resources on the Web that will enable me to set up a Watch List for VNQ. First, I can use a portfolio manager with a watch list capability. I discuss this type of resource in detail in Chapter 11. Second, I can simply use the site at finance.yahoo.com to set an alert on my investment.

To do so, I go to the site at finance.yahoo.com and enter VNQ in the *Get Quotes* box and a summary page for the investment will appear. Just below the thumbnail chart is a link with the title *Set Alert for VNQ*. Upon clicking this link, a page appears that enables me to enter prices for VNQ at which I want to be alerted by e-mail.

Price alerts can be set above the current price and below the current price. They can also be specified as dollar changes or percentage changes.

Now that I have the alert tool identified, I need to decide at what prices I want to be alerted with an e-mail. Let's again consult the price chart. I will use the support and resistance prices defined during my analysis of the chart to set up the following listed alerts, one above the current price and one below the current price.

A Watch List Alert Plan.   After studying the price chart, I will set the following price levels for VNQ that will cause an e-mail alert to be sent to me.

- Send e-mail alert when VNQ price goes up to $68 (at the resistance price)
- Send e-mail alert when VNQ price goes down to $55 (just below the support price)

I implement this alert system using the Yahoo! site as illustrated in Figure 8.3 that shows a screen capture of the site's alerts capability implementation.

Should I receive the $68 alert, I will investigate to see if positive things are happening in the real estate market and if the price chart is showing signs of a price breakout to the upside. Should I receive the $55 alert, I will investigate to see if a bottom is forming in the chart and I may wish to trade in and out of the ETF to make money even while its long-term trend is sideways. The PPM trading plan enables me to easily do this.

In either case, alerts will not automatically buy the ETF. I will simply get an e-mail prompting me to revisit my Real Estate investment decision. If after investigating the situation I still decide not to invest, I will adjust the Watch List alert prices accordingly.

Symbol	Price falls to	Price rises to	Percent Decrease	Percent Increase
VNQ	55	68	-- ▼	-- ▼

Figure 8.3 Setting Price Alerts on VNQ

Reproduced with permission of Yahoo! Inc. ® 2008 by Yahoo! Inc. YAHOO! and the YAHOO! logo are trademarks of Yahoo! Inc.

You can readily see that even though I have decided at this time not to include the Real Estate Building Block, VNQ, in my sample portfolio it is still constantly being monitored. I need only take action when I receive an e-mail alert. This is the beauty of the PPM approach. *All* Target Market Building Blocks are constantly being monitored, whether I own them or not!

Refer to the Appendix at the end of this book for a detailed example of how the Real Estate investment discussed here moved in and out of an actual portfolio that I managed during 2007. You will be interested to see how the PPM trading plan and watch list enabled me to actually earn a significant return on my Real Estate investment in a very negative market.

An Alternative, Shorting the Real Estate Market.   In the face of the current real estate market price downtrend I could have also decided to buy an ETF that shorts the real estate market. This is one option available to you under the Perfect Portfolio Methodology as described in Chapter 4. An example of an investment that enables me to do this is the Proshares UltraShort Real Estate ETF with the symbol of SRS. Its price goes up when the DOW Jones Real Estate Index goes down! Should I decide to buy this ETF I would then implement the normal PPM trading plan to manage its risk.

The use of short ETFs is discussed in more detail in Chapter 12 under the heading Adding Doomsday Building Blocks. There you will learn that you can short most of the PPM Building Blocks with an ETF and make money when the related asset or market is falling. This is yet another element of the PPM that makes it uniquely powerful.

Building *Your* Perfect Portfolio!

Now it is time for you to look for a Real Estate investment and decide if you want to include it in your Perfect Portfolio at the time you read this. First make sure that you understand real estate investing and REITs. If you need more detail than is presented in this chapter, then go to the online supplement of this book, log in and click on *Links by Chapter,* and then on *Chapter 8.* Look for the education links presented there. I do not want you to make a decision related to a Real Estate investment until you thoroughly understand what you are buying.

Then, go through the steps presented in this chapter for identifying and analyzing REIT candidates using the Target Market Building Block Worksheet found in the online supplement and the Web resources referenced here.

Current data may show that Real Estate is rebounding. By the time you read this book, you will know if the middle of 2008 was a good buying opportunity for this class of assets or not.

Chapter Summary

You learned in this chapter about investing in commercial Real Estate using Real Estate Investment Trusts. You studied what REITs are and how you can use multiple types of vehicles to invest in them. You also learned the factors that affect the price of this asset type.

The data collected in this chapter have painted a rather gloomy picture of the current Real Estate market. This is the first Target Market Segment Building Block discussed that does not have a price that is in an uptrend. This is not necessarily a bad thing. PPM Building Blocks were designed to be unique and to provide diversity to a portfolio. It would be very unusual for all of the Target Market Segment asset types to be moving up, or down, at the same time.

At the time this chapter was written, Gold, Energy, and Agricultural Commodities were moving up. Real Estate was moving down. So I left Real Estate out of my sample portfolio for the time being. Yet it is not out of the Perfect Portfolio model by any means. It is on a Watch List where its price is still constantly monitored. I will be automatically alerted when its price moves up (or down) and deserves further consideration.

This chapter has illustrated an important point. There will be times when the Perfect Portfolio does not hold all of the defined Target Market Building Blocks. The portfolio would not have held a Real Estate component for most of the year 2007, and my current analysis, at the midpoint of 2008, is still keeping this asset on the sidelines. *This frees up money to be allocated to the other Target Market Building Blocks that are faring much better.*

Real Estate will make a comeback and the PPM will be right there to take advantage of it.

We complete our construction of the Target Market Segment with an Emerging Markets Building Block discussed in the next chapter.

CHAPTER 9

Adding Emerging Market Stocks to Your Portfolio

SEARCHING THE WORLD FOR EXTRAORDINARY RETURNS

We complete the Target Market Segment with a Building Block dedicated to Emerging Markets. The first four Target Market Building Blocks related to "goods" such as gold, oil, food, and property. This Building Block targets "places" such as China, Russia, Brazil, India, and other countries and geographic regions. The one thing these geographic areas have in common is that they have economies that are growing and emerging onto the world stage.

In Chapter 3, we built a Core Segment containing thousands of stocks, both domestic and foreign. What makes Emerging Market stocks special? The answer is that, as a group, they fit the profile of a PPM Target Market Building Block, not a Core Building Block. Emerging Market stocks offer the potential for extraordinary returns, they provide significant portfolio diversification, they can be easily traded, and they are volatile, meaning they need to be placed under the watchful eye of a trading plan.

You will learn in this chapter what Emerging Market investments are, the factors that influence their price, how they can be purchased, how to identify promising investment candidates, and how to implement a trading plan for any that you decide to buy. As you look at the historical performance of Emerging Market investments in the pages that follow, you will see that they are a distinctly different asset type that deserves a place among the elite group of asset classes that make up the PPM Portfolio Building Blocks.

Now we begin the process that will result in the selection of an Emerging Market investment for the sample portfolio I am building. The process starts with understanding this type of investment in more detail.

Step 1: Understanding Emerging Markets

Countries around the world can roughly be placed into one of three categories that describe the state of their economies and thus their equity markets. The categories are: undeveloped, developing, and developed. Countries or regions of the world that are transiting between developing economies and developed economies are referred to as Emerging Markets.

Examples of emerging market countries include China, India, Russia, Mexico, Brazil, Peru, and Chile. Examples of emerging market regions include Asia, Latin America, and Eastern Europe. Recently, parts of Africa and the Middle East have been added to the list. It is difficult to think of a region as wealthy as the United Arab Emirates as an emerging market, but the qualifications for this status depend more on the profile of a country's political structure and trade policies than the money in its coffers.

Countries must have an economic and political structure that allows for free trade with the outside world to be considered on the path to becoming a developed economy. Until the fall of the Soviet Bloc, many Eastern European countries could not trade freely with the rest of the world. China entered the world markets only when the total Communist control of its economic power was eased. Thus, admission into the club of emerging markets takes more than wealth; it takes the market infrastructure and the political willingness to do business with other developed countries.

Investing in Emerging Markets means buying stocks in companies that are based in these markets. Thus, an emerging markets country must have a stock exchange and a set of rules for creating, listing, and monitoring the companies that issue stocks. We, in the United States, assume at times that stock exchanges like the NYSE and NASDAQ exist around the world. They do not. Also, many countries have stock exchanges, but there is little regulation or oversight of the companies that are listed. In other words, they don't have their own version of our Securities and Exchange Commission (SEC).

Without rules and oversight similar to that provided by our SEC, it is virtually impossible for the public to get verifiable information about a company. This makes it difficult, if not impossible, for individual investors to search for and evaluate stocks of companies in emerging markets. We must therefore leave it to experts to put together baskets of stocks that enable us to participate in the growth of emerging market economies. I discuss the types of investment vehicles available for this purpose later in this chapter.

Factors that Influence Prices of Emerging Market Investments

One reason that Emerging Markets is a PPM Building Block is because the value of this asset type is affected by a unique set of market catalysts and it therefore provides valuable diversity to the Perfect Portfolio. You need to understand what these influences are so you can decide whether to include this Building Block in your portfolio and, if so, which country or region to buy. Price influences can be both local to a country or region or in general to the entire foreign investment market. Here are several of the primary factors that affect the prices of Emerging Market investments.

- *Governments:* The type of government a country is ruled by has a significant influence on the world's willingness to invest in its economy. Countries with strong central governments that strive to control all aspects of the economy impede the ability of market forces to determine company values and related stock prices. Investors are reluctant to invest in companies whose fortunes depend on decisions made by governments for reasons totally unrelated to maximizing shareholder value. Of particular concern to investors are countries that are moving from free markets to nationalized markets. Venezuela comes to mind as an example.
- *Trade Policies:* When looking at the desirability of a country's stocks for investment, experts evaluate its trade policies. Embargoes, subsidies, and excessive trade tariffs all limit the ability of the market to determine the true value of the

companies in a specific country. The freer the trade environment, the more international capital a country can attract.

- *Intellectual Property Rights Protection:* Some countries are all too
  eager to copy things that they buy, whether it be a missile,
  a song, or a book. Without copyright and trademark pro-
  tections in place, a country will be shunned by many of its
  potential trading partners. Sellers do not want their buyers to
  instantly become competitors after buying one of their products. China struggles with this problem.

- *Political Unrest:* A country may have a trade-friendly government in place but the question must be asked: How stable is
  its government? When looking at emerging markets in which
  to invest, experts must look at the potential that the current
  rulers may be overthrown. For example, Nigeria is a country
  with vast natural resources, including oil and diamonds, yet
  its economic development is severely undermined by political
  unrest and uncertainty. It seems to be constantly engaged in
  civil war. Thus, Nigeria is found on almost no one's Emerging
  Markets investment list today.

- *Natural Disasters:* Weather and other forces of nature can
  affect the economies of entire countries and thus the prices
  of company stocks in these countries. When this chapter was
  written, floods and earthquakes were ravaging China and
  shares in China-based companies were dipping. We have
  seen the devastating effects of tsunamis in Southeast Asia.
  Droughts can wipe out the agricultural base of entire countries. Companies in countries prone to natural disasters can
  be risky investments indeed.

- *Value of the U.S. Dollar:* Any foreign investment, including
  those in our Core Segment's Foreign Stock Building Block,
  is subject to risk associated with the value of the dollar.
  Foreign stocks are valued in local currencies. When the dollar strengthens against these currencies, the value of these
  investments to U.S.-based investors, who will eventually sell
  them for dollars, goes down. This works both ways. When
  the dollar weakens, the value of these holdings to U.S.-based
  investors goes up.

- *Marketing Hype and Speculation:* As with all investments in the
  Perfect Portfolio, but particularly those in the Target Market
  Segment, prices are influenced by speculation and marketing

hype. Forces such as hedge funds and speculators can artificially drive up prices using a variety of manipulation tactics that have nothing to do with the fundamentals of the underlying asset. Marketing hype has also caused the prices of such assets as China stocks to soar, based on nothing more than slick sales pitches.

The first five price influences listed here are primarily country-specific. We can virtually eliminate the risk posed by these influences by diversifying our Emerging Market investment among many countries. Instead of buying the stock of a company or basket of companies in one country, a better strategy is to buy a basket of stocks from a *basket of countries.* The last two price influences on this list are not country specific, so diversification cannot eliminate the risk of their effects. We can only attempt to manage the risk they present, and we will do so with the PPM trading plan discussed in this chapter.

Emerging Market Investment Levels

Emerging Markets is a broad and often confusing field to navigate. A unique structure must be used to enable us to make informed and effective decisions in this area of investing. One element of such a structure comes in the form of dividing the Emerging Markets field into four types or levels of investment, based on the geographic area covered. The following are the four levels that we will consider when looking for an Emerging Markets investment.

1. *Single Country:* Investments exist that enable you to buy a basket of stocks from a specific country. For example, you can buy a China ETF that contains stocks of multiple companies based in China. Single-country investments are the most risky because they are exposed to the full force of the specific country risk factors listed earlier. I will avoid single-country investments in the sample Perfect Portfolio I am developing in this book because of those higher risk factors.
2. *Region:* The next Emerging Markets level is the regional investment. You can buy mutual funds and ETFs that hold stocks in multiple countries in a specific geographical area. Examples are Latin America, Southeast Asia, and Eastern

Europe. Buying a regional investment significantly reduces single-country risk. I will consider this type of investment for my sample portfolio.

3. *World:* At the highest level of Emerging Market investments are funds and ETFs that scan the world for Emerging Market investments. They are free to hold stock in companies that are based in multiple regions of the world. I will evaluate this type of investment for the sample portfolio.

4. *Select Countries:* Finally, there are investments that hold a select group of the most promising emerging market countries and combine them in a fund or ETF. Examples are investments that include only the countries of Brazil, Russia, India, and China. You will see these referred to as BRIC investments. Those that also include Mexico are referred to as BRICM investments. I will evaluate this type of investment for the sample portfolio.

I will take these levels into consideration in Step 2 of the process when I look for Emerging Market investment candidates.

Extra Credit

Learning More about Emerging Markets

Needless to say, there are entire books written on the subject of foreign and Emerging Market investments and investing. The information presented here should be sufficient to enable you to understand the basics of this investment type and to effectively evaluate and select an Emerging Market investment for your Perfect Portfolio.

You may wish to learn more about this unique type of investment and you can do so by referring to links presented in the online supplement to this book. Go to the site, log in, click on *Links by Chapter* and then on *Chapter 9* to access these links.

How to Invest in Emerging Markets

The investment vehicles I will consider when searching for an Emerging Markets component for my sample portfolio are mutual funds and Exchange Traded Funds. Mutual funds can be either index funds that are passively managed or actively managed funds for which a fund manager decides the stocks to include. ETFs are almost exclusively based on an Emerging Markets index.

Emerging Market indexes are created by several companies, most prominent among them being Morgan Stanley Capital International (MSCI) and Standard & Poor's (S&P). These companies define indexes for a variety of market sectors by establishing a set of rules for the companies to be included. When an index is defined, these companies then continuously monitor the stocks included and change the holdings on an as-needed basis. The companies that create the indexes license them to other organizations in the financial industry that use them to create ETFs and mutual funds. For example, MSCI may define and maintain an index that they license to Vanguard to create an ETF based on it.

As you look for investment candidates in the Emerging Markets arena, you will find that many of them have virtually identical returns history because they track the same index. What does this mean to us as individual investors? Quite simply, it means that most of the time it doesn't matter from whom we buy an Emerging Markets fund for a specific region. Regardless of the name of the index mutual fund or ETF, it will probably track the same index. Any performance difference, therefore, will be largely due to different expense ratios.

Thus, our most important choice when looking for an Emerging Markets investment is between buying an index-based investment or an actively managed mutual fund. These are the vehicles I will use in the following investment identification and evaluation process.

Choosing an Emerging Markets Level and Region.   Unlike the process used to find investment candidates for other Target Market Building Blocks, for Emerging Markets we will use a two-part process. First, we will collect and evaluate data that help us determine what level and region of the Emerging Markets universe is performing best. Once we have decided on a level to work with, we will then collect and evaluate data so we can find the best specific investment for that level.

I start the process of finding an investment for my sample portfolio by collecting data related to the Emerging Market levels discussed earlier in this chapter. For the regional level, I will look at the two most prominent Emerging Market Regions at the time this chapter was written. These are the Pacific Region and the Latin America Region. For each candidate, I will use the site at finance.yahoo.com to collect historical performance data. This is a very high-level analysis. My goal is simply to determine in which part of the world Emerging Market investments are currently performing best.

Table 9.1 shows ETFs that track indexes for various Emerging Market levels and regions. I found these ETFs by browsing the Web site at finance.yahoo.com/etf. On this site click "View ETFs" in the left menu. Then select the categories labeled "Diversified Emerging," "Diversified Pacific/Asia," and "Latin America." I get lists of ETFs including several that focus on Emerging Markets.

Because these ETFs track widely used indexes, I can legitimately use them as proxies for determining the performance of the entire targeted geographic area. To collect the data shown in Table 9.1, I used the Web site at finance.yahoo.com as discussed in previous chapters and I recorded this data using the Emerging Markets Data Collection Worksheet that you can print from the online supplement. To find this worksheet log in, click on *Links by Chapter* and then on *Chapter 9*. The data were collected in the middle of 2008 and will obviously be different by the time you read this.

Data Analysis and Level Selection. A quick scan of these data tells me that Emerging Markets just about everywhere have been extremely profitable for one-year and three-year periods. The year current as of this writing, though, shows that they are cooling off. The region least affected by this drop seems to be Latin America.

Table 9.1   ETFs and Performance Data for Emerging Market Levels

Emerging Mkt. Level/Region	ETF Symbol / Company	Annualized Returns		
		2008 YTD	1 year	3 years
World	EEM: iShares MSCI EM	−10.59%	16.82%	27.33%
Region/Pacific	GMF: S&P Asia/Pacific EM	−12.02%	26.89%	N/A
Region/Latin America	ILF: iShares S&P Latin America EM	1.44%	43.50%	47.90%
Specialty/BRIC	BIK: S&P BRIC 40	−12.79%	N/A	N/A
Country/China	FXI: FTSI/Xinhua China 25	−20.72%	33.49%	37.28%

Note 1: EM in the ETF name stands for *Emerging Markets*.
Note 2: N/A means *Not Available,* indicating the investment is too new to have the data.

Also of interest in these data is the dramatic drop-off of the single-country investment for China. This illustrates the extreme volatility of single-country investing.

Based on these data, I will select the Regional Latin America level for my sample Emerging Markets Building Block. Other people looking at the same data may come to a different conclusion. It is possible that Latin America has experienced a bubble that is about to burst. It is also possible that those areas currently showing a steep decline represent a good buying opportunity. Always keep in mind when considering these possibilities that the PPM monitors any investment purchased for the Target Market Segment of the portfolio with a trading plan. The trading plan protects us from disastrous price declines resulting from the bursting of bubbles.

An Alternative Method for Finding Performance Data.   Table 9.1 uses ETF proxies for finding the performance of various emerging markets. As an alternative method for finding these data, go to the site of Morgan Stanley Capital Investments at mscibarra.com. Look for the index performance area. Here you will see performance data for more than a dozen Emerging Market indexes. These are the indexes upon which many Emerging Market ETFs and funds are based. If this Web site reference changes, it will be updated in the online supplement.

The next task is to find investing candidates for the Emerging Markets level and region I have selected.

Step 2: Identifying Emerging Market Investment Candidates

Part 1 of the investment identification process directed me to look at Latin America for the Emerging Markets component of my sample portfolio. Now, in Step 2 of the process, the goal is to find specific candidates for investing in this geographic area. I will use the same methodology and Web tools described in previous chapters.

- *A Fund Family Candidate:* I start my search with the Core fund family I established in Chapter 3, Vanguard. Using the *Funds by Family* area of the finance.yahoo.com/funds site, I scan the Vanguard list for a Latin America Emerging Markets fund.

I don't find one, so I move to my second fund family choice, Fidelity. Here I find *Fidelity Latin America,* with the symbol FLATX. This is an actively managed fund as opposed to an index fund. It will be my first evaluation candidate.

- *A Top Performer Candidate:* I next look for a Top Performer using the Yahoo! site. Here I find a Latin America fund that is in the top performers' list for one, three, and five years. It is T. Rowe Price Latin America, with the symbol PRLAX. This is also an actively managed fund. It will be my second evaluation candidate.
- *An ETF Candidate:* Now I need an ETF for comparison purposes. I could go to the ishares.com Web site or to finance .yahoo.com/etf and browse for Latin America ETFs. But I have already identified one in Table 9.1. This is the iShares S&P Latin America Index ETF, symbol ILF. This fund tracks an S&P index, and it will be my third candidate.

I have two actively managed funds and an index ETF as evaluation candidates. It will be interesting to see if active management makes a difference in this area.

Step 3: Collecting and Analyzing Data

With three Latin America Emerging Market candidates, I am ready to move forward to the data collection and analysis phase.

I use the site at finance.yahoo.com to collect the data presented in Table 9.2 and I use the previously mentioned Emerging Markets Data Collection Worksheet to document it. As described in previous chapters, I simply enter the investment symbol where designated on the Yahoo! site and use the *Return, Risk,* and *Profile* menu items to find the needed data. Always keep in mind that the

Table 9.2 Emerging Markets Data Collection Worksheet

Company / Fund	Symbol	Annualized Returns			Risk: Std. Dev.	Expense Ratio
		1-year	3-year	5-year		
iShares ETF	ILF	43.50%	47.90%	49.53%	21.89%	.50%
Fidelity	FLATX	36.83%	51.56%	49.11%	22.49%	1.76%
T. Rowe Price	PRLAX	38.89%	54.97%	50.15%	23.79%	1.76%

data used in these examples are valid only as of the time this chapter was written.

Comparison and Selection

The returns listed in Table 9.2 are astounding. Could this be a bubble about to burst? Perhaps, but if it is, I can still ride the trend upward while it exists. I will protect myself with the PPM trading plan from a potential bubble burst.

The returns data for the three investments are similar and not a basis for choosing one over another. Risk data are also virtually the same. The big difference is in expenses, where ILF has a major advantage. The ETF is also easier to trade.

Now I will illustrate why it is important to know which index an ETF tracks. My original conclusion was to choose ILF as my Emerging Markets Portfolio Building Block. But when I checked the share price of ILF, it was a whopping $280 per share! I don't like to buy investments with this high a price. If I have only a few thousand dollars to allocate to this portfolio component, then I will have a very difficult time meeting the exact percentage allocation I determine (as discussed in Chapter 10). So, I first note that ILF tracks the S&P Latin 40 Index. Then I looked for another ETF that tracks the same index. I find an ETF that does so on finance. yahoo.com/etf with the symbol GML. Table 9.3 shows the data I collect as an extension to Table 9.2.

GML is a relatively new ETF and has very little data. But I don't need more data. It tracks the same index as ILF and I already have five years' worth of data for this index. This investment is more reasonably priced at $89 per share. My final conclusion is that GML will be my selection.

Step 4: Price Chart Analysis

The next step of the evaluation process is to look at a price chart to decide if now is a good time to buy my ETF selection. Figure 9.1

Table 9.3   Extension of Emerging Markets Data Collection Worksheet

Company/Fund	Symbol	1-year	3-year	5-year	Std. Dev.	Exp.
S&P Latin America EM	GML	39.64%	N/A	N/A	N/A	.60

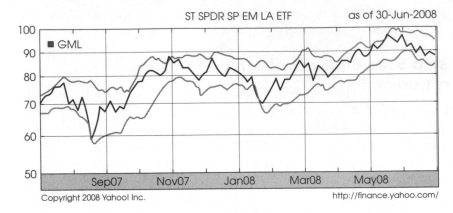

ST SPDR SP EM LA ETF   as of 30-Jun-2008

Figure 9.1   One-Year Price Chart for GML

shows this price chart with Bollinger Bands included. These data are not current as of the time you read this and your chart will look different.

Here are factors to look for on the chart.

- *Current Price:* The current price is $89 per share.
- *Price Trend:* The long-term trend is up, the short-term trend is down but approaching the bottom of the Bollinger Band channel. This could indicate that a bounce up is possible in the near future.
- *Support:* By simply eyeballing the chart, it seems that a support price level exists at around the $80 dollar level.
- *Resistance:* A point of resistance is not obvious on this chart. The price has recently moved up to the mid-90s and back down, but the price line has not hit this level multiple times, so no resistance level has been formed. Still, I would want a take-profit alert at $95 so that I can assess the situation just in case the mid-90s does turn out to be a resistance level.
- *Volatility:* The Bollinger Bands are neither widening nor narrowing at the current time, meaning that price fluctuations are relatively predictable. This tells me that I should not get whipsawed out of the position if I place a stop loss trigger at $80, which is below the bottom Bollinger Band. Normal, daily

fluctuations in price should not bring the price down to this level and then go back up.

Step 5: Purchase Decision and Defining a Trading Plan

I am prepared to add GML to my sample portfolio. But before doing so, I need to look closely at the market environment to determine whether conditions are favorable for this type of investment.

I look at a chart of the dollar versus the euro and do not see a major strengthening trend. If I had, it would have been a red flag as stocks denominated in foreign currencies lose value when the value of the dollar rises. I see no news headlines about disasters or political coups in Latin America, so this does not stop my decision. I also read in news headlines for GML that one reason that Latin America Emerging Market investments are doing better than other areas of the world is that they have a heavy emphasis on natural resources. I know from analyzing Oil and Agricultural Building Blocks in previous chapters that these assets are on the rise. This is another positive input to my decision.

I am ready to commit to the decision to place GML in my portfolio.

My decision, based on all of the information collected, is to buy GML at this point using the following simple trading plan.

- Place a Market Order at $89.
- Place a Trailing Stop to automatically sell the position if the price drops $9 or more from the highest point it reaches while I own it.
- Place a take-profit Alert at $95 that will send me an e-mail when this price is hit. At that point, I will perform additional research and decide whether to sell to take profits or to simply move up my take-profit alert price and tighten my tighten my Trailing Stop to perhaps a drop of $3.

This simple trading plan is based on both subjective and objective analysis. The data tell me that the price trend for Latin America Emerging Markets may still have legs. I may not know all of the reasons for this, but I don't need to. The fact is that for five years the trend has been up and there is no fundamental information that tells me that the trend is about to be reversed. If it does, my stop loss trigger protects me.

The decision of how much money to allocate to this investment in the portfolio is discussed in Chapter 10.

The Special Case of Getting Stopped Out for Emerging Markets

I discuss in Chapter 11 the monitoring and management of the Perfect Portfolio after it is implemented. I detail in that chapter what to do when the trading system you put in place for an investment in the Target Market Segment either automatically sells or prompts you to sell a position in order to stop losses or to take profits.

For the first four Target Market Asset Building Blocks discussed previously, the answer is to stay away from an asset type that you sell until prospects for further growth improve. I have explained how a Watch List can assist you in this process.

The investments chosen in previous chapters for Gold, Energy, Agriculture, and Real Estate represent relatively monolithic markets. For example, Gold prices are either trending up or down. Oil prices are either going up or down. The same holds true for the prices of food and property.

But the Emerging Markets category of assets is not monolithic. There is no one asset upon whose price this investment Building Block depends. So, for example, if I get stopped out and sell my Latin America investment, this does not mean I should stay out of Emerging Markets altogether. No, it means that I should simply repeat the process presented in this chapter to look for another area of the world where things are booming. This is a unique aspect of investing in Emerging Markets and selecting an investment for this Building Block.

Building *Your* Perfect Portfolio!

Now it is time for you to find an Emerging Markets investment for your Perfect Portfolio using the same process described in this chapter.

Use the worksheets, the process, and the Web sites referred to in this chapter to collect and document current data. The worksheet for this Building Block is different from the one used for other Target Market assets. It is titled the *Emerging Markets Data Collection*

Worksheet. It incorporates the two-step process for finding an investment in this area. To access and print this worksheet, go to the online supplement, click on *Links by Chapter,* and then on *Chapter 9,* where you will see a link to this worksheet.

The worksheet shows my example ETF proxies for the various Emerging Market levels. You may wish to analyze other markets. To do so, go to finance.yahoo.com/etf and find an ETF for other areas or regions of the world and insert them into a blank worksheet.

Chapter Summary

Regardless of what U.S. equity markets are doing, there is almost always someplace in the world where stocks are booming. Stocks in the developed areas of the world such as the United States, Europe, and Asia as a whole typically move in the same general direction. Globalization has linked the major economies to such an extent that the U.S. market influences them all. So, to find rays of light amid general gloom, you need to look at economies that are influenced by more localized factors. You need to look in the area of Emerging Markets to find these economies and pockets of stock prosperity.

You learned in this chapter how to add an Emerging Markets component to the Target Market Segment of your portfolio. You saw that Emerging Market investments come in many forms. The most conservative play is to buy an investment that holds stocks from Emerging Markets across the world. The most volatile play is to buy a single-country investment such as China or Brazil. Between these extremes are regional Emerging Markets, such as Latin America, and specialty Emerging Markets, such as a BRIC investment, which holds stocks from Brazil, Russia, India, and China.

You learned in this chapter that many factors affect the prices of Emerging Market stocks. Among these factors are local politics, trade policies, country instability, natural disasters, and the quality of local stock exchanges. Another factor that affects all foreign investments is the strength of the U.S. dollar.

As mentioned earlier, the beauty of Emerging Market investments is that regardless of what is happening with the U.S.

economy, there is almost always a country or a part of the world that is booming. Whereas developed countries may consider a boom to produce returns in the range of 12 to15 percent, a boom in Emerging Markets can bring returns of 30 percent, 40 percent, 50 percent, and higher.

There exists in developing countries tremendous untapped potential and room to grow that does not exist in developed economies. With such returns, however, comes risk, and that is why an Emerging Markets investment must be monitored and sold to stop losses and to take gains. That is why this Building Block is in the Target Market Segment where it is under the watchful eye of the PPM trading plan.

My Sample Portfolio's Target Market Segment

With the selection of an Emerging Markets Building Block, I have completed my sample Target Market Segment. The investments I have selected in Chapters 5 through 9 are summarized in Table 9.4.

If you are creating your own Target Market Segment, then use the *Target Market Segment Design Worksheet* to document your own selections. To access it, go to the online supplement, click on *Links by Chapter,* and then on *Chapter 9* to find a link to this worksheet in PDF format and print it.

You can also access the *Target Market Segment Calculator* to determine an estimated return for the entire segment by assigning Expected Returns and Allocations to each investment you plan

Table 9.4   My Sample Portfolio's Target Market Segment

Building Block	Investment	Symbol	1-Year Return
Gold	iShares Gold ETF	IAU	37.73%
Energy	Dow Jones Energy ETF	IYE	24.39%
Agricultural Commodities	Powershares Agriculture Fund ETF	DBA	46.68%
Emerging Markets	S&P Latin America Emerging Markets	GML	39.64%

to buy. This process is explained more fully in Chapter 10. For now, just do it for fun. You will find this calculator in the online supplement along with the Design Worksheet.

We are now ready to start Part III of the book, which shows how to bring the Core Segment and the Target Market Segment together into a total Perfect Portfolio. The fruits of your labor are about to be realized!

PART
III

CREATING AND WORKING WITH YOUR PERFECT PORTFOLIO

At this point in *The Perfect Portfolio* you have nine unique asset classes in your investing toolkit. You have a good understanding of the characteristics of each asset type and of the market factors that influence their prices. You also know how to find specific investments for adding each of these asset classes to your portfolio. In short, you now have in place the Building Blocks for designing and creating a Perfect Portfolio. Here in Part III I first show you how to combine these Building Blocks in a manner that matches your goals, your investing style, and current market conditions. The purpose of Chapter 10 is to show you how to design your unique Perfect Portfolio and to give you the tools and resources to do so.

Then I discuss in Chapter 11 how to put into place a structure, a process, and Web resources for monitoring your Perfect Portfolio on an ongoing basis. Your portfolio will be dynamic. It will change as your personal investing profile and market conditions change. The Perfect Portfolio Methodology (PPM) gives you the tools needed for easily adjusting your investment mix to rapidly and effectively respond to these changes. I show you in Chapter 11 exactly how this is accomplished.

Chapter 12 provides information that no financial adviser will give you. It shows you how you can increase the returns of your Perfect Portfolio by increasing your involvement in the investing process. I highlight here areas where you can take an active role in your portfolio's success and strive for returns that are limited only by your willingness to exchange time and effort for wealth. The PPM gives you the vehicle for channeling your involvement into productive actions and thus higher returns.

Finally, in the book's Summary, I review the major revolutionary elements of the PPM that make it superior to any other personal investing approach in the market today. I also give you an idea of the challenges I face when teaching the PPM to students who have never been exposed to anything outside the box of traditional investing concepts. Then I relate a story told to me by one of my students who confronted a professional adviser with her Perfect Portfolio design. I believe you will find this conversation to be both interesting and revealing. I conclude the book by asking you to consider what you have learned in *The Perfect Portfolio*. I hope what you have learned here will inspire you to be proactive in your investing activities and to do so with both confidence and enthusiasm!

CHAPTER

10

Designing Your Perfect Portfolio

BUILDING A POWERFUL PORTFOLIO
THAT MEETS YOUR UNIQUE NEEDS

At this point in the book you have defined two Perfect Portfolio Segments and nine Asset Building Blocks. The beauty and the power of the Perfect Portfolio Methodology are that one investment for each of these Building Blocks is all that you will ever need in your portfolio! To review, the nine Portfolio Building Blocks are as follows:

Core Segment

- Cash
- Bonds
- U.S. Stocks
- Foreign Stocks

Target Market Segment

- Gold
- Energy
- Agricultural Commodities
- Real Estate
- Emerging Markets

If you have been building your Perfect Portfolio along with me as we moved through the previous chapters, then you have selected a specific investment for each of these Building Blocks and are now fully prepared to create your own unique Perfect Portfolio.

But what is a Perfect Portfolio? Does there exist one combination of the assets listed here that is "perfect"? The answer is no. A Perfect Portfolio does not exist in the absolute sense. It only exists within the context of your unique goals, your investing style, and current market conditions. The Perfect Portfolio for you will be different from the Perfect Portfolio for anyone else. So, the first task you must undertake in defining *your* Perfect Portfolio is examining, understanding, and documenting those elements that make you the unique type of investor you are. Thus, before defining your Perfect Portfolio you need an Investing Plan. The first part of this chapter is devoted to this task.

With an Investing Plan in place, I will then walk you through a process for allocating investment money to each Portfolio Segment and to each Asset Building Block to help you meet the goals of your Investing Plan. These allocations will completely define the risk-return profile of your portfolio and match it to your individual investing style as well as current market conditions. When you finish this chapter you will have a design for a Perfect Portfolio that is customized for you.

You should note that in this chapter I will make extensive use of worksheets and calculators as I illustrate various activities. Each of these is available in the online supplement. You access them by going to the supplement Web site, logging in, clicking on *Links by Chapter,* and then on *Chapter 10.* You can, however, create the worksheets and perform the required calculations on your own, if you wish.

Defining Your Investing Plan

In my 10-plus years of teaching, the biggest problem I have seen is that students have no specific investing goals and no structured approach to investing in general. In short, they have no Investing Plan and as a result, they are essentially investing at random.

I am not just speaking here only of my younger students right out of high school or college. I am also speaking of people in the middle of their working careers as well as people who are well into their retirement years. Far too many individuals have just not taken the time to set specific investing goals and work toward them in a structured manner.

These same people are also unsure of how much money they have, how much they earn, how much they spend, and how much money will be required in the future to maintain a comfortable lifestyle. These are all questions that must be answered to be an effective investor. These are all questions that are addressed in an Investing Plan.

Almost as serious as not having an Investing Plan is letting a third party create one for you. I have seen far too many people simply turn over their portfolios to advisers or brokers who produce a plan that is nothing more than a cookie cutter, computer generated framework for selling commissioned funds. You can't afford to allow your financial future to be dictated by an uninterested third party. You are unique and you must have a unique plan created by and for *you*.

If creating an Investing Plan was a massively complex endeavor I could understand people not having one, or hiring a third party to produce one. But it is just not that difficult a task. You simply need to know the steps involved, the data to be collected, and the questions to be answered. This is what I provide in the discussion that follows.

I would urge you to devote an hour or two to creating your Investing Plan using the process, resources, and tools that follow. The task will not be difficult but it will take some of your time and attention. This is the first step in a journey that will end in the creation of your unique Perfect Portfolio by the end of this chapter!

Defining the Scope of Your Investing Goals

Without investing goals, it is virtually impossible to make informed and effective investing decisions. These goals don't need to be complex. Your goal may be as simple as maximizing return in the current market environment. Or you may have longer-term goals that aim for a target amount of money at a specific time in the future, to buy a house or to retire comfortably, for example. No matter how simple or involved your goals, you must define them, document them, and work toward them.

Maximizing Current Returns

An integral part of my teaching plan for many years has been to teach people how to develop long-term investing goals. This process includes defining goal amounts, setting time horizons, determining risk tolerance levels, and more. I walk you through this process here.

But my students are often retirees having time horizons that are basically *now*. Their investing goals are simply to increase the current return of their portfolios within their risk tolerance limits. As a result, many of my students did not feel that the full planning process applied to them. In many cases, they were correct.

So, if your goal is focused on maximizing the current returns of your portfolio then the following Investing Plan development process may not completely apply to you and you can move to the section titled "Beginning the Perfect Portfolio Design Process" that is presented next in this chapter if you wish. But I don't recommend that you do this. There are elements of the Investing Plan development process that you will benefit from knowing, whether you use them in the exact manner presented or not.

Setting Longer-Term Goals

If your investing activities are directed toward goals that are more than a few years in the future, then you need to work through a simple process that will result in a structured Investing Plan. For example, perhaps you are currently 45 years old and you want to have a sum of $2,000,000 by the time you are 60. For this type of goal you need a specific plan, one that will guide and inform the design of your Perfect Portfolio.

The Steps listed here show you how to build an Investing Plan with a time horizon of five-plus years. They make liberal use of tools available in the online supplement of this book found by logging in, clicking *on Links by Chapter* and then on *Chapter 10*. If you prefer not to access the supplement, then simply perform the tasks described on your own. Let's begin.

Step 1: Set Your Goal or Goals.   The first step in the process is to take some time and set one or more investing goals. You may be investing for retirement. Perhaps you have set up a college investment fund for a child. There are any number of goals you can set, but common among them must be the following factors.

- Name of the goal
- Target dollar amount of the goal
- Time horizon for reaching the goal amount

- Initial amount of money you will dedicate to the goal
- Amount of money you are willing to contribute monthly to the goal

For the purpose of designing a sample portfolio using the PPM Building Blocks identified in this book, I will use the following factors as the starting point for building my Investing Plan:

- *Name:* Retirement Goal
- *Target Amount:* $2,000,000
- *Time frame:* 15 years
- *Initial Investment Amount:* $100,000
- *Monthly Contribution:* $300

I suggest that you initially set a Target Amount that is higher than you may currently think is possible. Steps 2 through 5 will bring you back to earth if it is not feasible.

Now go to the online supplement to this book and print out a blank *Investing Plan Worksheet.* You will find it by first going to *Links by Chapter* and then *Chapter 10,* where it is presented in PDF format. You could also simply make your own worksheet using the templates that I use in the following illustrations.

Step 2: Determine Your Current Financial Profile.   You probably can answer the first four parameters in your goal definition fairly easily. But what about the monthly contribution? Do you know how much you earn and how much you spend? Do you know how much money you have available to contribute to your goal? Surprisingly, most people do not. You need to determine how much discretionary income you have at the end of each month and then make a decision that will be fundamental to your financial future. You will need to decide how much of this positive cash flow you are willing to dedicate on a monthly basis to reaching your overall investing goal.

You need to document your income and your expenses to determine what your monthly cash flow is. My strong recommendation is that you go to the online supplement of this book and use the worksheets and calculators provided there. These will include the National Association of Online Investor's *Hidden Expenses Worksheet* and related calculator along with the *Cash Flow Worksheet* and related calculator.

The result of using these resources will be your monthly cash flow after expenses. With this information, you will then be able to decide how large a monthly contribution to your investing goals you can afford. Fill in this number on your Investing Plan Worksheet.

If you are not using the online supplement, simply subtract your average monthly expenses from your monthly income. The online tools provided in the supplement walk you through this process, but you can, if you wish, do it on your own.

Step 3: Determine Your Required Portfolio Return. With your goal defined and your monthly contribution specified, you now have the data you need to determine whether the parameters for your targeted goal are feasible.

The next step is to use a specialized calculator designed by the National Association of Online Investors that shows you the annual rate of return required by a portfolio to meet your target goal amount. This calculator is available in the online supplement. Figure 10.1 is an example of its use using my sample goal parameters. Note that I have assumed that my portfolio is held in a tax-deferred account such as an IRA so the tax entry in the calculator is zero.

You can see that this set of parameters requires an exceptional rate of portfolio return of approximately 21 percent for each year for 15 years. The stock market has averaged a return rate of about 12 percent for decades. Using this as a comparison point, a 21 percent return would require an excessive amount of risk. So I will need to change some parameters.

Step 4: Making the Target Goal Amount Realistic. I need to lower the Return Required for my Investing Plan to make it feasible. There are various parameters that I can change. I can lower my

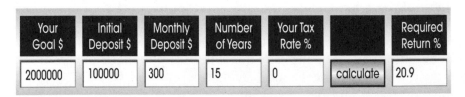

Your Goal $	Initial Deposit $	Monthly Deposit $	Number of Years	Your Tax Rate %		Required Return %
2000000	100000	300	15	0	calculate	20.9

Figure 10.1   The Required Return Calculator
Reproduced with the permission of the National Association of Online Investors (NAOI.org).

goal, increase my monthly contribution, or extend my time horizon. The calculator shown in Figure 10.2 illustrates the effects of these changes with one test set of parameters per row. Note the changes that are made in each row and the new Required Return rate that results from each change.

Work with your parameters until you get a set that results in a Required Return rate of around 17 percent or less. Your target return rate is one input that you will use when designing your Perfect Portfolio as discussed later in this chapter. You can always come back to this step and make further changes if you are not able to design a portfolio that meets your targeted Return Rate.

These steps are applicable for individuals with longer-term goals. They give you a target return to shoot for, which will affect your Perfect Portfolio design. Individuals who simply want to maximize returns from their current portfolio will place less emphasis on this process. It is useful for all investors, though, to work through the exercise.

I will choose the parameters shown in the second row of the calculator in Figure 10.2 for my sample Investing Plan. My Required Return Rate is therefore 17.9 percent. This is the target I will aim for when designing my sample Perfect Portfolio later in this chapter.

Step 5: Complete Your Investing Plan Now complete your Investing Plan Worksheet. The steps discussed here have enabled you to fill in each data field. The Target Return from this worksheet will be one input in the design of your Perfect Portfolio, and the completed Investing Plan provides information such as initial contribution and monthly investing contributions that will be required to meet your investing goals.

Your Goal $	Initial Deposit $	Monthly Deposit $	Number of Years	Your Tax Rate %		Required Return %
2000000	100000	300	15	0	calculate	20.9
2000000	100000	350	17	0	calculate	17.9
2000000	100000	300	20	0	calculate	15

Figure 10.2 Testing Multiple Parameters Sets

Reproduced with the permission of the National Association of Online Investors (NAOI.org).

Beginning the Perfect Portfolio Design Process

Finally! The time has come to start designing a complete Perfect Portfolio on the basis of all of the work done up to this point. In the following pages, I will design a portfolio that meets my investing goals. I will use the sample data collected throughout this book to illustrate the portfolio design process. This is the same process that I suggest you use to design your own Perfect Portfolio.

The goal of the Perfect Portfolio design process is to combine the PPM Building Blocks in a manner that meets your investing goals, your unique investing style, and current market conditions.

The PPM Profile Dials

The Perfect Portfolio Methodology is designed to enable you to easily design a portfolio that meets your unique requirements. For this purpose, it provides multiple *dials,* which I first referred to in Chapter 2. These dials allow you to efficiently adjust the profile of your portfolio as your personal circumstances and market conditions change. They are described in this section and their use is illustrated on the pages to come.

- *The Core Asset Allocation Dial:* The first set of decisions you will make in the portfolio design process relate to the percentage allocations of investment money you assign to each of the Core Building Blocks, these being, Cash, Bonds, U.S. Stocks, and Foreign Stocks. I discussed this Segment in Chapter 3 and you know that this is an area where relatively conservative investments are placed. You increase the risk-reward profile of the Core Segment by allocating more money to stocks and less to cash and bonds.
- *The Target Market Allocation Dial:* The second portfolio profile dial involves the money allocations you assign to each Building Block in the Target Market Segment. You learned about this Segment in Part II. These are more volatile investments that have the potential for returns that are significantly higher than market averages. You make allocation decisions here primarily based on current market conditions and current price trends of the various Building Block investments. The allocations you assign here will also affect the risk-reward profile of your portfolio.

- *The Segment Allocation Dial:* The third portfolio profile dial is your allocation of money to each of the two Portfolio Segments. You increase the risk-reward profile of the portfolio by increasing the allocation to the Target Market Segment. Your decisions here will be based on a number of factors, including your willingness to become involved in the process of monitoring your portfolio.

There are multiple moving parts in this design process, and each affects the expected return of a portfolio that you design as well as its risk profile. A structure is needed that enables you to test various allocation parameters so you can find a set of allocation percentages and dial settings that match your unique investing style, return needs, and current market conditions. Providing you with this structure is the purpose of the Perfect Portfolio Design Worksheet and Calculator that I introduce next.

The Portfolio Design Worksheet and Calculator

To add structure to the portfolio building process, you will use the *Perfect Portfolio Design Worksheet.* You can find this worksheet in the online supplement to this book. Simply log in to the supplement, click on *Links by Chapter* and then on *Chapter 10.* Here you will find the worksheet in PDF format and a companion *Portfolio Design Calculator.* You will record on the worksheet the performance data collected throughout this book and test multiple allocation scenarios to find one set of parameters that fits your unique requirements.

I suggest that you go now to the online supplement and print at least one copy of the Portfolio Design Worksheet in preparation for the discussion that follows. Or you can simply create your own worksheet based on the illustrations that follow.

Elements of the Worksheet

What follows is a description of the elements of the Portfolio Design Worksheet that is shown in Figure 10.3 and the corresponding calculator. Some are input fields and some are calculated fields as indicated in the definitions presented here. I will show you how to define these fields for your Perfect Portfolio in the pages that follow. For now let's just understand what these worksheet fields are.

| Total Investment Amount: | $ 100000 | | | |

| Core Segment | Allocation: 40 % | Dollars: $ 40000 | | |

Building Block	Expected Return	Allocation	Contribution	Dollars
Cash	3 %	5 %	0.15 %	$ 2000
Bonds	5 %	15 %	0.75 %	$ 6000
U.S. Stocks	10 %	40 %	4 %	$ 16000
Foreign Stocks	12 %	40 %	4.8 %	$ 16000
Core Segment Totals >>		100 %	9.7 %	$ 40000

| Target Market Segment | Allocation: 60 % | Dollars: $ 60000 | | |

Building Block	Expected Return	Allocation	Contribution	Dollars
Gold	20 %	30 %	6 %	$ 18000
Energy	20 %	25 %	5 %	$ 15000
Agriculture	20 %	25 %	5 %	$ 15000
Real Estate	0 %	0 %	0 %	$ 0
Emerging Markets	15 %	20 %	3 %	$ 12000
	0 %	0 %	0 %	$ 0
Target Market Totals >>		100 %	19 %	$ 60000

| Portfolio Totals >> | | 100 % | 15.28 % | $ 100000 |

Figure 10.3   The Perfect Portfolio Design Worksheet/Calculator

- *Initial Fields.* The first two fields on the worksheet and the calculator relate to the amount of actual dollars you will dedicate to this portfolio and the amount you will dedicate to the Core Segment. They are as follows:
  - *Investment Dollar Amount (input):* This is the dollar figure of the amount of investment money you will dedicate to your entire Perfect Portfolio. This number should come from your Investing Plan Worksheet, discussed previously in this chapter. If you have not completed an Investing Plan, then just use a number for test purposes.
  - *Core Segment Allocation (input) and Dollar Amount (calculated):* The first of these fields is the percentage of your total portfolio you decide to allocate to the Core Segment. The Design Calculator will then calculate the dollar amount represented by this percentage.
- *Core Segment Building Blocks:* This section of the worksheet is dedicated to the asset Building Blocks that we worked with in Chapter 3 for the Core Segment of the portfolio. The following worksheet fields relate to each Building Block.
  - *Allocation (input):* This is the percentage of Core investment money that you will allocate to each Core Building Block. This is your decision and how you make it is discussed later in this chapter. I would expect you to try multiple allocation sets.
  - *Expected Return (input):* This is the return that can reasonably be expected from each Building Block based on the data collection and analysis performed in Chapter 3. This will typically be the three-year average annualized return that was documented on the Core Building Block worksheets completed in Chapter 3. But you can use your own judgment as to the return figures that you believe to be the most probable.
  - *Contribution (calculated):* This is simply the allocation percent times the expected return percent for each Building Block. This is the amount of return contributed by the associated Building Block to the total Core Segment return. For convenience, you can use the Portfolio Design Calculator to perform the math and document the results on the Portfolio Design Worksheet.

- ◆ *Core Totals (calculated):* This row shows the Total Expected Return from the Core Segment as you have configured it as well as the total dollar amount dedicated to this Segment. The numbers here are derived by simply adding the figures in the associated columns. The Design Calculator will do the math for you or you can do it on your own. Note that the "Total Core Allocation" must be 100 percent or you will get an error if you use the calculator.
- *Target Market Building Blocks:* The data in this section relate to the asset Building Blocks discussed in Part II.
  - ◆ *Target Market Allocation (input) and Dollar Amount (calculated):* The first field is the percentage of your total portfolio you decide to allocate to the Target Market Segment. The Design Calculator will then give you the Dollar Amount this represents based on the Total Investment Amount you entered at the top of the worksheet.
  - ◆ *Target Market Building Block Rows:* The definitions of the fields in this area are the same as described previously for the Core Segment. These, however, relate to the Target Market Segment. You will note that there are more rows available on the Worksheet and Calculator than there are Building Blocks defined for this Segment. They exist to enable you to add your own Building Blocks as discussed in Chapter 12, if you wish. Most people will leave these rows blank.
  - ◆ *Target Market Totals (calculated):* This row shows the Total Expected Return from the Target Market Segment as you have configured it, as well as the Total Dollar Amount dedicated to this Segment. The numbers here are derived by simply adding the figures in the associated columns. The Design Calculator will do the math for you or you can do it on your own. Note that the Allocation numbers within the Target Market Segment must add up to 100 percent or you will get an error if you use the calculator.
- *Portfolio Totals:* On this final row of the worksheet and calculator, you will see the Total Expected Return from the entire portfolio as you have designed it along with a repeat of the total number of dollars you have decided to commit to this portfolio. The total dollars number is the same as the one

you input in the first field of the portfolio worksheet. It is simply repeated here.

The Total Expected Return is the sum of the Core Return Total times the Core Allocation percentage plus the Target Market Return Total times the Target Market Allocation percentage. *This is this number that you are seeking to match to the Required Return number you calculated for your Investing Plan.*

The Issue of Portfolio Risk

The Portfolio Design Worksheet gives you a specific number for expected return. But where is the corresponding specific number for risk in terms of Standard Deviation? This number is very difficult to calculate. You cannot simply add the Standard Deviation numbers for each asset type and divide the sum by the number of asset types to get an average. Why? Because each asset has a different correlation with all of the other assets in the portfolio and consequently interferes with the calculation.

There certainly are Web resources that will give you a number for the risk of a portfolio. I have studied portfolio theory for years and to me these numbers are of little practical use when using the Perfect Portfolio Methodology. They *do not* take into account that you are substantially reducing risk by implementing a trading plan for each of your Target Market Building Blocks. And they *do not* factor in your willingness to become involved in the investing process so you can make more informed, and thus less risky, investing decisions. Involvement is a factor that I discuss in more detail in Chapter 12.

Risk numbers as represented by Standard Deviation here simply confirm the obvious: the higher the expected return, the higher the risk. So don't feel cheated that the PPM does not give you a specific risk number for various portfolio designs. *You* control risk by how you design and monitor your portfolio and by how much effort you are willing to devote to the investing process.

Using the Portfolio Design Worksheet and Calculator

I have described the Perfect Portfolio Design Worksheet and the Perfect Portfolio Design Calculator. Figure 10.3 shows a screen capture of the Calculator that you will find in the online supplement. The Worksheet has the same fields and looks similar. Use the Worksheet to document your work and the Calculator to perform the calculations.

The Worksheet and Calculator combination is an incredibly powerful tool for designing your Perfect Portfolio. It enables you to test various allocation scenarios in an effort to reach a Total Portfolio Return that matches the Required Return for the Investing Plan you created at the beginning of this chapter.

You can also test various Expected Return parameters for each of the PPM Asset Building Blocks that you have studied in previous chapters.

You will want to test multiple scenarios. Observe the effects of increasing and decreasing allocations for the three portfolio profile dials described earlier. These are Segment allocations, Core Segment Building Block allocations, and Target Market Building Block allocations. You will see that Segment allocation has the greatest effect on overall portfolio return. Allocations among the Building Blocks within each Segment enable you to fine-tune the risk-reward profile of the portfolio.

Next, we put these resources to work as we begin the process of creating a final design for the Perfect Portfolio.

Designing a Perfect Portfolio

Now we are ready to actually use the Perfect Portfolio Design Process to create a portfolio. If you are using the online supplement go to the Web site, log in, click on *Links by Chapter* and then on *Chapter 10.* Find a listing for the Perfect Portfolio Design Worksheet and print one or more copies. If you are not using the supplement, then simply create your own worksheet with the fields shown in the illustrations presented here.

I illustrate in the following pages the design process by using the data that I have collected throughout the previous chapters. I suggest that you use this same process for the Perfect Portfolio that you are building.

Defining Perfect Portfolio Expected Returns

The first set of data that I will complete on the worksheet is the Expected Returns for each Portfolio Building Block. I will use the nine Building Block Worksheets that I have created in the course of the book for this purpose.

The first question is which numbers to use as the Expected Returns in the Design Worksheet. For the Core, long-term holdings, I will use the three-year historical returns average I collected in Chapter 3 as my initial basis for estimating the Expected Returns for each of these Building Blocks.

For the shorter-term holdings in the Target Market Segment, I will use as my initial basis for estimating the Expected Returns the one-year returns I collected in Chapters 5 through 9. In this Segment I am more interested in recent performance as an indicator of future short-term performance.

I will then condition these estimates on the basis of my analysis of current and future market conditions for each asset. Table 10.1 shows historical returns that I have collected for each Building Block and the Expected Returns I estimate for next year, which are based on these numbers. These are Expected Return numbers that I feel are conservative, but I would rather estimate low than high. Your personal market outlook at the time you read this will color your analysis and the numbers you select.

I enter these numbers on my Portfolio Design Worksheet. These percentages will also be used in the related Portfolio Design Calculator.

Table 10.1 Portfolio Building Block Historical and Expected Returns

Portfolio Segment	Building Block / Symbol	3-Year Return	Expected Return For Next Year
Core	Cash / VMMXX	4.48%	3.0%
	Bonds / VBMFX	5.43%	5.0%
	U.S. Stocks / VTSMX	6.19%	10.0%
	Foreign Stocks / VGTSX	15.53%	12.0%
Target Market		1-Year Return	
	Gold / IAU	37.73%	20.0%
	Energy / IYE	24.39%	20.0%
	Agriculture / DBA	46.68%	20.0%
	Real Estate / VNQ	−17.60%	15.0%
	Emerging Mkts. / GML	39.64%	15.0%

The next task is to determine the all-important allocations to each Building Block, which will define the portfolio's complete profile.

Defining Perfect Portfolio Allocations

Now we have come to the most critical aspect of the portfolio design process, assigning allocations to the two Segments and to each Building Block within the Segments. The work you do here and the allocations you assign will determine the portfolio's returns potential, its risk profile, and how much time and effort you will need to devote to the investing process.

Always keep in mind as you move through this process that there exists no one set of "best" allocation parameters. There exists only a set that best meets your unique investing goals, your investing style and current market conditions.

You also need to understand that assigning allocations is an iterative process. It starts with you defining an initial set of allocations, entering them into the Design Calculator, and viewing the resulting Expected Return from the portfolio. You will then likely revise the allocations multiple times in order to obtain a result that closely matches your unique investing profile and market outlook. Using the Portfolio Design Calculator makes testing multiple allocation scenarios a very simple process. Be prepared to spend some time on this effort, though.

Defining allocations is not simply a matter of randomly picking numbers. Throughout this book you have obtained knowledge and tools that enable you to make informed decisions. Each allocation number you enter is the result of the knowledge you gained and the data you collected for each PPM Building Block.

I next discuss the factors that you should take into consideration when determining the three sets of allocations for your Perfect Portfolio.

Defining Core Segment Allocations

I discussed the Core Segment of the Perfect Portfolio in Chapter 3. You learned there that its purpose is to provide a stable foundation for the total portfolio. In this Segment, you will purchase investments for Cash, Bonds, U.S. Stocks, and Foreign Stocks. You will go through the PPM evaluation process for each to find one investment that enables you to own the entire related market or asset class. Thus, in the Core Segment you will own only a maximum of four securities. These are buy-and-hold investments that you will likely own for years.

You adjust the risk-reward profile of this Segment through allocations to the four Core Building Blocks. More returns potential is added by increased allocations to the two Stock Building Blocks. This also adds risk, of course. You decrease returns potential and risk by increasing allocations to Bonds and Cash.

The main factors that need to be considered when making allocation decisions in the Core Segment include the following:

- *Your risk tolerance:* First, consider your tolerance for risk. If the portfolio is funding your current lifestyle, then your risk tolerance will be less than if your portfolio is targeted at buying a house many years from now. The more risk you are able to tolerate in exchange for higher returns, the more you should allocate to the two Stock Building Blocks.
- *Your time horizon:* The longer you hold stocks, the less risky this asset class as a whole becomes. History has shown that while stocks will have short-term ups and downs, they have in the long run trended upward for decades. So if your portfolio time horizon is five years or more, you should feel safe in allocating more of your Core money to the Stock Building Blocks. If your time frame is shorter, then you should allocate more to the Cash and Bond Building Blocks. (Some experts recommend for retirement portfolios that the sum of the allocation percentages to your Cash and Bond assets equal your age.)
- *Your view of the current economy:* While Core Segment holdings are intended to be buy-and-hold investments, this does not preclude you from making judgments and adjustments based on current economic conditions. To inform your Core Segment allocations look at current trends for the stock market, interest rates, inflation, gross national product, energy prices, and the state of world affairs. These factors will give you a sense of the health of the economy. The more robust the state of the economy, the greater should be your initial allocation to stocks. If stocks are diving or stagnate when you design your initial portfolio then either allocate more money to Cash and Bonds in the Core Segment and/or allocate a

greater percentage of your total portfolio money to the Target Market Segment. Macro economic factors will influence your initial Core Segment allocation choices. I present resources for assisting you in determining the health of the economy in the online supplement. To access them, log in, click on *Links by Chapter* and then on *Chapter 10.* Look for the appropriately labeled link.

Sample Analysis and Core Segment Allocations.   At the time that I created my sample portfolio, interest rates were at about 2 percent. I regularly read the business news and the Federal Reserve was not signaling that they planned to introduce rate hikes any time soon. The subprime mortgage crisis caused me concern as I did not believe that we had at the time completely understood or yet realized the full extent of its negative affects on equity markets. And, of course, the looming presidential election was injecting a significant degree of uncertainty into the markets.

As a result of this quick analysis, I formed a neutral-to-slightly negative view of then-current economic conditions. I also took into consideration that my sample portfolio time horizon was 15 years and this relatively long time horizon mitigated some of my short-term stock market concerns. These factors guided my decision to assign the following allocations in the Core Segment of my sample portfolio:

- *Cash:* 10 percent
- *Bonds:* 30 percent
- *U.S. Stocks:* 30 percent
- *Foreign Stocks:* 30 percent

This is a relatively moderate allocation. Sixty percent of the Core is invested in stocks. This may seem high when facing an equity market that could have the potential for a significant downturn in the near future. But the fact that I plan to hold these investments for many years substantially reduces the risk of holding stocks and I want to take advantage of the returns potential of the Stock asset class in the long-term. Cash and Bonds are defensive investments, and my assessment of the economy told me that an allocation of 40 percent to these Building Blocks is appropriate for protecting my Core Segment value should short-term trends move downward.

Keep in mind that the initial percentages assigned within the Core Segment are not intended to remain the same for the life of the portfolio. I will review these percentages at least once per year and readjust them to account for changing conditions, both personal and in the market environment. I discuss periodic portfolio reviews and the factors to consider in Chapter 11.

I will add these allocation numbers to the Portfolio Design Worksheet. But they are not at this point set in stone. Later in this chapter, after defining my Target Market allocations, I will test the overall portfolio Expected Return results. I may revisit and change these allocations as a result of these tests.

Defining Target Market Allocations

The purpose of the Target Market Segment is to add a returns boost to my portfolio. I do this by taking advantage of asset classes that are currently experiencing price uptrends. You learned about Target Market Building Blocks in Part II and how to use price charts to decide if now was a good time to buy.

A simple and valid allocation method here would be to just allocate an equal amount to each of the asset types that I chose to include in the Target Market Segment. This would mean in my sample an allocation of 25 percent of my Target Market money to Gold, Energy, Agricultural Commodities, and Emerging Markets. You will recall that I decided to not include a Real Estate component at this time because its price was falling.

A more finely tuned allocation set, however, would include a review of each price chart and the allocation of more money to those Building Blocks that show the strongest price uptrend. The following is my sample analysis related to how I determined allocations for my sample portfolio.

Sample Analysis and Target Market Segment Allocations. Figure 10.4 shows the price charts for each of the Target Market Building Blocks I selected in Part II. Before assigning allocations, I will view current price trends and use my knowledge of the factors that influence each asset's price to determine an allocation for each.

The following are the allocations I will give to each Target Market Building Block based on the data that I have previously collected. The price charts for each are repeated in Figure 10.4. The data were current at the time this chapter was written in the

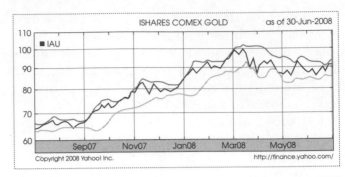

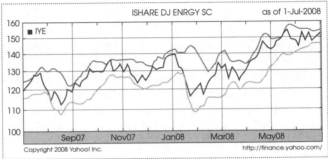

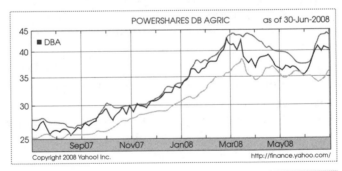

Figure 10.4   Price Charts for Target Market Investments

middle of 2008. I also provide a short explanation of the rationale for each of my decisions.

Gold: 30 percent. The price chart shows an uptrend at the current time. Stocks continue to struggle as uncertainty exists in the market related to financial stocks and how they will handle the credit crisis. My assessment is that while I believe stocks will eventually recover in the long term, there exists in the short term a good likelihood that stocks may trend lower. I will give the largest allocation in my Target Market Segment to my Gold investment on the basis of these observations and my knowledge that this asset type is a safe haven investment when stocks are declining.

Energy: 25 percent. My reading of financial news tells me that while there is some thought that current energy prices have risen to a point of irrationality, there may still be room for further price appreciation. I know that OPEC has recently decided to not increase oil production. I also read that the U.S. Congress is gridlocked on the subject of opening up new sites for drilling here in the United States and thus limiting potential new domestic sources of supply. I am also realistic enough to know that alternative energy technologies will not become economically feasible for years to come. The price line on the chart for my Energy investment looks strong, so I will allocate 25 percent of my Target Market money to this Target Market Building Block. I do this with the assurance that if energy prices are currently experiencing a bubble, my Target Market trading plan will protect my downside from catastrophic loss.

Agricultural Commodities: 25 percent. The factors that have driven up prices for this asset class are still in place. Corn and sugar are still being shunted off to make biofuels. Energy costs are driving the prices of food transportation higher, and the trend of this investment's price chart looks strong. These factors give me the confidence to allocate 25 percent of my Target Market money to my agriculture investment. As with Energy, if Agricultural Commodities are currently experiencing a speculative bubble, my PPM trading plan will protect my downside in this investment.

Real Estate: zero percent. While this chart is not shown in Figure 10.4, you will recall that in Chapter 8 we analyzed Real Estate and the chart was in a definite downtrend. Real Estate will make a comeback in the long term. But it is not showing signs of a recovery right now, and right now is the only time period I am concerned with for setting Target Market Segment allocations. I will not risk any of my investment money on this asset now. I will, however, put the investment symbol in a Watch List, as explained in Chapter 8. I illustrate how my trading plan worked for Real Estate in the calendar year 2007 in the Appendix to this book.

Emerging Markets: 20 percent. I like the story behind my Emerging Markets selection related to Latin America. The factors that have made it such a phenomenal investment in the past several years are still in place. But the price trend line makes me cautious. It is starting to turn down but this may be a temporary pause in the uptrend. I will allocate only 20 percent of my Target Market money to this investment and will watch it closely through the trading plan I put in place for it. If this investment turns sour, I will exit quickly and automatically.

I will add these allocations to the Portfolio Design Worksheet. and test the resulting portfolio's expected return later in this chapter in order to determine its total Expected Return. I may come back after that determination and revisit these allocations.

Defining Segment Allocations

The final allocation decision is between the Core Segment and the Target Market Segment. The allocations to the Building Blocks within each of these Segments can be viewed as fine-tuning dials. The allocation to each Portfolio Segment is a major-tuning dial, which will perhaps be the largest determinant of the portfolio's total risk-reward profile.

To review:

The Core Segment is designed to add stability to the portfolio. It will not produce spectacular returns but it has a lower risk profile. History tells us that its price trend should be up in the long term. This Segment will have expected return rates in the 8 to 12 percent range over time periods of five years or more.

The Target Market Segment is designed to supercharge the returns of the portfolio by investing in narrowly focused investment types. There is more risk here but constant monitoring and a trading plan for each investment mitigates this risk. This Segment will have expected return rates of 20 percent and above.

You can consequently see that the allocation of investment money between these two Segments is the prime driver of the risk-return profile of the portfolio. It is therefore critically important to understand the factors that need to be considered when making this all-important decision. The major factors are as follows:

- *Goal Amount:* I started this chapter with a short discussion of how to create an Investing Plan. In this plan you set a Target Goal Amount and various other parameters related to your unique profile. You then determined a Required Return Rate that will enable you to reach the goal amount at the end of your specified time horizon. The higher this Required Return Rate, the more money you will need to allocate to the Target Market Segment of the portfolio in order to realize it.

- *Involvement Level:* You must assess your willingness to become and stay involved in the investing process. If you are a relatively passive investor, then you will want to allocate more money to the Core Segment, where minimal trading will take place and very little of your ongoing attention to these investments will be required. If you are a more active investor and willing to dedicate more time and effort to the investing process, then you should allocate more money to the Target Market Segment. This Segment enables you to translate increased involvement into higher returns. How can you increase returns by increasing your involvement? I tell you in Chapter 12.

- *Current Economic Conditions:* You took into account the state of the general economy when you determined allocations to the various Building Blocks within your Core Segment. The gloomier the outlook, the less you allocated to stocks. Another way to counter a falling stock market is to increase your allocation to the Target Market Segment where you can invest in Gold, which is a safe haven in times of market turmoil, and other asset types that have a low or negative correlation with stocks.

Allocation between the Core and the Target Market Segments is the classic trade-off between risk and reward. You will need to allocate more to the Target Market Segment to reach higher returns goals. This means, of course, higher risk exposure, but this will be mitigated by the trading plans you implement for each Building Block and your willingness to stay involved in the investing process.

Sample Segment Analysis and Allocations.   I described my outlook for the economy in the previous two allocation examples. My analysis tells me that stocks will recover in the long term but will not fare well in the short term. This tells me to allocate more to the Target Market Segment right now. Also, my sample Investing Plan has a Required Return Rate of 17.9 percent, and I must allocate more to the Target Market Segment to have the potential of reaching this number. And finally, I am willing to spend a couple of hours per week working with the Target Market Segment investments in ways that I explain in Chapter 12. Taking all of these factors into consideration, I will make the following Portfolio Segment allocation assignments for my sample portfolio.

- *Core Segment:* 40 percent
- *Target Market Segment:* 60 percent

I will enter these numbers on the Portfolio Design Worksheet.

The Practical Effects of Segment Allocations.   The Portfolio Segment allocation numbers determine how much of my total investment money will be devoted to the Core Segment and to the Target Market Segment. Building Block allocations within each Segment then apply only to the amount of money dedicated to that Segment.

As an example, if I start with $100,000 of investment money and allocate 40 percent to the Core, then I have $40,000 to spread out among the four Core Building Blocks. If I allocate 15 percent to Bonds, then my total dollar figure allocated to bonds is $6,000, which is 15 percent of $40,000. Therefore, the dollar figure that is allocated to each Asset Building Block is determined by not only the allocation percentage assigned to that Building Block but also by the allocation percentage assigned to its Segment. This will become evident as we work through the final Portfolio Design Worksheet.

Keep in mind that all of these allocations are subject to change after I view the results they produce using the Portfolio Design Worksheet and Calculator. Testing my initial set of allocations is where we go next.

The Final Perfect Portfolio Design

All of the data have been assembled. It is now time to fill in the Portfolio Design Worksheet for my sample portfolio and use the companion Calculator to test the results.

In the online Portfolio Design Calculator found in the supplement, I fill in the *Total Investment Amount* with $100,000. This comes from the Investing Plan I formulated at the beginning of this chapter. The remaining calculator data fields are filled in on the basis of work done earlier in this chapter and book.

Table 10.2 shows the Portfolio Design Worksheet entries and results from the Design Calculator.

My original test design has resulted in a remarkably diverse portfolio with an Expected Return of 14.7 percent. Keep in mind that this total return is calculated by multiplying the total return from each Segment by that Segment's allocation and then adding the two figures. Thus the calculation for the Portfolio Total Return is $(40\% \times 8.4\%) + (60\% \times 19\%) = 14.7\%$. The online Portfolio Design Calculator does this math for you.

Testing Multiple Scenarios

It would not be uncommon for your first set of parameters to result in a total Expected Return that does not match the Required Return Rate goal of your Investing Plan. My sample Investing Plan had a target rate of 17.9 percent and my portfolio design predicts 14.7 percent. In my case, this is close enough, and I will stick with my original allocation decisions. I believe that my personal involvement in the investing process can result in higher returns for the various Target Market Building Blocks than I predicted earlier.

If your portfolio design leaves you well short of your goal, then you may want to adjust your various allocation dials to obtain a more acceptable result. Let's look at the effects of doing so.

Adjusting Segment Allocations. The Segment allocation dial has the most effect on the risk-reward profile of the portfolio.

Table 10.2 The Perfect Portfolio Design Worksheet

Investment Dollar Amount: $100,000

Core Segment Allocation: 40%

Dollars: $40,000

Building Block:	Investment Symbol	Expected Return	Allocation	Contribution	Dollar Amount
Cash	VMMXX	3%	10%	.3%	$4,000
Bonds	VBMFX	5%	30%	1.5%	$12,000
U.S. Stocks	VTSMX	10%	30%	3.0%	$12,000
Foreign Stocks	VGTSX	12%	30%	3.6%	$12,000
Totals			**100%**	**8.4%**	**$40,000**

Target Market Segment Allocation: 60%

Dollars: $60,000

Building Block:	Investment Symbol	Expected Return	Allocation	Contribution	Dollar Amount
Gold	IAU	20%	30%	6.0%	$18,000
Energy	IYE	20%	25%	5.0%	$15,000
Agriculture	DBA	20%	25%	5.0%	$15,000
Real Estate	VNQ	0%	0%	0%	$0
Emerging Markets	GML	15%	20%	3.0%	$12,000
Totals			**100%**	**19%**	**$60,000**
Portfolio Totals				**14.7%**	**$100,000**

I allocated 40 percent to the Core Segment and 60 percent to the Target Market Segment in my sample portfolio. Let's assume that I wanted to increase the Expected Return of my portfolio design. To do so, I could change my Segment allocations to the following:

- *Core:* 30 percent
- *Target Market:* 70 percent

Plugging these figures into the Portfolio Design Worksheet and Calculator gives me the following calculation and Expected Return.
$$30\% \times 8.4\% + 70\% \times 19\% = 15.8\%$$
This sample allocation would allow me to come closer to the goals of my Investing Plan with slightly increased risk.

Adjusting Core Building Block Allocations.   You can also increase your returns potential and/or lower risk by fine-tuning the less sensitive dials related to Building Block allocations within the Core Segment. Allocating more to Stock Building Blocks increases both expected return and risk, but these adjustments have less effect on the total portfolio risk-reward profile than adjusting the Segment allocations.

Adjusting Target Market Building Block Allocations.   Changing allocations within the Target Market Segment will not adjust the risk profile of the portfolio because each of the Building Blocks in this Segment has virtually the same risk level. Here you adjust the portfolio return profile by changing your prediction of the expected return of each asset type. For example, in my test portfolio, I have estimated a return of 20 percent for the Emerging Market Building Block. Further analysis and market developments may enable me to change this estimate to 25 percent. This has the effect of increasing the Expected Return of the Target Market Segment and to a lesser extent increasing the Expected Return of the total portfolio.

The *Perfect Portfolio Design Worksheet and Calculator* give you the tools you need to easily see the effects of any change you make to your allocation decisions and to your individual Building Block expected return predictions. Use these resources to model different scenarios before settling on one that you feel best balances your expectations of the market, your predictions for the returns potential of each asset type, your Investing Plan goals, and your investing style.

Building *Your* Perfect Portfolio!

Here are the ten steps you now need to take to design your unique Perfect Portfolio:

1. Create your Investing Plan as described at the beginning of this chapter. Derive a Required Return Rate for meeting your goal amount using the NAOI Return Required Calculator found in the online supplement. Print your Investing Plan Worksheet.
2. Print one or more copies of the Portfolio Design Worksheet from the online supplement or create your own based on the tables presented in this chapter.
3. Determine how much money you will devote to this portfolio. Fill in the corresponding blank on the Portfolio Design Worksheet.
4. Consult the Building Block Worksheets that you created as you moved through this book for each of the Portfolio Building Blocks. For the Core Segment, find the three-year historical return data, and for the Target Market Segment, find the one-year historical return data. Use these numbers and your current market analysis to determine Expected Returns for each asset type. Enter these numbers on your Portfolio Design Worksheet in the column titled Expected Return.
5. Enter the data you have collected for each Building Block into the online Portfolio Design Calculator.
6. Determine your initial set of allocations as discussed in this chapter and enter them on your Portfolio Design Worksheet and then into the online Portfolio Design Calculator. After entering all input fields for this calculator, click on the Calculate button and get the results needed to complete your Design Worksheet.
7. Compare the Total Expected Return as calculated in Step 6 to the Required Return from your Investing Plan.
8. Adjust the various input factors to find an allocation set that you feel best fits your needs. You can adjust both expected returns and allocations.
9. Print out your final Perfect Portfolio Design Worksheet.
10. Combine your Portfolio Design Worksheet with the Building Block Worksheets you have completed throughout this book. This is the investing packet that will guide the implementation of your Perfect Portfolio in Chapter 11.

Chapter Summary

I showed you in this chapter how to design a total Perfect Portfolio.

I started this chapter by emphasizing the need for an Investing Plan. You simply cannot build an optimal portfolio without setting goals and understanding your financial profile. I then walked you through a step-by-step process for combining the Portfolio Building Blocks in a manner that takes into consideration the return requirements of your Investing Plan, your risk tolerance levels, your willingness to become involved in the investing process, and your current view of the market.

To define the risk-return profile of your portfolio, I showed you how to adjust percentage allocations in three areas: between Portfolio Segments, among Core Building Blocks, and among Target Market Building Blocks. This is a revolutionary approach to portfolio design. It is simple, intuitive, and a process that all investors can understand. It also enables you to change the profile of your portfolio rapidly in response to changing market conditions.

I also discussed in this chapter the factors that will guide your allocation decisions. Among these factors are your investing goals, your time horizon, your view of the economy, your investing style, and your short-term outlook for each asset class in the Target Market Segment. Your portfolio design is *not* based on a set of generic rules that you robotically follow. It is, instead, a process that enables you to transform your knowledge and market analysis into a portfolio configuration that has the potential to significantly outperform market averages without excessive risk.

Finally, you were given in this chapter a 10-step action list for creating your Perfect Portfolio. If you have completed the assigned tasks in this chapter, you are to be congratulated! You have done significant work and have laid the groundwork for a new, exciting, and more profitable investing career. But this is no time to rest on your laurels. You are not done yet. Now you need to understand how to implement your Perfect Portfolio and how to monitor and manage it. This is the topic of Chapter 11.

11

Implementing, Monitoring, and Managing Your Perfect Portfolio

KEEPING YOUR PORTFOLIO ON COURSE IN CHANGING CONDITIONS

Y ou learned in previous chapters of a radically new way to invest. You have studied a portfolio design methodology that requires you to buy no more than nine investments. You designed in Chapter 10 a Perfect Portfolio customized for your unique goals, your investing style, and your view of current market conditions. If you have been building your own Perfect Portfolio as you moved through the book, you have done a lot of work and you are to be congratulated. Here is what you have accomplished.

- You have identified specific investments for each of the nine PPM Building Blocks
- You have defined a trading plan for each Target Market Building Block
- You have created your unique Investing Plan
- You have designed your Perfect Portfolio

You are now ready to start your new and improved investing career by implementing, monitoring, and managing your Perfect Portfolio. I show you how in this chapter by discussing the following action items.

- *Implementing your portfolio:* This action consists of identifying an online broker, buying the investments you have selected, and putting into place the trading plan you have defined for each investment in the Target Market Segment.
- *Monitoring your portfolio:* This topic involves a discussion of how to react to the various alerts and sell actions that can result from the trading plan you have implemented for each of your Target Market Building Blocks.
- *Managing your portfolio:* I discuss here how to make adjustments to your portfolio as certain factors change. Portfolio management includes not only responding to alerts but also periodically reassessing your goals, your investing style, your portfolio mix, and your view of current market conditions.

The knowledge you gain, the tools you identify, and the work you do in this chapter will make the day-to-day monitoring and management of your portfolio easy and effective. The PPM approach is designed to automate these activities so you are not required to spend hours in front of your computer on a regular basis.

It is critical, however, that you spend time up front putting into place the appropriate structure, procedures, and resources to develop the environment in which your portfolio can run smoothly and effectively. A concentrated effort here will make your future investing activities flow with the efficiency of a well-oiled machine.

You will be empowered to transform your Perfect Portfolio design from theory to reality after completing this chapter. You will also know how to build an ongoing support system that keeps your portfolio as relevant tomorrow as it is today.

Implementing Your Portfolio

Implementing your portfolio means taking it from concept to reality. It means taking what you have on paper and translating it into actual investments. There are several implementation steps you must perform. The first is to find a good online broker. With your broker in place, you can then start to buy your investments and implement your trading plans.

Finding an Online Broker

The first task in the portfolio implementation process is to actually buy the investments you have selected as you moved through this book. For this purpose, an online broker is needed. You may already have one that you like and will be happy to continue working with. If you don't, the goal of the following discussion is to help you identify a good online broker for implementing your Perfect Portfolio.

Since as an individual investor you can't go directly to the stock exchanges and buy investments you must find a broker that can perform this task for you. Two general types of brokers exist. There are full-service brokers that will buy stocks and funds for you and there are online brokers that enable you to make these trades on your own using your computer and the Web. You need an online broker for the purpose of implementing the Perfect Portfolio. Why? Because you want low trading commissions, you want the ability to set up your own automated monitoring system, and you want to be able to make adjustments to your portfolio at any time, day or night, weekday or weekend.

You may still use a full-service broker to manage a portion of your total investments, but an online broker is essential for implementation of the total Perfect Portfolio. For example, you may use a fund family such as Vanguard for the Core Segment of the portfolio and a separate online broker such as TD Ameritrade for the Target Market Segment. Implementation and management of your Perfect Portfolio is more efficient, however, if you use the same broker for both Portfolio Segments.

You have a simple choice within the universe of online brokers. You can use a broker that is also a fund family such as Fidelity or Vanguard, or you can use an online broker that is not linked to specific funds and may offer a fuller array of stock and ETF analysis capabilities. Examples of the latter are TD Ameritrade and Scottrade. Most of these online brokers allow you to buy funds from a variety of fund families. I suggest Web resources in this section that enable you to compare online brokers. Let's discuss first what to look for when searching for one that meets your needs.

What to Look for in a Broker. If you currently have an online broker that you like, you are fortunate. But you need to make sure that they offer the features listed here, which are essential to implementing and monitoring your Perfect Portfolio. If you do not have an online broker, use this list in your evaluation process.

An online broker should offer the following:

- *Reasonable Trading Commissions:* You should not have to pay more than $12 for a trade. At the time this book was written, the industry average commission price for a trade is just under $7.
- *Multiple Order Types:* The broker should offer a full range of order types, including Market Orders, Stop Orders, and Trailing-Stop Orders.
- *Triggers and Alerts:* The broker should offer order triggers where one event automatically triggers the execution of another. An example would be the automatic sending of an e-mail to you triggered by a stock reaching a price point you have defined. These capabilities are covered in more detail in the section titled Implementing Your Trading Plans later in this chapter.
- *Fund Purchases:* The broker should give you the ability to purchase a full range of no-load funds with no transaction fees. You may have selected one or more specific funds for your portfolio as you worked through this book. Make sure the online broker you select offers them.
- *User-Friendly Web Site:* The broker should provide a user-friendly Web site that is intuitive and easy to navigate.
- *Responsive User Support:* Call the help line of any online broker you are evaluating and see how long you have to wait. Ask a question and note how accurate and polite the person answering the call is.

In general, I would suggest that you consider only the major online brokers. Included in this list are TD Ameritrade, Schwab, Scottrade, E*Trade, Vanguard, Fidelity, and the like. I would be leery of an organization that offers gimmicks such as free trades or access to super-duper trading systems.

Using Fund Purchase Information to Identify a Broker. In Chapter 3, I looked for one fund family to purchase all of my Core Building Blocks from. Since these total-market funds are all so similar regardless of the fund family, it just made sense to buy them all from one company, making it easy to transfer money among them. In the Target Market Segment, however, you may wish to buy funds from different families.

When searching for Target Market investments, you have a choice between traditional mutual funds or ETFs. In my sample portfolio, I chose all ETFs for the reasons discussed in the selection process for each. I can buy ETFs from any online broker because they trade like stocks, so finding different fund families was not a consideration for my design. You, however, may have chosen a traditional focused mutual fund for one or more of your Target Market Building Blocks. If so, and it is not offered by your Core Fund Family, you need to know where to buy it.

The finance.yahoo.com site can help. It has a menu item for each fund you evaluate titled *Purchase Information*. When you click this menu entry, you will be shown a list of the online brokers through which you can buy this fund. This information can influence your selection of a broker. If you are going to use focused mutual funds in the Target Market Segment of your portfolio, do your best to find one broker that can provide them all.

Broker Evaluation Resources.   The Web offers multiple resources that evaluate and compare online brokers for you. I offer links to several of these sites in the online supplement. I suggest that you use them. To do so, log in to the supplement site, click on *Links by Chapter* and then on *Chapter 11*. Look for the appropriate heading. Or you can also simply go to a Web search engine and enter "Online Broker Ratings for 2008 (or the current year)."

You will find in the reviews of these sites ratings for both intangible (for example, customer satisfaction) as well as tangible (for example, trading commissions) offerings.

Using Multiple Online Brokers.   I have mentioned this briefly before, but it is worth repeating. To completely implement your portfolio in the most effective manner, you may need to use more than one broker. While this is not ideal, you should not sacrifice significant returns for the sake of convenience. For example, you may find it beneficial to work with a fund family to buy your Core Segment mutual funds and a nonfund-based broker for trading ETFs and focused mutual funds in the Target Market Segment.

For example, it would not be unusual for you to decide to use both Vanguard and TD Ameritrade to implement your portfolio, taking advantage of the benefits of both a fund-focused broker and a stock-focused broker. It is common, however, for fund families to also offer ETF and stock trading capabilities, but make sure the ETF trading capabilities the fund family offers meet the requirements listed earlier in this chapter for an online broker. Again, do not sacrifice power for convenience.

Broker Identification Summary.   Take the process of selecting an online broker seriously. Dedicate the time required to analyze multiple candidates in depth. Go to the sites of several online brokers and look for demo sections. Browse the tools offered and get a feel for the user-friendliness of the site. Don't compromise your Perfect Portfolio by using a broker that is anything but the best.

Buying Your Investments across Account Types

Taking maximum advantage of your Perfect Portfolio requires that you take into consideration the tax implications of the PPM approach. Part of this approach requires buying and selling investments so you can take advantage of current market conditions. This will result in taxable events. You therefore need to implement your portfolio in a manner that minimizes this factor. You can do this by spreading your portfolio investments across multiple investment account types.

When you open an account with an online broker, you will be given the option of opening different account types. Among these will be a regular trading account, an options trading account, and a retirement account (an IRA, for example). To maximize the return of your Perfect Portfolio you need to carefully plan in which account to buy your investments.

The Target Market Segment of the portfolio is designed to include investments that you regularly buy and sell to realize returns that can significantly exceed market averages. This could result in a substantial tax bill at the end of the year. To address this issue, I strongly suggest that you place as much of your Target Market Segment as possible in a tax-advantaged account such as an IRA or a SEP retirement account. By doing this, you can defer paying taxes on your trading gains until you retire, at which time they will be taxed as ordinary income when you withdraw the money. Note that this does not work with Roth IRA accounts, where you pay taxes when you earn the money (because these accounts are nondeductible), not when you withdraw it upon retirement.

The Core Segment of the portfolio consists of buy-and-hold investments. You will not be realizing capital gains on these investments on a regular basis because trading them should happen only infrequently. They can therefore be placed in a regular trading account without serious tax consequences.

Implementing Your Trading Plans

The PPM approach calls for you to implement a trading plan for each of the investments you have selected for your Target Market Segment. The trading plan puts the investments in this Segment under constant and automatic surveillance. It frees you from spending virtually any time in front of the computer monitoring your most volatile investments.

The Building Block Worksheet that you created for each Target Market investment in Part II contains the trading plan for that investment. You documented on this worksheet the price levels at which you want action to take place. This action will either be an automated sale of your position or the sending of an e-mail prompting you to pay attention to the investment. You derived the action price levels by examining each investment's current price chart.

You should immediately implement your trading plan when you buy each of your Target Market investments. The following are the tools that your online broker should offer that enable you to do so.

Trailing Stops. Central to the PPM trading plan is setting a Trailing Stop for all orders placed in the Target Market Segment. Figure 11.1 shows an example screen of how your broker should enable you to buy an investment while at the same time adding a Trailing Stop.

I have implemented Figure 11.1, one component of a trading plan for the Energy Building Block ETF with the symbol IYE. In this case, the Trailing Stop is the Order Type. This transaction assumes that the purchase is a Market Order that will be executed immediately. It also automatically places a floor on losses should IYE go down 5 percent from the highest price it reaches while I

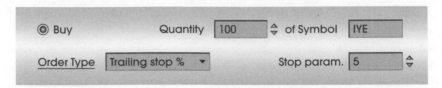

Figure 11.1   Trailing Stop Order Example

own this ETF. Note that I could have specified a dollar amount drop instead.

Thus, if I bought IYE at $100 and it immediately started to sink, the system would automatically sell 100 shares of IYE when the price hits $95. Yet, should the price start to go up, the sell price moves up with it. Should the price move up to $120 with no 5 percent drops during the climb, the automated sell price would move up to $114, which is a 5 percent drop from $120. Thus, a Trailing Stop locks in the highest profit I reach minus 5 percent.

E-Mail Alert Triggers.   Instead of automatically selling my position, I could have set a trigger that sends an e-mail alerting me to when a stop-loss price target is hit. Upon receipt of such an e-mail, I can then do further research to help me decide what action to take, if any. While a Trailing Stop *sell* action will incur a trading commission if triggered, a trailing stop e-mail trigger will be free of charge.

Profit Alerts.   Not all alerts or triggers are negative. As discussed in Part II, I can also set a price level at which I will be happy to consider taking a profit. Therefore, in addition to the Trailing Stop already mentioned, I can also set an e-mail alert trigger *above* the purchase price. Thus, in this example, I might request that the plan I implement trigger an e-mail to me if IYE goes up to $110.

Should I get such an e-mail, I would check the price chart and news headlines related to IYE. If I felt that the uptrend was still strong, I might decide to simply set another take-profit e-mail alert above the current price. I might also decide to tighten my Trailing Stop trigger to lock in more profit. I could decrease my Trailing Stop parameter from 5 percent to 3 percent, for example.

Traditional Mutual Fund Alerts.   My experience with online broker sites is that most offer triggers for the automated selling of stocks and ETFs but not for traditional funds. You will therefore need to use a separate set of tools for implementing an automated trading plan for the mutual funds that you may buy in your Target Market Segment and perhaps even for those in your Core Segment. You will simply buy your funds using a market order. Then look on your broker's site for an area where you can set alerts on the funds that you buy. This capability may be available in the site's portfolio section or there may be a watch list section. If all else fails, call the broker and ask how to set e-mail alerts on funds. There will in most cases be a way, but it may not be obvious.

You can also use the site at finance.yahoo.com to set alerts for funds that you buy. Simply go to the home page, enter your fund symbol, and you will see a menu selection for setting alerts below the thumbnail price chart. Thus, while your online broker should offer alerts capability for funds, if it doesn't, you can always use this alternative.

The alert capability that you use will enable you to set price levels both above and below your purchase price at points where you want to be notified in order to consider taking action. The fund alert e-mail will be your trigger to investigate what is happening with the fund so you can decide whether now is the time to sell to either stop losses or take profits.

The fund alert process is not as automated or as convenient as the process for ETFs, but it still serves the purpose of constantly monitoring your fund investments. Don't let this discourage you from buying a focused fund for a Target Market Building Block if its performance is clearly superior to an ETF in the same category.

Broker Implementations May Differ.   Be aware that different brokers will handle Stops, Triggers, and Alerts in different ways. *Always* check with the broker you are evaluating for details on how to implement these essential components of a PPM trading plan. If you don't see on their site how to implement these features, then ask the broker support staff for help. Describe exactly what capabilities you need to implement your trading plans. If the broker doesn't offer them, look for another broker. It is that simple.

Portfolio Implementation Summary

With a broker selected and a full understanding of how to place various order types, triggers, and alerts, you are now ready to implement your Perfect Portfolio by purchasing the investments you have identified. You are also prepared to put into place a trading plan for each Building Block in the Target Market Segment. Now is the time for action and you are fully prepared!

I am sure that you will feel a great deal of satisfaction after implementing your portfolio. You will have put a portfolio into place with tremendous upside potential and limited downside risk. You have significantly decreased your dependence on advisers and the noise that rules the personal investing environment today. You are taking the first step toward regaining personal control of your portfolio and thus your financial future.

Monitoring Your Portfolio: Reacting to Triggers and Alerts

With the selection of a good online broker, you will have at your disposal the tools to set triggers and alerts for your trading plan. But knowing how to most effectively use these tools is a completely separate topic. It is therefore beneficial to discuss in more detail the art and science of setting triggers and alerts and how to respond to them.

As a part of the discussion of the Target Market Building Blocks in Part II, you looked at price charts and determined price levels at which you wanted automated actions to occur. In addition to the price points, you had an additional choice to make. Should you set triggers to automatically sell your position (often called a *hard stop*) or to send you an e-mail (often called a *soft stop*)? The answer to this question depends in large part on your investing style.

When you put in place a trading plan that includes the automatic selling of your investments, there is a risk involved. Prices of ETFs and funds that you have put in your Target Market Segment have long-term trends and short-term fluctuations. The goal of an effective sell strategy is to ride the trend up without being stopped out by normal daily price changes. This latter effect is called being "whipsawed" out of a position. The danger is that on any given day, the price for an ETF you own could drop to a point where your stop-loss trigger sells your position and then the next day, or even during the same day, the price recovers and continues on its merry way upward.

In our discussions of where to place stops, we looked at the normal volatility of a stock by using Bollinger Bands. I showed you how to use this simple technical indicator to determine the volatility of an ETF and thus the extent of its normal short-term fluctuations. Then we set stop prices that took into consideration this normal range so as to avoid a whipsaw-induced sale. This is not a foolproof methodology, of course, and there is always the potential of being stopped out of a position by a short-term price drop regardless of how much up-front price analysis is performed.

One way to avoid being whipsawed out of a stock is to implement your trading plan with soft triggers that simply send you an e-mail when a sell price is reached. This e-mail prompts you to research what is happening with your investment and allows you the option of deciding whether a sale of the position is appropriate or not. A disadvantage of a soft stop, however, is that time can elapse between when the e-mail is sent and when you receive it and do your investigations. The investment price could continue to drop during this period. With a hard stop, you would be out of the position immediately when the sell price is hit. These are the trade-offs when choosing between the use of a hard stop and a soft stop.

The type of trigger, hard or soft, that you use will depend on your desired level of involvement in the investing process. If you are in a position where you can check your e-mail regularly and are willing to perform stock research at a moment's notice, then soft stops makes sense. If you are not interested in interrupting your work on a regular basis or you don't find doing the research required to be an enjoyable activity, then hard stops make more sense.

One advantage of hard stops is that they take emotions and indecision out of the equation, and for a large majority of investors this is a positive thing. When a stop price is hit, your position is sold. End of story. If you are a hands-off kind of investor, then this is the type of stop for you.

One advantage of soft triggers is that you can set your stop prices tighter than if you use hard stops. The closer to the purchase price you set the stop, the more e-mails you will get and the more research you will be prompted to perform. This is a good thing if you know what you are doing and enjoy doing it. If you are a hands-on kind of investor, then this is the type of stop for you.

I want you to be very aware of the trade-offs between hard and soft stops. And you may decide to use different types of stops for different investments. Your investing style will determine which is more appropriate for your unique trading plans.

Responding to Triggers and Alerts

Setting effective triggers and alerts is critical to a successful trading plan. Knowing what to do when a trigger is pulled is equally critical. Let's discuss how to respond to triggers and alerts when they happen.

Responding to Hard Stops.   As discussed earlier, a hard stop is a trigger that automatically sells your position when the price point you set is hit. For example, suppose you buy 100 shares of the Gold ETF with the symbol IAU at $100 per share and set a $5 trailing stop. Now let's assume that luck isn't with you and the price immediately starts to drop. When the price of IAU hits $95, your broker's system automatically places a market order to sell your 100 shares. But there is no guarantee that you will get a price of $95. You will get the price that IAU is selling for when your order is actually executed. Your order may be in line behind other market orders. If the price continues to drop, you may get only $94.50 or $94.00 when your order is executed. The bottom line is that you will get out of the position, hopefully at $95 or close to it.

When you sell a position, you create a hole in your Target Market Segment. In the example just discussed, you don't now own a Gold investment. But this is okay. Nothing in the PPM approach says you must hold all of the Building Blocks at all times.

After selling a position, you must decide what to do with the money from the sale. In the example discussed above, you have approximately $9,500 of additional cash in your portfolio's Cash Building Block. Cash is not a high-return investment. So your next step is to scan the price charts of the other Target Market Building Blocks in your portfolio and look for those that are in an uptrend. You need to put your cash to use by buying more shares in asset classes that are on the rise if any exist.

In my sample portfolio, after selling a position, I may buy more shares in my Emerging Market ETF or I may buy more shares of my Energy ETF. Or, if everything is going down, perhaps the best action is to do nothing and put the proceeds from my Gold sale into my Cash account. Cash is not at risk of losing principal, and is always available for reinvestment when conditions start to improve for any Building Block. If everything is going down I also have the option of buying a "short" ETF for any Building Block as discussed in Chapter 4 and again in Chapter 12.

A second action you need to take when you sell a Target Market investment is to place the investment in a Watch List. This is a resource that all brokers should offer, and a Watch List capability is often included as a feature of a portfolio manager. (I discuss portfolio managers in more detail later in this chapter.)

In a Watch List you can put price alerts on an investment you do not currently own and automatically monitor its price movements. Therefore, when you are stopped out of a position at a certain price, place the investment in a Watch List with an e-mail alert at the same price at which you sold it or higher. You will then be automatically notified via e-mail when the investment's price begins to rise again. When you get this alert, look at the investment's chart again and investigate what is happening. If you were whipsawed out of the position on the basis of a short-term price dip, then perhaps you should just get right back in if you think the upward price trend is still intact. If you buy back in to the position, set your stops further away from your purchase price in order to avoid another whipsaw sale. Learn from each instance of being stopped out.

If the price continues to drop after you get stopped out, of course, you will not get a Watch List alert and your trading system will continue to function as it was designed to. You have limited your losses on an investment that is heading south.

Refer to the Appendix for a detailed description of how a Watch List capability can be used as an integral part of a trading plan.

Responding to Soft Stops.   Now let's discuss what happens if you have set a soft stop and get an e-mail informing you that one of your sell price points has been hit. Nothing will happen unless you take action. Unlike the hard stop discussed earlier, your position is not automatically sold. You are simply informed that the price is moving down into potentially dangerous territory. It's now up to you to take action.

If you have set soft stops in your portfolio, you should be checking your e-mail on a regular basis so that you are able to react to alerts within a reasonable time. Here are some of the things that I suggest you do in response to a soft stop e-mail:

- Use your favorite investment Web site, such as finance.yahoo. com, to look at the price chart for the investment involved. If the price has moved back above your stop alert, then you may decide that the dip was a short-term fluctuation and that the long-term uptrend is still intact. In this case, you will probably decide to keep the investment in your portfolio and no action is required.

- Price moves are more significant if they are accompanied with high volume. If the price drop that caused the e-mail alert is associated with very little volume compared with the average daily volume for that investment, you may decide that the price change is not the result of a fundamental problem and you may decide not to sell.
- Look at news headlines for the investment. Perhaps you will find the reason for the downward price movement here. If so, determine whether the news represents a temporary price influence or a long-term price influence. For example, if my Gold ETF price is dropping and I find that the cause is an announcement that the Federal Reserve is cutting interest rates, I would see this catalyst as one having a long-term effect on gold prices. I would probably decide to sell in such a case.
- If you sell the investment on the basis of your research, then you should place its symbol in a Watch List as discussed just above for hard stops.
- If you decide not to sell an investment when you receive an e-mail alert, then you will need to reset the alert. Once an alert trigger is fired, it ceases to exist. It must be rearmed.

You can see that soft stops enable you to become more involved in the process. They alert you to do research before deciding whether to sell. This takes more work than an automated sell generated by a hard stop, but it may enable you to avoid being whipsawed out of a position that is still in an uptrend. The downsides of soft alerts include that you need to react quickly to the alert e-mail, you will need to do some research, emotions can get in the way, and you may still make the wrong decision. You must determine whether the activities related to soft alerts fit your investing style.

Managing Your Portfolio Using Online Resources

Triggers and alerts are intended to monitor and manage each individual investment in the Target Market Segment of your portfolio. You also need a tool for managing your total portfolio on an ongoing basis. For this purpose, you need to use a full-featured online portfolio manager. Finding and evaluating the best such managers on the Web is the topic of the next discussion.

Not too many years ago portfolio managers offered by online brokers were a joke. They simply listed your positions and the dollar value of each. The quotes in the portfolios were often a day old! This has changed. Online brokers are now offering very capable portfolio managers. So the first place you should look for a portfolio manager is with your online broker.

Don't be discouraged, however, if the portfolio manager offered by your online broker does not offer all of the features you need. Several nonbroker sites offer very powerful portfolio managers. Among the sites you will want to review when searching for a full featured online portfolio manager are the following:

- morningstar.com
- moneycentral.com
- finance.yahoo.com

If other good portfolio manager sites appear or if these recommendations change, updates to this list can be found in the online supplement by logging in, clicking on *Links by Chapter*, and then on *Chapter 11.*

On each of these sites simply look for the *Portfolio* section and investigate the capabilities offered. A list of features to look for is provided just below. Compare the offerings on these sites to those offered by your online broker. The advantage held by the portfolio manager offered by your broker, of course, is that your purchases and sales are automatically recorded in the portfolio. You may have to enter them manually when using a third-party portfolio. You need to decide if the extra effort is worth it.

What to Look for in a Portfolio Manager

A good portfolio manager does more than list your holdings and show you a price. The following is a list of other features that you should look for when evaluating a portfolio manager:

- *Basic Data:* For each of your holdings, you should be able to see the investment name and symbol, price updated on an intraday basis, your purchase price, and your purchase date. You should also be able to click on the symbol of an investment in the portfolio and be able to access full data for that security, including charts, news, fundamental data, and more.

- *Performance Data:* For each holding, you should be able to view daily price changes in both dollars and percentages. The best portfolios will also show you year-to-date performance, annualized performance, and accumulated capital gains or losses.

- *Alerts:* The portfolio manager should allow you to set a full range of alerts for any of your holdings. You should be able to place alerts on individual securities and on the portfolio as a whole. You should be able to set alerts on the basis of price changes and news events.

- *Analysis:* A good portfolio manager will enable you to perform multiple types of analyses on your holdings. Among these are asset allocations, geographic allocations, industry or sector allocations, and more. Some may even give you a risk grade for your portfolio, although this is neither common in most portfolio managers nor a necessity.

- *Watch List:* Your portfolio manager must enable you to build a Watch List as described earlier in this chapter. A Watch List is a special type of portfolio that allows you to monitor equities that you have not purchased but rather are simply watching. Perhaps you are waiting for a certain fund or ETF to reach a lower price before buying. Perhaps you are interested in receiving news alerts on a specific ETF that you don't own yet. For these purposes, you would place them in a Watch List and set alerts that will send you e-mails when activated.

- *Multiple Portfolios:* The portfolio manager should enable you to create more than one portfolio and at least one Watch List. You may wish to create separate portfolios for different investing goals, or divide your Perfect Portfolio into two portfolios, one for the Core Segment and one for the Target Market Segment so that you can track each separately. Your portfolio manager should enable you to do this.

Life is much simpler if the broker you select offers a full-featured portfolio manager that provides these capabilities. If it doesn't, take a look at the third-party portfolio managers listed above. Don't sacrifice power for convenience. A portfolio manager is essential to the ongoing operation and maintenance of your Perfect Portfolio.

Scheduled Portfolio Reviews

It is certainly nice to know that your portfolio is being constantly monitored by an automated system and that you don't need to spend hours in front of your computer to check it on a regular basis. But you periodically do need to fire up the computer and review your holdings without being prompted.

Alerts and triggers can tell you when you need to pay attention to specific investments. But they don't tell you how your entire portfolio is performing in comparison to your Investing Plan. And they don't tell you when global adjustments to your portfolio are warranted based on market factors or changes in your lifestyle. You should therefore review your entire portfolio at least once a month. Here is what you should look for during these reviews:

- *Portfolio Performance:* Use your portfolio manager to check the performance of your entire portfolio against the Investing Plan and the Portfolio Design Worksheet that I showed you how to create in Chapter 10. Your Portfolio Design Worksheet includes Expected Return numbers for each of your investments, for your total Core Segment, for your total Target Market Segment, and for your total portfolio. Your portfolio manager should give you the information you need to see whether each of these portfolio elements is meeting its performance goals. If not, you may want to make adjustments by moving money from lower-performing PPM Building Blocks to higher-performing Building Blocks.
- *Asset Allocation:* The portfolio you designed in Chapter 10 specified percentage allocations for each Building Block investment and for both portfolio Segments. These allocations will change as time goes by and prices change. Your portfolio manager should have an "analyze" feature that shows you these allocations as they currently exist. If any have strayed significantly from your original allocation, you may then decide to move money among investments to reestablish your original percentage allocations.

If the allocations are close to the originals, then I wouldn't worry about it because moving money between investments involves selling and buying, and this activity can result in trading commissions and taxable events. But for an investment that has recently thrived, its allocation may become top-heavy and as a result increase the risk of your portfolio to unacceptable levels. You must periodically consider rebalancing your portfolio.

- *Time Stops:* Here is a factor you must monitor that you won't typically find in any book on investing. You need to look in your Target Market Segment for time stops. What are these? A time stop occurs when you are holding an investment that is essentially doing nothing for an extended period of time. Perhaps you have purchased a Gold-related ETF that has been trading in a narrow range for three months. It is not hitting your stop price or your take-profit price and is also failing to meet your expectations for returns. It is essentially dead money. You cannot afford idle money in your portfolio if it is to reach its return goals. You therefore need to define a time stop for each investment in your Target Market Segment.

  No portfolio manager or alert system that I know of currently allows you to implement an automatic alert trigger for a time stop as I have defined it. You need to proactively review your investments to spot these nonperformers. The time period you set is up to you. In my opinion, three months is a reasonable time period. If during this time the investment is not moving up, look for a better PPM Building Block to add money to.

- *News Review:* During your investment review period, quickly scan the news headlines for each of your investments. If you have received no alerts from your various trading plans, then probably nothing earthshaking has happened. But you should have a general awareness of what is currently going on in the economy, in the market, and in the financial world that could affect your portfolio. This news review is not difficult or time consuming. The PPM approach gives you the advantage of having only nine investments to review. Each one is related to an investment that is understandable. Let's face facts: It is easier to understand what factors are occurring that can affect Gold or Latin America than what factors are affecting a mid-cap value fund.

But a word of warning is needed. Don't be overly influenced by what you read in the news. I warned you in Chapter 1 that much of what is printed in the financial press is simply filler or contains a good deal of biased opinion. Pay attention to verifiable facts such as interest rate trends, inflation, the strength of the dollar, and current events. Do not take the opinions and projections of experts too seriously. So, read the news but don't tinker with your portfolio because of the regular noise of the daily news cycle.

Monthly reviews of your portfolio don't need to take a lot of time and they are not difficult to perform. Web tools that are available to you in the form of portfolio managers and investment Web sites make reviewing and researching your investments extremely simple. In fact, because you have a portfolio of your own creation, it should actually be fun to check on. So, at least once a month, just do it. It will give you a great feeling of control and personal satisfaction. Your investments will cease being the "black box" that they probably are now.

Your Portfolio Implementation and Management Action Checklist

An incredible amount of critical information has been packed into this short chapter. You may find it beneficial to have it all summarized in a checklist of action items as follows:

1. *Assemble your portfolio action packet:* Pull together the PPM Building Block Worksheets that you have created throughout this book along with your personal Investing Plan and the Perfect Portfolio Design Worksheet that you completed in Chapter 10. This packet of worksheets specifies the investments you will buy and the trading plans you will implement for each. This is your action packet.

2. *Identify one or more online brokers you will use:* Go through the evaluation process described in this chapter to identify one or more online brokers that provide the capabilities you need to implement, monitor, and manage your Perfect Portfolio.

You are ahead of the game if you already have an online broker that you like.

3. *Place your orders:* After setting up an account with the broker you identify, place your investment orders as specified on your Perfect Portfolio Design Worksheet. Remember, try to put your Target Market Segment investments in an IRA or other tax-advantaged account if you can. Your Core Segment investments can go anywhere.

4. *Put your trading plan for each Target Market into place:* When you place your Target Market orders, also enter trailing stops at the same time as discussed in this and previous chapters. You decide whether to make them hard stops that automatically sell your position or soft stops that send you an e-mail prompting further research. Your decision will depend on your investing style and willingness to become involved in the process.

5. *Find a full-featured portfolio manager:* Locate an online portfolio manager that has the features described in this chapter. It would be good if it is the portfolio manager provided by your online broker. If not, go to the third-party sites listed earlier and explore their offerings.

6. *Configure your portfolio manager:* If you are using a third-party portfolio manager, enter your investments into it. If you are using your broker's portfolio manager, they will be entered for you. Use the portfolio manager features to set price alerts for any funds you have included, as most brokers will not allow you to set trailing stop triggers for funds. Also set up a Watch List and enter any investments that you are simply monitoring without owning.

7. *Check your e-mails for alerts:* Plan to check your e-mails on a regular basis for portfolio alerts. Most brokers and portfolio managers will also have the option to send alerts by text messages to your cell phone if you wish. Develop an online environment for doing quick research if you are using soft stops.

8. *Schedule monthly portfolio reviews:* Get out your calendar and set dates for a periodic review of your portfolio. Once a month should be fine. Remember, your PPM trading plan will automatically alert you if anything in your portfolio needs more immediate attention.

9. *Revise your Individual Investing Plan once per year:* In Chapter 10 you created an Individual Investing Plan for your unique

needs. This plan took into account your goals, your time horizon, the amount of money you will devote to your investments initially, and the amount you are willing and able to contribute to the plan each month. Based on this information, you derived an annual return rate required of your portfolio and you used this as one input when designing your Perfect Portfolio. Well, with each year that passes most, if not all, of these factors will change. So at the end of each year that your portfolio is in existence, use the worksheets and tools found in Chapter 10 to update your Individual Investing Plan. The results may prompt you to update the design and allocations of your Perfect Portfolio.

10. *Continue to learn:* I have suggested throughout this book that you use the online supplement. You will find Web sites there that provide additional information in a number of areas. You will find at least one Web site where you can learn more about each Target Market asset type. While the information presented here will enable you to construct a powerful portfolio, you should seek to understand more about Gold, Energy, Agricultural Commodities, Real Estate, and Emerging Markets. The PPM has allowed you to narrow your investment universe to just a few highly rewarding areas. You should embrace the task of learning all you can about each one because the PPM approach enables you to directly transform knowledge into increased returns and additional wealth.

Also continue to learn from experience. I have stated many times that defining a trading plan for each of your Target Market investments is both an art and a science. The science part you can read about and learn. Understanding the "art" of this activity comes from experience. Every time you get whipsawed out of a position, learn from it. Every time you should have taken profits but didn't, learn something. And every time you make exactly the right call, learn from that as well.

This is obviously a checklist that you will not complete in one day. Give yourself perhaps a week or two to complete the specific action items detailed in items 1 through 6. Items 7 through 10 will remain relevant throughout your investing career.

Chapter Summary

This chapter has given you specific action items for implementing, monitoring, and managing the Perfect Portfolio that you designed in Chapter 10.

It is important to realize that designing your Perfect Portfolio was only the first step to investing success. The next step is transforming your conceptual portfolio into reality by actually buying and implementing trading plans for the investments you have selected. This chapter has given you the knowledge, structure, and resources for doing so.

Some of you will want to start using the Perfect Portfolio Methodology by committing only a portion of your portfolio to this new approach. For example, if you have $500,000 of investment money, then perhaps you will want to begin by committing only $100,000 to the Perfect Portfolio approach. You can then add money as you see the results. This is a perfectly reasonable approach and one that I suggest to my students.

You are now empowered to embark on a new way of investing that you have probably never considered. Take your time and carefully consider each step in the Action Checklist presented here. Then commit to taking action and becoming involved in the investing process.

The next and final chapter shows you how to maximize the effectiveness of your Perfect Portfolio through your increased involvement in the investing process.

12

Maximizing the Potential of Your Perfect Portfolio

TRANSFORMING YOUR PERSONAL INVOLVEMENT INTO WEALTH

We have put into place throughout this book a powerful portfolio using a revolutionary methodology. The portfolio we have created has the potential for incredible returns. It is protected from downside risk by a series of trading plans. It is flexible to meet changing market and economic conditions. It is customizable to fit our unique investing goals and style. And its incorporation of an automated alert system to tell us when investments need attention means that we do not need to spend hours in front of the computer monitoring it. These are among the reasons why I have dubbed what we have created here *The Perfect Portfolio.*

The Perfect Portfolio Methodology (PPM) offers another incredibly valuable feature. It enables you to translate your involvement in the investing process directly into higher returns. Showing you how this is done is the purpose of this chapter.

In the personal investing classes that I teach at the college level, I find that my students are willing and eager to dedicate time and effort to the investing process in order to achieve higher portfolio returns. Yet they are frustrated when they can't find a way to convert this involvement into additional wealth. Their efforts often include investing activities that are based on newsletter advice, attending investing seminars, signing up for trading systems, and looking for recommendations in the financial media. Energy expended in this manner is typically wasted as these are essentially random activities with no focused goal or comprehensive plan of action in mind.

The PPM approach to investing is different. It provides a structure that does enable you to channel time and effort into effective action. I have discussed previously how the risk-reward profile of your Perfect Portfolio can be defined by adjusting various *dials* relating to allocations of money to Segments and Building Blocks. There exists yet another dial that you can adjust to define your portfolio's profile. This is the dial related to your level of personal involvement in the investing process. Using the PPM the higher you set this dial, the higher will be the potential of your portfolio for generating wealth. You will learn how this works in this chapter.

Many of you will be perfectly satisfied with the relatively minimal level of involvement discussed and illustrated in previous chapters. The PPM approach was designed specifically to be simple to implement, easy to monitor, and require little of your time on an ongoing basis. You do not need to become heavily involved in the investing process to produce a powerful portfolio.

Others among you will be motivated to devote more time and effort to the process to achieve even higher returns and reach even higher investing goals. I discuss areas of the PPM approach in this chapter where additional involvement can produce these higher returns. After reading about and understanding each, you can decide if and where you will be willing to exchange effort for additional wealth.

Selecting Investments

The first activity you can consider for increasing returns is devoting more time and research to selecting each of the specific investments in your portfolio.

I provide in this book a streamlined methodology for selecting individual investments for nine Portfolio Building Blocks. In the sample portfolio I constructed, my preference was simply to buy index funds in the Core Segment and an Exchange Traded Fund for each asset type in the Target Market Segment. For this purpose, I identified, evaluated, and compared data for a minimum of three candidates before selecting one. The process was simple, easy to perform, and took very little time. Yet, it was effective.

More involvement directed at finding additional investment candidates and evaluating each in more detail could possibly have allowed me to achieve a few more percentage points of return. The following sections discuss several actions I could have taken to select potentially better investments, particularly in the Target Market Segment.

Learn More about Each Asset Type

I provide in this book a brief education related to each asset type in the Target Market Segment. For each of these Building Blocks, there is a lot more that can be learned. The more you know about each asset type, the more informed your decisions will be. You can expand your knowledge related to each asset by going to the online supplement and following the links presented for Chapters 5 through 9. They point to sites that will give you further education, insights, and news related to the five Target Market asset types. Experience has shown me time and time again that increased returns correlate directly with increased knowledge of the assets in which you are investing.

Identify and Evaluate More Candidates

I suggested for each portfolio Building Block that you identify and evaluate at least three investment candidates. In the sample portfolio built in this book, I looked for an ETF, a fund from the fund family I was using for other investments, and a top-performing fund for each Target Market Building Block. I showed you how to find these candidates using free Web resources. I could have added to my evaluation and comparison list more candidates from other fund families. I could have looked at more ETFs that track different indexes for an asset class. I could have widened the scope of my candidate search.

When searching for a Gold investment, for example, I could have also included in the comparison investments that combined gold with other precious metals such as silver and platinum in their holdings. If you are willing to dedicate more time to the process of identifying and evaluating additional candidates for each PPM asset class, you increase your chances of finding the most promising investment available.

Using Third-Party Help

Another action you can take that has the potential to improve your investment selections is to use third-party assistance. There are numerous newsletters and Web sites, for example, that offer analysis and recommendations for the best investments in each PPM asset category. You can also ask a financial adviser for recommendations if you are currently working with one. Specialized knowledge from third parties can be particularly helpful in an area such as the Emerging Markets asset class, where there are significantly more variables to consider than, say, the Gold asset class.

For the purpose of getting assistance in making your specific investment selections for each Portfolio Building Block, I have listed sites and resources in the online supplement. To access them, log in to the supplement site, click on *Links by Chapter* and then on *Chapter 12.*

Always keep in mind that you need to be careful with third-party advice. Don't be taken in by newsletters or any other third-party resource that promises quick riches by following the advice presented. Only consider recommendations that are well reasoned, and provide both the pros and cons of any investment profiled.

Buying Multiple Investments for a Building Block

You can also consider buying more than one investment for a particular asset type. This will, of course, require more time dedicated to understanding the asset type, finding candidates, and evaluating them. As an example, for the Energy Building Block, you may decide after extensive analysis that instead of just buying an ETF that tracks an oil-based index, you may also want to buy one that tracks an alternative energy index or a nuclear power index. This does not break the rules of the PPM approach. You will still have nine PPM Building Blocks. But you may have more than one investment for each. Doing so simply requires that you become more involved in the investing process.

Expanding Your Awareness of the Market

This area of involvement deals with expanding your study of market conditions and how they can affect the asset classes in your portfolio. Doing so has the potential of enabling you to make more timely and accurate adjustments to your portfolio and as a result increasing its returns and reducing its risk.

Part of understanding an asset class is learning the factors that influence its price. I have provided an overview of these factors for each asset class discussed in this book. For example, higher interest rates have a negative effect on the Stock asset class. A disruption in oil production causes Energy-related investments to spike. World unrest tends to drive up the price of Gold.

If you understand how various market events influence the price of your investments, you can increase portfolio returns potential by monitoring the market on a regular basis and recognizing when these events occur. The PPM structure then enables you take advantage of these events by simply adjusting the allocations in your portfolio accordingly.

To take advantage of market events, you need to set up a market information environment that enables you to plug in to current events. There are many resources you can use for this. Simply scanning the *Wall Street Journal* on a daily basis, in print or on the Web, will help you accomplish this goal. You can also use one of many Web sites that can send you market update e-mails on a regular basis. You can access one such site, appropriately named MarketWatch, at marketwatch.com. You can select from a number of e-mail newsletters on this site covering such topics as broad as the total market or as narrow as an update on the gold market. There are other such sites and I list several in the online supplement in Chapter 12 of the *Links by Chapter* section.

Be very careful with this area of increased involvement however. One purpose of the PPM is to remove information overload from your investing life. Look only for major market events before adjusting your portfolio on the basis of the information you review on a daily basis. As I mentioned in Chapter 1, most financial news is simply noise and not worthy of your attention. Select only one, or a very few, news resources to monitor on a regular basis and then scan only for news that has the potential to affect the prices of the nine Perfect Portfolio asset classes.

Knowing How to React to Market Events

The second key to successful portfolio adjustment, based on monitoring the market, is to understand the effects that events have on the various asset types in your portfolio. You must know what to adjust in your portfolio to take advantage of market news.

The following are a few examples of major market and world events, the assets affected by them, and the appropriate portfolio adjustments to consider. These examples are greatly simplified and are intended only to illustrate the thinking process you should engage in when scanning the news.

- *Interest Rate Changes:* Increased interest rates suppress capital expenditures and in general slow down business growth. This typically results in the stock market declining. Increased costs of loans also dampen the real estate market. When you see interest rate increases looming, consider decreasing allocations to the Stock and Real Estate Building Blocks. Consider increasing allocations to Gold and Agricultural Commodities. When you believe that interest rates will go down, consider doing just the opposite.
- *Major Weather Events:* Significant weather events can affect assets in your portfolio in the short term. Frosts in the Sunbelt can affect the supply of produce such as orange juice and vegetables. Droughts and floods in the Plains states can affect the supply of legumes and grains such as soybeans, corn, and wheat. In the face of catastrophic weather events, you may want to consider increasing your allocation to the Agricultural Commodities component of your portfolio. As another example, hurricanes in the Gulf of Mexico can affect offshore drilling operations and temporarily disrupt the flow of oil. This may prompt you to increase your allocation to the Energy component of your portfolio. These are temporary catalysts and you should be prepared to take profits as their effects abate.
- *Dramatic Oil Price Changes:* Oil prices are unpredictable and there is great debate as to what causes them to spike. I discussed this issue in Chapter 6. When oil costs do spike, this catalyst typically has a negative effect on the entire stock market. When facing the prospect of significant increases in the price of oil, you may wish to consider increasing your allocation to Energy and decreasing your allocation to Stocks. If you feel that oil prices are due for a drop, perhaps in response to a decrease in consumer demand, then the opposite adjustments may be appropriate.

- *Weakening Dollar:* When the U.S. dollar weakens against major foreign currencies, the stocks denominated in these currencies are worth more dollars solely on the basis of the exchange rate. A weak dollar also allows foreign companies and consumers to buy American goods more cheaply. If you see a major trend toward a weaker dollar, you may want to consider increasing your allocation to Emerging Markets and Foreign Stocks. A stronger dollar, on the other hand, bodes well for U.S. Stocks, but not so well for foreign investments.
- *Major World Unrest:* Investors run for cover when events such as terrorist attacks or the threat of a major war are looming, like between Israel and Iran, for example. The most frequently used safe-haven investments in your portfolio are Cash, Bonds, and Gold. You may wish to consider increasing allocations in these areas in times of turmoil. When such events threaten oil supplies, then consider increasing your allocation to Energy. World unrest typically has a negative affect on Stocks.

These are just a few of the major events and trends that you can spot if you pay even casual attention to the news on a daily basis. When you recognize these market catalysts, you should understand the effects they can have on the prices of the various components in your portfolio. Your PPM portfolio is designed to enable you to easily adjust Segment and Building Block allocations so you can take advantage of market catalysts that can move the prices of the Asset Building Blocks in your portfolio.

But be careful not to overdo this activity. Act only on significant events that have the potential to affect widespread markets. Portfolio adjustments have a cost in terms of commission charges and taxable events. Do not make portfolio changes based on localized or transitory events. And certainly do not act only on the basis of opinions or projections of experts. If you have spent the time to study each PPM asset class closely, as is recommended in this book, you should be able to separate significant events and catalysts from those that are irrelevant or short-lived. Your skills in this area will increase with experience.

Also keep in mind that the trading plan you put into place for each of your Target Market Building Blocks is automatically watching the price of your investments. The trading plan either sells your investment when prices go down or sends you an e-mail when prices go down *or* up. If you are a less hands-on investor, then the level of market monitoring provided by your automated trading plans may be sufficient.

Having said this, however, you should realize that an alert from your monitoring system is a reaction to events that have already occurred. Your personal news monitoring environment enables you to get ahead of the event and the potential asset price changes. In doing so, you have the opportunity to pick up additional returns by allocating more money to assets that are poised to react positively to events and decreasing allocations to those poised to react negatively.

Market Monitoring Summary

There are both costs and benefits to increasing your involvement in the investing process by monitoring the market on a regular basis. If you enjoy reading about markets and you are confident in your ability to interpret the tea leaves, then the PPM approach enables you to translate this involvement into potentially higher returns. If regular market monitoring is a chore you would rather not do, then rest assured that your Target Market trading plans are performing this task for you.

Enhancing Your Trading Plan Skills

As mentioned many times in this book, a key component of the Perfect Portfolio Methodology is the implementation of an automated trading plan for each investment held in your Target Market Segment. Trading plans mitigate the risk associated with these investments that offer the potential for significantly higher returns. Designing trading plans for each Target Market investment is another area where you can increase potential returns through more personal involvement in the process. The following discussion explains how.

In Part II of *The Perfect Portfolio* we defined sell and alert price points by viewing a price chart for an investment. We plotted on the chart both a price line and Bollinger Bands. The price line showed trends and levels of price support and resistance. Bollinger Bands showed volatility. Using this information, we were able to determine investment price exit points to either stop losses or to take profits.

The process discussed for setting price alerts was not difficult to understand or to implement. We simply eyeballed the chart and set our stops based on several quick observations. There is nothing wrong with this simple methodology. It is very effective and knowing that the process is easy to do means people will use it.

By using additional technical analysis indicators, however, you can potentially make your trading plans more effective. This is another area where your increased involvement can translate into additional returns without additional risk.

Using Additional Technical Indicators

Technical analysis is the art and science of predicting future price movements of an equity based on price chart patterns. Technical indicators are tools that enable you to derive information from price movements and transform this information into action. If you are willing to become more involved in the investing process, then you may be able to profit by using one or more technical indicators when creating and reacting to your trading plan triggers and alerts. I present one suggestion here.

I have previously discussed the advantages of placing hard stops that automatically sell your position when a sell price point is reached. You can also set soft stops that simply send you an e-mail when a sell point is hit. This e-mail will prompt you to do additional research before deciding if you will sell the investment at the current time. This research can include looking at the investment's fundamentals, news headlines, and one or more technical indicators on a price chart.

There are dozens of technical indicators in addition to the Bollinger Bands discussed previously that you can use to analyze the price chart of an investment you are researching. One that I find to be simple to use and that provides valuable information is discussed next.

The Relative Strength Indicator (RSI). The RSI is a technical momentum indicator that compares for the equity you are investigating the magnitude of recent gains to recent losses in an attempt to determine overbought and oversold conditions. This indicator is illustrated in Figure 12.1 and is shown just below the price chart.

The RSI number ranges from 0 to 100. An asset is deemed to be overbought once the RSI approaches the 70 level, meaning that it may be getting overvalued and is a good candidate for a price pull-back. Likewise, if the RSI approaches 30, it is an indication that the asset may be getting oversold and therefore likely to be on the verge of a price rebound. The RSI line moving above 50 is seen as a bullish sign. Also be aware that the RSI signals are most relevant when a security's price is trending in a sideways direction as opposed to being in the middle of a significant uptrend or downtrend.

Let's look at an example of where to get RSI information and how to interpret it.

Assume you purchase the Real Estate ETF with the symbol VNQ and at the same time set a stop loss e-mail alert. You will recall from Chapter 8 that we looked at this investment and decided not to put it in the sample portfolio. But assume you did buy it and the price falls to the stop price you have set. You will get an e-mail alert and this will prompt you to research what is happening with the ETF.

When you get the alert, you can investigate the price action by going to a Web-based charting resource that provides technical indicators. The site at finance.yahoo.com will do the job. On this site, simply enter the investment symbol and click on the menu item titled *Basic Technical Analysis*. You want to analyze the Relative Strength Index for VNQ so on the resulting screen, click on *RSI* in the menu above the chart. You will get a display that looks like Figure 12.1.

The RSI indicator is displayed below the price chart. The vertical axis of the indicator ranges from 0 to 100 and the horizontal axis is the same time line as the price chart. You can see that the RSI line for VNQ on this chart moves in a pattern that closely matches the price line. The current RSI is approximately 45. This tells us that VNQ is neither oversold nor overbought at this point. A mere few days ago, however, the RSI touched the 20 level, which indicated an oversold condition. You can see that the price line bounced up at this point. As you look at one year of trading for this ETF, you will see several instances where the overbought line has been touched and the price has bounced up at least temporarily.

If I were performing this analysis in response to a stop loss e-mail alert, I would go ahead and sell VNQ. The RSI is not telling me that VNQ is oversold at this point and due for a price rebound upward. If either the RSI was close to 20 or if the RSI was moving

Figure 12.1   VNQ Price Chart with RSI Indicator

Reproduced with permission of Yahoo! Inc. ® 2008 by Yahoo! Inc. YAHOO! and the YAHOO! logo are trademarks of Yahoo! Inc.

above 50, then I might hold off my decision to sell and instead, reset my alert trigger to a lower level. But neither of these conditions exists, so I would sell to avoid further losses. Others, viewing the same information, may come to a different conclusion.

The same type of RSI analysis applies to profit alerts. When you get a take-profit e-mail alert, bring up a price chart with the RSI displayed. If the RSI is approaching 70, then the investment is in overbought territory, which is a signal that a price decrease may be imminent. So, go ahead and sell to take your profit. If the RSI is below 50, then there may be further room for the price to grow, in which case you may consider simply tightening a stop loss trigger you may have set, say from a price drop of $8 to $5, and resetting your take-profit alert to a higher level.

Using Technical Analysis Summary.   When you get a soft alert in the form of an e-mail or text message, then you can make more informed action decisions by using technical analysis (TA) indicators. The RSI is one example of many. The online supplement points you to resources where you can learn more about TA if you find this field to be interesting and if you are willing to put in the work required to learn how to use it. To find these references, log in to the supplement, click on *Links by Chapter*, and then on *Chapter 12.*

Using TA is an area where you can increase the potential returns of your portfolio by increasing your involvement in the investing process. This activity is completely optional, however. The effectiveness of the PPM does not depend on you using TA other than the simple Bollinger Bands we have used to determine volatility and thus price stops for the Target Market trading plans. Using additional TA indicators does have the potential, however, to enable you to boost portfolio returns using the PPM approach.

Resources For Enhancing Your Trading Plan Skills. A host of resources, some free and some that incur a fee, are available that have the potential to increase the effectiveness of your trading plans. After completing this book you will be perfectly capable of implementing effective trading plans with the knowledge and tools you have gained here. However, if you are willing to dedicate additional time, effort, and perhaps money to honing your skills in this area, log in to the supplement, click on *Links by Chapter*, then on *Chapter 12* and look for the link related to trading plan resources.

Creating Additional PPM Building Blocks

I am often asked by students in classes where I teach the Perfect Portfolio Methodology if they would be violating the rules by adding more Asset Building Blocks to the portfolio over and above the nine defined in this book. You may be asking the same question.

The first part of my answer is that I don't believe you need to. The nine Building Blocks as defined cover virtually the entire spectrum of asset classes available in the market. Owning all nine Building Blocks gives you a portfolio that includes thousands of stocks and bonds in virtually all parts of the market.

The second part of my answer is that yes, you can, if you wish, add Portfolio Building Blocks, as long as you define and work with them using the Perfect Portfolio Methodology described in this book.

The purpose of the PPM approach is not to limit your choices of investments. As a unique individual investor, you may have a specific interest in, or knowledge of, focused markets not included in the nine Building Blocks defined here. For example, perhaps you work in the medical field and you would like to take advantage of your specialized knowledge in this area by including a Healthcare Sector Building Block in your portfolio. Or perhaps your analysis of the market tells you that adding a Technology Sector Building Block makes sense at this time.

The PPM allows for such additions within certain constraints. You must use the same structure and work with these new Building Blocks using the same resources and methods as used for the original ones. You will note from Chapter 10 that I have left several blank lines in the Portfolio Design Worksheet and Calculator for Building Blocks that you may wish to add.

Here are the steps for adding your own Building Blocks to your unique Perfect Portfolio.

1. *Identify a Target Market of Interest:* This should be a market segment that you have identified because you have specific knowledge of it or because your analysis tells you that it is poised for significant growth. Do *not* select a market segment based on third-party opinion or speculation. Do *not* select a market segment based on a news item related to a transitory event. And do *not* select a market segment based on rosy projections for an individual stock in that segment. Make sure that there are good, sound reasons for including a new Building Block in your portfolio.
2. *Identify an Index and an ETF:* The target market you select should be tracked by at least one major index. The PPM approach requires that Building Blocks be purchased with one investment that holds a basket of stocks in the target market you have identified. This eliminates company risk and doing so is a key principle of the PPM approach. Look for an ETF that tracks your chosen target market on sites such as ishares.com and finance.yahoo.com/etf.
3. *Review a Price Chart:* After finding an ETF that tracks the market segment of interest, pull up its price chart and study its performance over at least the past two years or the longest time period available if the ETF has not been in existence for two years. You will be able to easily see if this market segment has a history of good performance, and more important, if it is performing well now. Don't include a market segment in your portfolio that is currently trending down. Remember,

Target Market investments are buy-and-sell holdings. The most recent trend is the most important.

4. *Use the PPM Process:* Follow the identification, evaluation, and selection process as discussed in Chapter 4 and illustrated in Chapters 5 through 9 of this book for the original Target Market Segment Building Blocks. The steps include:

    ◆ Identifying at least three candidates for evaluation
    ◆ Collecting, analyzing, and comparing data for these candidates
    ◆ Selecting one investment that has the best mix of historical return, risk, and expenses
    ◆ Defining a trading plan using a price chart, stop loss triggers, and take-profit alerts

Examples of just a few potential PPM Building Block markets and ETFs that track them are the following:

- Biotech: IBB
- Healthcare: IXJ
- Telecom: IXP
- Tech Sector: IYW

These markets are not recommendations and there are dozens more you can consider. But let me stress again, the original set of nine Portfolio Building Blocks was designed to provide full market coverage and full risk-reducing diversity. The beauty of the PPM approach is that it has so few investments for you to have to deal with. This advantage fades as you add more Building Blocks.

For those of you who do wish to search for and define additional Building Blocks, I have presented resources that enable you to do so in the online supplement. To access them log in to the site, click on *Links by Chapter* and then on *Chapter 12.*

Adding Doomsday Building Blocks

The standard nine PPM Building Blocks give you plenty of areas to play defense when the stock market is declining. The most common areas to run for cover are Gold and Cash. There is a category of ETFs, however, that enables you to go on offense when the stock market or any asset class is behaving badly. These are *short* ETFs that I call the "Doomsday" versions of the PPM Building Blocks. I first mentioned them in Chapter 4 and I explain their use in more detail here.

First, let's look briefly at the activity of *shorting*. If you think the price of a certain stock is poised to move lower, you can make money if your prediction is right by shorting the stock. To short a stock, you first borrow shares, typically from your broker, and sell them at the current market price. You receive the money from this sale immediately and it is automatically deposited in your brokerage account. Then, if you are right and the stock price goes down, you can buy the stock at market price, give back the shares you borrowed, and pocket the price difference.

With individual stocks, this is a very risky strategy because if you guess wrong, you may have to cover your short position by buying the stock at a higher price than you sold it for in order to return the borrowed shares. There is theoretically no upper limit on how high a stock price can go. So, unless you already own the stocks you are shorting, you are facing unlimited risk.

But the risk of shorting stocks, or market indexes, through buying ETFs is not unlimited. At worst you can lose only the price of each ETF share you buy. So when markets are trending downward, it is not unreasonable to consider buying an ETF that shorts the entire stock market or any of the more narrowly focused asset classes defined as PPM Building Blocks. Two such investments that allow you to take advantage of a drop in the stock market are described here to illustrate the concept.

If you believe that the S&P 500 Index (which is a good proxy for the entire stock market) is poised to drop in the near future, then you can make money on this prediction by purchasing one of the following ETFs:

- *ProShares Short S&P 500—Symbol SH:* This investment seeks daily investment results, before fees and expenses, that correspond to the inverse of the daily performance of the S&P 500 Index. In other words, for every point that the S&P 500 Stock Index goes down, the price of this ETF will theoretically go up by the same amount.
- *ProShares Ultrashort S&P 500—Symbol SDS:* This investment seeks daily investment results, before fees and expenses, that

correspond to twice the inverse of the daily performance of the S&P 500 Index. This ETF provides a stronger reaction to a drop in the stock market. It will theoretically go up two points for every one point that the S&P 500 Index drops.

These are the ultimate stock market Doomsday Building Blocks. Study them more closely using your favorite investing Web site. Employ them carefully and only if you are convinced that the stock market, represented by the S&P 500, is ready to plunge. And if you buy either, make sure you put it under the watchful eye of a PPM trading plan to lower the risk of owning it.

Figure 12.2 illustrates how each of these short investments performed from the middle of 2007 to the middle of 2008. On the chart, SDS is the top line, SH is in the middle, and the S&P index labeled ^GSPC is the bottom line.

Note that this is not a price chart. It is a chart that compares the performance over time of the same amount of money invested in each investment at the beginning of the chart. Shown are the relative performances for each of the short ETFs discussed earlier compared to the performance of the S&P 500. The results are as advertised. During the time shown on the chart, the S&P 500 lost 20 percent, SH gained 20 percent, and SDS gained 40 percent.

These are not the only short ETF investments available to you. There are ETFs that go up when the price of oil goes down. There are ETFs that go up when the price of gold goes down. In fact,

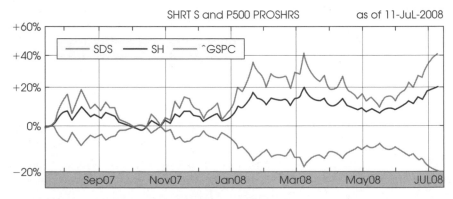

Figure 12.2 Shorting the Market with ETFs

there are short ETFs for just about all of the PPM Building Blocks. To find a list of them, log into the supplement, click *Links by Chapter* and then *Chapter 12*. Look for the link related to *Short Investing*. With these tools in your investing arsenal now you have three choices when viewing a price chart for a PPM Building Block investment that you are considering. If the price trend is up, you will want to buy. If the price trend is down, you can decide to not buy at this time and put it in a Watch List. Or, in a downtrend you can buy a short ETF for the Building Block and actually make money as the underlying market index or asset type declines. You can see that the PPM gives you the potential to make significant returns in *all* market conditions.

What about Adding Individual Stocks?

Buying individual stocks is not part of the Perfect Portfolio Methodology approach. Remember why the PPM approach was developed in the first place. It was designed so that you, the average investor, would not be subjected to the complex analysis and enormous risks associated with trading individual stocks.

When you buy an individual stock, you face the full force of company risk in addition to market risk. Company risk includes such factors as failed products, lawsuits, bad management, missed earnings predictions, and factors that go on behind the scenes that we as individual investors have no access to. When I was writing this chapter, I was thinking about the recent fiasco at Bear Stearns where corporate officials were announcing to the public that the company was strong and had plenty of cash to ride out the sub-prime credit crisis. This very public announcement was spread worldwide by the media unquestioned and convinced many people to buy at what seemed to be a bargain price of around $30 per share. Two days later, the stock was valued at $1. While the take-over price eventually paid by JPMorgan Chase ended up around $10 per share, I use this example to illustrate the incredible risks of owning an individual stock regardless of how much research you have done.

Individual stocks also expose you to the full force gales of marketing hype, adviser bias, and stock manipulation by hedge funds and short sellers. I discussed all of these problems in Chapter 1. One goal of the PPM approach is to eliminate these factors by mandating as the basic investing unit mutual funds or ETFs that hold baskets of company stocks. These investments are sufficiently diversified to virtually eliminate the risks associated with individual stocks.

The PPM does not therefore accommodate investing in individual stocks. Does it forbid you from buying them? It absolutely does not. You do not have to dedicate all of investment money to your Perfect Portfolio.

I have discussed throughout this book the power of adjusting allocations of money to various portfolio segments and assets to change its risk-reward profile. The highest allocation dial discussed was the allocation between the portfolio Core Segment and the Target Market Segment.

There is yet a higher allocation dial that you can put into place. This is the allocation of your investment money between the portfolio you build following the PPM approach and any investments you hold outside of your Perfect Portfolio structure. For example, it would not be out of the question for you to start by allocating 50 percent of your investment money to the PPM approach and 50 percent to more traditional approaches with which you may currently be more comfortable. In your traditional portfolio, you can buy stocks, work with an adviser, and continue to operate as usual. Then, as you see better results from the PPM approach, you can gradually turn up this dial to incrementally increase the allocation of your total investment monies to your Perfect Portfolio.

Monitoring and Trading Your CORE Segment

The last area of involvement that I discuss is implementing PPM trading plans for your Core Segment funds. I don't usually recommend doing this because the Core investments are buy-and-hold investments that you should own for years. History has shown over the long term that these investments will trend upward even though they will have ups and downs in the short term. The purpose of the Core Segment is diminished if you start to trade it.

However, there are two main reasons why you may want to treat your Core Portfolio Building Blocks in the same manner as you treat your Target Market Building Blocks. The first is if your portfolio time horizon is less than three years. This length of time does not enable you to take full advantage of stock price appreciation in the long-term that history tells us is the rule. A second reason for monitoring and trading your Core Building Blocks is if you are willing to do additional work in order to squeeze out every point of additional return from your Core investments possible.

If either of these conditions applies to you then by all means feel free to buy ETFs for the Core Building Blocks and place them under the watchful eye of a trading plan in the same manner as has been described in this book for your Target Market Building Blocks. Doing so would have certainly protected you from the crushing stock market losses suffered during the market crash of late 2008.

Also remember that if you are planning to trade your Core investments, try to also place them in a tax-deferred account such as an IRA.

Learning from Experience

The PPM is a new and original approach to investing. It allows for little involvement on your part or a lot. You decide how much to involve yourself in the investing process on the basis of your investing goals and investing style. If you decide to become involved, start slowly and learn from the results of each of your actions.

For example, implementing a trading plan and setting price action points is as much an art as a science. You will initially set some hard stops too close to the purchase price of an investment and get whipsawed out of the position before the uptrend is over. You will probably also set some soft stops too close to the purchase price of an ETF or fund and be inundated with e-mail alerts for which no action is required. In either case, you need to learn from experience what works and what doesn't. Experience will be your best teacher and you will get better and better at implementing, monitoring, and managing your Perfect Portfolio as time goes on.

Chapter Summary

Let's call this chapter extra credit. If you had stopped reading this book at the end of Chapter 11 you would be fully prepared to put into place an extraordinary portfolio, one that is probably far better than the one you currently own. However, after reading this chapter, you know that you can do even better if you are willing to become more involved in the investing process.

The purpose of this chapter has been to show you that the Perfect Portfolio Methodology gives you the potential for higher returns if you are willing to work for them. In this chapter I showed you areas where increased involvement can result in increased returns. The ability that the PPM gives you to transform your involvement into higher returns is a powerful feature indeed.

The bottom line is that the PPM approach enables you to be the type of investor you want to be. If your investing style is more passive, the PPM gives you a very powerful portfolio that requires only occasional attention. If, however, you are aiming for higher returns, then you can enhance your chances of obtaining them through increasing your involvement in the investing process. I have shown in this chapter what this involvement looks like. You choose the areas where you want to participate. To borrow a phrase from an army recruitment promotion, your increased involvement in working with the Perfect Portfolio Methodology enables you to make your portfolio "all that it can be."

The Perfect Portfolio Summary

REVIEWING, TEACHING, AND EXPERIENCING THE PERFECT PORTFOLIO METHODOLOGY

I have introduced you to a revolutionary approach to personal investing in *The Perfect Portfolio*. You have been presented with a lot of new ideas, tools, and methods, many in direct contradiction to what you have been taught about investing in the past. So, it is time to reflect on what you have just read through several short discussions presented in this summary.

In the first discussion, I will review the breakthrough concepts of the Perfect Portfolio Methodology (PPM) that merit this approach to personal investing being called "revolutionary." In the second, I will discuss the very interesting reactions I get in the classroom when teaching the PPM. Then I relate a real-life story told to me by one of my students who implemented the PPM for her own investments. I end the summary with a final note of encouragement to take action.

Why Is the Perfect Portfolio Methodology Revolutionary?

I have called the Perfect Portfolio Methodology revolutionary. This is a strong term that is used far too often to describe approaches to investing that simply apply a new coat of paint to old and tired concepts. I believe that the PPM merits this adjective based on the following six breakout ideas and methods. These are among the reasons why I truly believe that what you have learned in this book is a revolutionary new way of investing.

- *The Use of Nine Asset Classes:* The PPM completely discards the traditional concept of there being only three asset classes. I have given you in this book *nine* clearly defined asset classes, each possessing a unique profile in regard to risk, reward, correlation, and reaction to market events. Nine asset classes provide the flexibility needed to model a portfolio that can thrive in all market conditions. Nine asset classes enable you to build a portfolio having the risk-reward profile that meets your unique goals and investing style. Under the PPM, portfolio design is no longer artificially constrained by the three-asset class straitjacket. This changes the nature of personal investing at its very core.
- *The Use of Total Market Investments:* The PPM advocates including in the portfolio only investments that hold baskets of stocks or bonds that represent entire markets or asset types. I discussed the use of Exchange Traded Funds (ETFs) and Index Funds in this book to include each of the nine asset classes in my sample portfolio. This approach virtually eliminates single-company risk from the portfolio. It also totally eliminates the need for you to sort through thousands of stocks, bonds, and fund styles trying to find the "best" individual investments. Imagine the time and aggravation this will save you!

  The PPM approach also shows that you can build a powerful and efficient portfolio using only a maximum of nine investments *and these are all that you will ever need.* The PPM is thus dramatically easier to implement, monitor, and change than traditional portfolio building methods.
- *Portfolio Design through Allocations:* The PPM enables you to define the risk-reward profile of your Perfect Portfolio by simply adjusting money allocation percentages to the nine PPM Building Blocks. You can use allocation adjustments to design a portfolio that matches your unique investing style, from conservative to aggressive and from passive to involved. And you can use allocation adjustments to configure your portfolio to thrive in any market environment from bearish to bullish.

The ability to change the profile of the portfolio through the simple adjustment of allocations among the investments that you already own means that you can react more quickly and effectively to changing conditions. This rapid response capability of the PPM gives you the potential to profit from current market dynamics in a manner that traditional buy-and-hold portfolios cannot.

- *Risk Management through Trading Plans:* Most traditional portfolio design models suggest that you simply buy and hold investments. This exposes you to maximum market risk and prevents you from buying investments that can produce extraordinary returns because, the models say, the risk is just too great. The PPM recognizes the value of buy-and-hold investing in its Core Segment. But it also embraces the advantages of buy-and-sell investing in its Target Market Segment. Here, you will buy high return, but volatile, investments and control their risk with a trading plan that stops losses and lets profits run. In other words, the PPM enables you to realize higher returns in your portfolio without incurring higher risks. This is unheard of in conventional portfolio design theory.

- *Risk Reduction and Return Enhancement through Involvement:* Traditional portfolio theory holds that risk is reduced only through investing in assets that have lower returns potential. The PPM believes there is another risk-reduction factor that is totally ignored by conventional wisdom. This is your involvement in the investing process. The PPM suggests that you can gain additional returns without additional risk if you pay attention to your investments and take informed actions on the basis of your recognition of market factors that can influence their prices.

  Traditional investing approaches assume that you are a totally passive investor. The PPM assumes that you are willing to trade time and effort for additional wealth and gives you the means for doing so.

- *Enhanced Portfolio Awareness:* The portfolios of many, if not most, of the individuals I meet in the course of my teaching activities are a mystery to them. They don't know what they own, they don't know how their investments are performing, and they don't know how to change their portfolio to meet changing personal circumstances or market conditions. The PPM is different. You own just a maximum of nine investments. You learned in this book what each one is and the factors that influence the price of each. As a PPM user, you are always completely aware of exactly what you own, why you own it, how it is performing and how to change the risk-reward profile of your portfolio when necessary. The enhanced awareness and renewed control of your portfolio provided by the PPM will undoubtedly enable you to sleep better at night.

In summary, you can see that the Perfect Portfolio Methodology does not simply tweak traditional portfolio building concepts and techniques. It blows them away!

The PPM dramatically simplifies the portfolio design and creation process. Using it, you only need to concentrate on nine investments. Under the PPM, your portfolio is constantly and automatically monitored 24 hours a day, 7 days a week, 365 days a year. The trading plan you implement for each investment will notify you when your attention to any investment is needed.

The PPM enables you to become a more involved and effective investor. It gives you the potential for incredible returns without excessive risk. And it enables you to ignore most of the noise and chaos that permeates the world of personal investing today as I illustrated in Chapter 1.

These are among the reasons why I feel justified in using the word *revolutionary* to describe the Perfect Portfolio Methodology.

Teaching the PPM: Untying the Gordian Knot

I have been teaching the Perfect Portfolio Methodology since 2006 and doing so is both a pleasure and a challenge. Students who attend my classes arrive with a host of preconceptions and expectations. Many have been taught for years, and some for decades, that successful personal investing involves such activities as analyzing individual stocks, choosing fund styles, diversifying a portfolio with three asset classes, and buying and holding as the preferred investing style. Most enter my classroom expecting more of the same. What they get in the PPM is something totally different, and many are literally stunned.

I try to soften the culture shock of what students are about to learn by starting my classes with the following story.

The Gordian Knot

In 333 B.C., as Alexander the Great was slashing his way through the city-states of present-day Turkey on his way to conquering most of the known world, he happened upon the city of Gordium. He encountered here an oxcart tied to a post with an intricate tangle of tree bark strands. This was the Gordian Knot. As the story goes, a prominent oracle of the day had decreed that the person who could free the oxcart would become the king of Asia.

Alexander studied the knot's intricate and complex nature. Then, instead of going through the almost impossible task of trying to untie the knot, he simply drew his sword and sliced through it. In this manner, he freed the oxcart and met the test of the prophecy. He then did go on to become the king of Asia.

This story illustrates what is now commonly called the *Alexander Solution*. It is a term used to describe the solving of an intractable problem with bold strokes.

The world of personal investing today is the public's Gordian Knot. It contains the overwhelming, confusing, and frustrating elements that I described in Chapter 1. I learned very early in my teaching career that it is extremely difficult to resolve the complexities of personal investing with the traditional methods that have been taught for decades.

Instead of trying to understand and untie the personal investing Gordian Knot, the Perfect Portfolio Methodology simply slices through it with a bold new approach. The PPM doesn't even attempt to deal with the tangled mess of analyzing stocks and fund styles. It simply sidesteps these incredibly complicated topics and suggests that students buy and work with only nine simple total-market investments. This is a bold, new, and vastly simpler, approach to personal investing. I have designed the PPM to be the Alexander Solution to personal investing. With this new perspective, students begin to understand that they need to start my classes with a clean slate and an open mind.

Still, as I begin to teach the PPM in the classroom, it is interesting to watch student reaction. They are at first wary. They wonder if this is some type of off-the-wall trading system that I am trying to sell them. As classes progress, they begin to understand the logic of the PPM's nine Building Block approach.

They then turn curious as they see the simplicity and elegance of designing a portfolio by combining Building Blocks. They are amazed at how they can design a portfolio that meets virtually any investing style and any market condition by simply adjusting allocations among the Building Blocks. Gone from the process is the need to sort through thousands of stocks and funds. Gone from the process is the need to go through the agonizing process of analyzing company financial statements and fund prospectuses.

Curiosity turns to excitement as they view with their own eyes the incredible returns potential of the various Target Market Building Blocks and how the risk of these relatively volatile investments is managed through simple and automated trading plans.

The final level that my students reach is one of enthusiasm when they realize that there is nothing in the PPM that they are not capable of understanding and there is nothing here that they cannot easily implement using free Web resources.

Most students are finally sold on the approach when I illustrate the exceptional returns produced by sample portfolios built using the PPM approach in previous classes. They see that these returns can be exceptional in markets that are both good and bad (refer to Appendix A for an example of good returns in a bad market). And they understand that the risk involved with higher returns can be significantly mitigated by their becoming more involved in the investing process, which they are willing to do.

How many of my students actually carry this enthusiasm into the real world and implement their own Perfect Portfolio? I have no way of knowing. I do occasionally hear from former students, however. One story stands out in my mind.

Gloria: The Beginning of Financial Independence

I started this book with a series of real-life stories from students in my classroom. They illustrated the problems faced by individual investors today and the need for a totally new approach to investing. I end this book with a more upbeat student story that illustrates how, in one instance, the Perfect Portfolio Methodology is working.

Gloria is a 64-year-old retired healthcare professional who attended one of my classes at Montgomery College in March 2007, where she learned the PPM approach to portfolio building. She told me at the time that she had approximately $600,000 to invest and that it was spread across a host of funds accumulated over many years. She admitted that she wasn't sure what she owned or why she owned it and that her portfolio performance was dismal. This was why she enrolled in my course.

She enthusiastically told me after completing the course that she was going to devote $100,000 of the total $600,000 to the PPM approach. If it worked, she would increase this total.

Gloria called me approximately a year later, in April 2008. She wanted to tell me about a recent meeting she had with a financial adviser at a major full-service brokerage firm. Her story is worth sharing.

The financial adviser involved in this story had been calling Gloria for many months trying to get her to come to the brokerage office for a discussion and complete review of her financial situation and portfolio. His calls had been persistent, so Gloria decided to go and see what he was offering. She had been working at this point with her PPM-designed portfolio for approximately 12 months. She scheduled an appointment.

Upon arrival at the broker's office she was ushered into a large and well-appointed conference room with a massive mahogany table, multiple types of refreshments on a sideboard, and several glossy brochures arrayed before her chair. It was all was very polished and professional-looking.

The impeccably dressed adviser greeted her, initiated the usual small talk about her family, the weather, and their latest vacations. Then, at a well-orchestrated time, the adviser asked Gloria to tell him about her investments. Gloria pulled out her Perfect Portfolio Design Worksheet and showed him the eight ETFs that she owned. She did not own a Real Estate investment at the time because the PPM trading plan had stopped her out of that asset in mid-2007.

The adviser glanced at the simple list and asked how she had decided on this portfolio. Gloria gave him a brief explanation of the PPM approach and told him that she had learned it in a class at Montgomery College. The following dialog ensued.

Adviser: This looks very simple. How did you decide to buy these investments?

Gloria: Based on a process I learned in the investing class, I first developed an Investing Plan where I determined my goals, examined my risk tolerance, and decided how much time I was willing to devote to the investing process. Then I assessed the current state of the market to design my Core Segment using the four Core Building Blocks you see on my worksheet. Then I learned about and looked at price charts for the five PPM Target Market Building Blocks to design that Segment of my portfolio. At the time I originally built my portfolio, all of the Target Markets were experiencing an uptrend. So I allocated money to each, giving higher allocations to those assets that had the strongest uptrend. You can see that I simply bought an index fund for each of my Core Building Blocks and an ETF for each of my Target Market Building Blocks.

Adviser (looking dubious): This portfolio seems very risky. Are you sure it matches your risk tolerance level?

Gloria: I think that you will agree that my Core Segment is not risky at all as it contains extremely broad-based index funds for each of four very diverse asset classes. You are probably referring to my Target Market Segment where I do have relatively volatile investments. I eliminated company risk in each Target Market investment by purchasing a basket of stocks through an ETF. In addition, for each asset type, I have managed my risk by implementing a trading plan that limits my losses to approximately 7 percent and lets my profits run.

Adviser (after learning details of the trading plan): Gloria, you know that trying to time markets is almost always a losing proposition. Investing based on charting and technical analysis is a very difficult method of investing and should be left to professionals.

Gloria: I am not simply timing the market. I have studied each asset class that I own. I know the factors that influence the price of each. And when I bought each investment, I knew from looking at its chart that its price was in an uptrend. My only use of charts was to first verify that the price was moving up and then to determine price points at which I will exit to stop losses or to take profits. In my opinion, this is a far less risky strategy than simply buying and holding a mutual fund as it moves up and down with no plan to sell.

Adviser (becoming uncomfortable): Yes, but my firm offers to you funds that are managed by financial professionals. Our managers interview company presidents and our analysts thoroughly research financial statements. We invest in only the best companies. Your portfolio with its index investments can't take advantage of this expertise.

Gloria: I don't really have the time or the desire to argue those points. Let's just compare results. I see you have some brochures for funds that you are planning to recommend. Can we use your computer to show me the one-year returns for at least one of them?

Adviser (not seeming very happy with this unexpected request): Well, I guess so. We can use the computer here in the conference room. Let's start with our flagship Large-Cap Value Fund. This is our most popular fund, and the manager has performed extremely well for the last five years. He is one of the best in the business. You can see the incredible performance from this chart in the brochure.

Gloria: Instead of using the seemingly random time period for the chart in the brochure, could we use the Web to see the fund performance for the calendar year 2007?

Adviser (hesitating): I don't see why not. Let me log on and pull it up. OK, it looks like it returned 5 percent in 2007, which isn't great, but this was about the market average for the year and this is an investment that is meant to be held for many years. Look again at the five-year chart in your brochure.

Gloria (making no move to look at the glossy brochure): I started my PPM portfolio in April of 2007 and it earned 17 percent for just a portion of the year ending in December of 2007.

Adviser: Maybe so, but you assumed a lot more risk.

Gloria: I respectfully disagree. The majority of my return came from my Gold, Energy, and Agricultural Commodity ETFs.

Each rose over 20 percent and my trading plan limited my risk to a 7 percent maximum drop on each. My risk is completely controlled. If I were to buy and hold your fund, it seems that my risk is out of my control and as a result, the risk to me is much higher because I have no idea of what your professional fund manager is doing or thinking.

Adviser: But you don't have the time to monitor your investments on a daily basis. We do. This is our only job and it is done by trained professionals.

Gloria: My Target Market investments are automatically monitored 24 hours a day, 365 days a year by Web resources. My simple trading plans either sell my position when an exit point is hit or send me an e-mail prompting me to do some research and make a decision. I spend almost no time watching my investments. I devote about one hour reviewing the portfolio every month on a scheduled basis and I research individual investments only when I get an alert e-mail. Other than that, if my trading systems don't come knocking, then I can rest assured that my holdings are either moving up or moving sideways. If they were falling, I would know it and take appropriate action.

Adviser (noticeably uncomfortable): Well, we have other funds I could have you look at.

Gloria (leafing through one of the glossy brochures): Am I reading this correctly? If I were to buy this fund, you would charge me a 1.8 percent annual management fee and a 5 percent load on top of that? This can't be right, can it?

Adviser (really struggling now): Well, an incredible staff of professional researchers spends a lot of time working on this fund and that effort is worth the management fee. As for the load, that goes down to zero if you hold the fund for five years, so it won't even come into play.

Gloria: So for a fund that returned 5 percent in 2007, you are taking 1.8 percent away in management fees every year and I paid you a load of 5 percent up front for the privilege of owning it? Have I got that right? All of this when the portfolio I own gave me a 17 percent return for 2007 with management fees on the order of 0.4 percent and no upfront costs other than several $9 trading fees?

Adviser: Well perhaps we should look at a different set of funds for you. Why don't I do some more work and let's get together again in the near future.

At this point the meeting ended. The next day she got a call from the adviser telling her that his schedule was extremely full and that he unfortunately could not take her on as a client at this time. Gloria could only smile.

Gloria did not go to this meeting to flaunt her knowledge or her results. She was genuinely interested in seeing if an adviser could contribute to what she was already doing with her PPM portfolio. She found that the adviser was not interested in much more than selling her commission-based mutual funds. Her simple approach did not fit his business model. There are thousands upon thousands of individuals who do fit his model. So, dismissing Gloria as a client was, to him, a sound business decision.

Is this an indictment of investment advisers? No, they perform a valuable service for many people. This story is more about the newly found power and confidence of an individual who took the time and effort to learn a totally new approach to investing and who had the motivation to implement it. The PPM was the vehicle for freeing herself from dependency on advisers, high investment fees, and mediocre funds. It was the vehicle that enabled her to unleash her innate potential for accumulating wealth on the basis of her own efforts.

Gloria's visit to the full-service brokerage firm did not discourage or even irritate her. It simply confirmed what she already knew: The best custodian of her investments was not some disinterested third party. The responsibility for her financial future and security was hers and hers alone. In the PPM, she had found the knowledge, structure, and tools needed to assume this responsibility with confidence. I believe you will as well.

A Final Note

Investing will never be easy, and I have not tried to convince you in this book that it is. There will always be risks and there will be times when investing decisions that you make using the Perfect Portfolio Methodology will lose money. Following the PPM does not make investing success a sure thing.

What it does is give you the comprehensive approach you need to significantly enhance your chances of succeeding in the world of investing as it exists today. It also enables you to take personal control of your investments and decrease your dependence on third parties.

In essence, I believe that the PPM brings the world of personal investing into the twenty-first century with new ideas, new ways of viewing the market, and new investing resources. World markets are changing rapidly and you should not have to confront new challenges with worn-out tools. The PPM gives you the new and sharper tools you need to thrive in today's markets and markets as they will exist in the future.

Some experts will look upon this book with disdain. They will give you any number of reasons why the PPM will not work. But these are people who profit when you depend on them for advice. You know now that by using the PPM, you can declare your independence from financial advisers, newsletters, the financial press, and other assorted Wall Street mavens. This is not good for their business, so listen to their criticism but understand where it is coming from and judge for yourself the merits of their arguments.

I feel that it is appropriate to end *The Perfect Portfolio* where we started, with a reference to a quote from the Buddha presented at the start of this book. When you first read it you may not have fully appreciated the wisdom it contained and its relevance to personal investing. Perhaps now, after completing this book, you will. So I suggest that you return to the front pages of this book and read it again.

Taking the Buddha's words to heart, you should not simply accept what I have presented to you in this book at face value. I encourage you to study, analyze, and question the Perfect Portfolio Methodology. I believe that after doing so you will find that it "agrees with reason" and that it is "conducive to the good and benefit" of your financial health.

As a graduate of *The Perfect Portfolio*, you now have the knowledge, the structure, and the resources to implement a portfolio that you can easily design and manage on your own. You are prepared to create a portfolio that can be an amazing source of wealth in good markets and in bad. In summary, you are now fully capable of taking personal control of your portfolio and your financial future. Now it is up to you to just do it.

I hope you do.

Appendix

A SAMPLE PPM BUILDING BLOCK
TRADING PLAN

I n Chapter 10, where I designed a sample Perfect Portfolio, one of the key factors in determining its returns potential for the next year was my estimate of the Expected Return for each Target Market Building Block. Here are the returns I estimated and as shown in Table 10.1:

- Gold—20 percent
- Energy—20 percent
- Agriculture—20 percent
- Real Estate—15 percent
- Emerging Markets—15 percent

I stated in Chapter 10 that I felt these returns estimates to be reasonable. As you viewed these numbers, you may have been skeptical that such returns could be achieved. And you would be right to think this if I planned to simply buy and hold these investments for a year. But this is not the case. For each of these investments, I implemented a Perfect Portfolio Methodology (PPM) Trading Plan as discussed for each Target Market Building Block in Chapters 5 through 9.

I want to show you in this Appendix the step-by-step process and the power of a PPM Trading Plan in action. I want to show you that the returns shown above are not unreasonably high and that they are, in fact, quite conservative.

To illustrate how an effective Trading Plan can make lemonade out of lemons, I will show you my trading plan used for the Real

Estate Building Block, VNQ, a REIT Exchange Traded Fund (ETF) that we discussed in Chapter 9. VNQ lost 19.5 percent in 2007. In a Perfect Portfolio that I managed during the calendar year of 2007 and that was under the watchful eye of a PPM Trading Plan, my VNQ holding gained 19 percent after trading commissions!

Below, I show a price chart of VNQ for 2007, and Table A.1 details the actions I took in managing VNQ in accordance with the PPM Trading Plan I had put in place for that year.

The Price Chart for VNQ

Figure A.1 shows the price chart for the Vanguard REIT Exchange Traded Fund (ETF), with the symbol VNQ for the calendar year 2007.

In addition to the price chart, I have also included the Relative Strength Indicator (RSI) shown below the price chart. I discussed how to use this technical analysis indicator in Chapter 12.

I used the site at finance.yahoo.com to create the chart shown in Figure A.1. After entering the VNQ symbol on the home page, I clicked on *Interactive* in the charts menu and specified that I wanted a chart for January 1, 2007 to December 31, 2007. I then clicked on the RSI menu selection above the chart to show the Relative Strength Indicator.

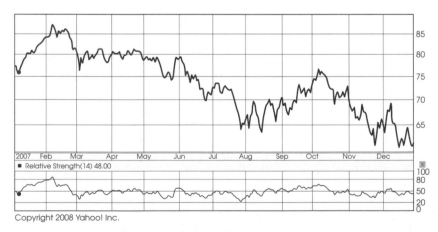

Copyright 2008 Yahoo! Inc.

Figure A.1   2007 Price Chart for VNQ

The PPM Trading Plan for VNQ

Table A.1 shows the actions I took in accordance with the PPM Trading Plan that I established for VNQ during the year 2007. Remember, ETFs trade exactly like stocks, so it was easy to buy and sell VNQ through my online broker for only a $9 transaction charge. If I had purchased a mutual fund for this Building Block, implementing a trading plan would have been slightly more difficult, but not impossible.

Let's take a look at the data in Table A.1. Each row shows an action that I took as a result of the PPM Trading Plan. Here I comment on each of the nine action steps in the table. These comments are listed in order by date as they are shown in the table.

- *1/2/2007:* I started the year on January 2 by purchasing 100 shares of VNQ at $77 per share. As the first step in developing a trading plan for my position, I viewed VNQ's price chart and decided to place a trailing stop trigger to sell should VNQ drop $7 from the highest point it reaches while I own it. The first stop price is obviously then $70. But remember, for a trailing stop, this sell price moves up with the market price of the investment. This is a hard-sell trigger, meaning that my broker's system will automatically sell my shares if the $7 drop condition is met. On the upside, I again looked at the price chart and set a take-profit alert at $84 that will send me an e-mail should this price be reached. This alert does *not* move up with the price of VNQ; it stays at $84 until I change it.

    I determined these stop and alert prices by looking at Bollinger Bands on the price chart as discussed in Part II of this book. I made sure that the stop loss price was far enough away from the purchase price so that daily volatility did not whipsaw me out of my position.

    With my initial Trading Plan in place I do nothing until the plan comes knocking on my door with an alert telling me that the ETF was sold to stop losses or had reached a profit price point and I should investigate.

- *2/1/2007:* On this date, I get a take-profit e-mail. The price has moved up to $84, triggering an e-mail alerting me to this fact. As a result of this e-mail, I look at VNQ's price chart and see that the trend of the price line is still moving up. I could have sold here with a nice profit but I want to take advantage of the potential that VNQ's price will continue to go up.

So, instead of selling, I simply tighten my stop loss trigger to a drop of $2 instead of $7. Now the system will automatically sell my shares if VNQ drops $2 from the highest price it reaches from this point forward. This action locks in profits of at least $5 but I am hoping for more. I also reset my take-profit alert to $87. And again, I wait for an alert.

- *2/7/2007:* This investment is moving fast. On this date, I get another take-profit alert e-mail. The price has reached $87. I quickly view the chart and decide that I am happy with a $10 per share profit in a little over a month and sell my 100 shares for $7,700. I have earned $1,000 in a little over 30 days and will not be greedy. Sure, the price may go higher but in a disciplined Trading Plan, taking profits of this magnitude is never a bad idea.

  I have sold my Real Estate investment, but I am not through with Real Estate investing so early in the year. My next step is to put VNQ in a Watch List and monitor it without owning it. Watch Lists were discussed in Chapters 4 and 11. I want to be alerted if the price of VNQ drops or rises significantly, at which time I will evaluate the situation and decide if I want to get back into the game. So in my Watch List, I set a low-price alert at $77 and a high-price alert at $90. These are large enough moves to stir my interest. The Watch List will send me an e-mail when either price is hit.

  Again, I will do nothing until I receive an e-mail for VNQ sent by my Watch List.

- *5/16/2007:* My Watch List sends me a low-alert e-mail. The price of VNQ has dropped to $76, which is below my low-price alert of $77. I view a price chart for VNQ and see that the price line is in a significant downtrend. I am not comfortable getting back into this investment now. So I simply reset my Watch List alerts to a low of $70 and a high of $80 and again wait.

- *6/25/2007:* I get a low-alert e-mail. VNQ's price has dropped to $70. I view the price chart and see that VNQ's price line is still heading south. I simply reset my Watch List alerts, $65 on the downside and $75 on the upside. I am looking for VNQ's price to start to go up again before investing in it.

- *7/27/2007:* I get yet another low-alert e-mail at a price of $64. This thing is dropping like a stone. I'm glad I don't currently own it. I simply reset the alert prices again, to $59 on the downside and $69 on the upside, and wait.

- *8/8/2007:* I finally get a high alert at a price of $69. This tells me that perhaps VNQ is oversold and ready for a rebound. I look at the price chart and the RSI Technical Indicator that I discussed in Chapter 12. This indicator tells me that VNQ is indeed in an oversold status with RSI recently being under 20. I determine that a recovery may be beginning and *buy* 100 shares at $69.

  I look at the Bollinger Bands on the price chart to determine volatility and set my stop loss trigger for a drop of $7 and my take-profit alert at $76. You can view these actions in Table A.1.

- *10/5/2007:* I get a take profit e-mail alert. The price has reached $76. I view the price chart and see that the price line is moving up. I want to lock in some profit and try to squeeze a few more dollars of gain out of my investment, so I do not sell. I simply tighten my stop loss trigger to a drop of $2 and reset my take profit alert to $80.

- *10/15/2007:* I get an e-mail telling me that my shares were sold. The price has dropped to $74 and my stop loss has been triggered. My broker's system automatically sold my 100 shares of VNQ for $7,400. I could now put VNQ back in the Watch List but decide, based on the news I am reading, that Real Estate is a very troubled market. So I take VNQ out of my monitoring system. I have made significant returns on this investment for the year 2007 and will start monitoring it again at the beginning of 2008.

The Results

If you follow the value of my Real Estate investment in the right-most column of Table A.1, you will see that I started the year with $7,700 and ended the year with $9,200. This occurred in a year where VNQ started at $77 and ended at $62.

Let's summarize the results of my PPM Trading Plan for VNQ during the year of 2007.

- *Number of Actions: nine*—After I purchased VNQ at the beginning of the year in 2007, I had to pay attention to it only eight more times during the entire year. Most of my actions simply consisted of viewing a chart and resetting my alerts. Thus, I spent no more than 30 minutes during the entire year working with this Real Estate investment.

- *Number of Trades: four*—I bought and sold VNQ twice during the year resulting in four trades. At $9 per trade commission, my transaction costs were $36.
- *Percent Return: +19 percent*—My Real Estate investment began on 1/2/2007 with a purchase of 100 shares worth $7,700. At the end of the year, my real estate account was worth $9,200. This is an increase of 19.4 percent! When subtracting $36 in commissions, this return is reduced to approximately 19 percent.
- *Percent Return for VNQ for 2007: –19.5 percent*—If I had simply bought VNQ at the beginning of the year at $77 and held it until the end of the year when the price was $62, I would have lost 19.5 percent of my investment as opposed to the +19 percent I earned using the PPM Trading Plan.
- *Amount of time holding VNQ during the year: 3.5 months*— Looking at Table A.1 you can see that I owned VNQ stock for only a little over three months. I was not exposed to real estate risk for most of the year because I was on the sidelines.

Trading Plan Example Summary

The intent of this example was twofold. First, I wanted to illustrate in detail how a PPM Trading Plan can be implemented and monitored in a real-life scenario. Second, I wanted to show you that the estimates I made for Expected Returns in Chapter 10 for the Target Market Building Blocks were not wildly optimistic. In fact, they were conservative.

In the example, I took an investment that had lost over 19 percent for the year and showed how by moving in and out of owning it, using very simple logic, I earned 19 percent for the year.

And I could have earned more. In the example, when I did not own VNQ, I assumed that the money I had allocated to Real Estate was kept in cash. If I had invested this money in other Target Market Building Blocks, such as Gold, it could have created additional returns. Then, when VNQ became attractive again, I could have sold some of whatever other Building Block I had bought and reallocated the money back to VNQ.

Table A.1   VNQ Trading Plan for 2007

Date	VNQ Price	Action	Stop-Loss Low Alert	Take-Profit High Alert	Acct. Value
1/2/2007	77	Buy 100 shares			7700
		Set Stop Loss Trigger	−7		Stock
		Set Take-Profit Alert		84	
2/1/2007	84	Take-Profit Alert			
		View Chart			
		Reset Stop Loss	−2		
		Reset Take-Profit Alert		87	
2/7/2007	87	Take-Profit Alert			8700
		View Chart			Cash
		Sell 100 Shares			
		Move to Watch List			
		Set Watch List Alerts	77	90	
5/16/2007	76	Low Alert			
		View Chart			
		Reset Watch List Alerts	70	80	
6/25/2007	70	Low Alert			
		View Chart			
		Reset Watch List Alerts	65	75	
7/27/2007	64	Low Alert			
		View Chart			
		Reset Watch List Alerts	59	69	
8/8/2007	69	High Alert			6900
		View Chart			Stock
		Buy 100 Shares			1800
		Set Stop Loss and	−7		Cash
		Take-Profit Triggers		76	
10/5/2007	76	Take-Profit Alert			
		View Chart			
		Reset Stop Loss	−2		
		Reset Take-Profit Alert		80	
10/15/2007	74	Stop Loss Triggered			9200
		Sell 100 Shares			Cash

Or, as a very real alternative I could have bought an ETF that shorted the Real Estate Market and made significant money during the down trends. Use of short ETFs is discussed in Chapters 4 and 12.

Another important benefit to point out is that I spent very little of my time working with this investment. The PPM Trading Plan was continuously monitoring it and alerted me only eight times during the year to take action, and these actions were simple and quickly executed. I viewed a price chart, looked at the trend, and decided whether to buy, sell, or do nothing. Most of my activity involved simply resetting alerts and triggers.

As an individual investor, you have limited time to devote to your investments. You are probably now spending most of this time looking for equities in which to invest. The Perfect Portfolio Methodology does not require you to spend time on this search and analysis effort. Your nine investments, once put in place, will not change. This frees up your time to work with the PPM Trading Plan you implement for each Target Market Building Block. And you have seen in this Appendix that just a little bit of effort devoted to this task can result in huge returns.

About the Author

Leland Hevner is a leading figure in the world of personal investor education and has been for more than 10 years. He teaches personal investing classes at the college level, has written 12 investor education publications, and is the founder and President of the National Association of Online Investors (NAOI).

Taking early retirement from a successful business career in 1992, Mr. Hevner became a full-time investor. These were the Wild West days of personal investing. The personal computer, the Internet, and the Web were rapidly entering homes across the United States and with them an incredible power for individuals to trade stocks on their own. While Mr. Hevner achieved a degree of success with his online trading activities, he also recognized that many individuals, tempted by the siren call of day-trading riches, were losing money hand over fist.

Individuals in the early 1990s had the power to invest, yet there existed virtually no education resources that taught people how to use this investing power safely and effectively. This was a problem. Power without knowledge is a dangerous combination and Mr. Hevner watched as thousands of people lost incredible amounts of money through uninformed and naïve trading.

Resolving to address this issue, Mr. Hevner founded the NAOI in 1997 to provide the public with the serious education they needed to become confident and successful investors. For this purpose, he created the nation's first comprehensive and academically rigorous investor education curriculum called the *NAOI Confident Investing Series*. This offering consists of five multimedia courses that were then, and continue to be today, the gold standard of personal investor education.

Thousands of students have graduated from Mr. Hevner's courses, accessed at www.naoi.org, and the NAOI has emerged as the nation's premier provider of college-level, investor education.

Mr. Hevner also teaches the art and science of personal investing in the college classroom in the Washington D.C. area and he continues to revise his curriculum content based on student input and his ongoing monitoring of market dynamics.

The national media have recognized Mr. Hevner's status as a leading authority in the field of investor education and as a strong advocate for the average person with money to invest. He has appeared on the three major commercial TV networks, ABC, CBS, and NBC, as well as multiple times on the CNBC business channel. He has also been interviewed extensively on radio stations across the United States and is often quoted in the national press.

Mr. Hevner holds a B.S. degree in Computer Science from the Rose-Hulman Institute of Technology and an MBA from Purdue University. He lives and works in Washington, D.C., where the National Association of Online Investors is based.

Index